The
NYSTROM
A★T★L★A★S
of
United States History

NYSTROM
DIVISION OF HERFF JONES, INC.

CONTENT REVIEWERS

Betty B. Franks, History Teacher and Department Chairperson,
Maple Heights High School, Maple Heights, OH

Jacqueline L. Frierson, Principal and former History Teacher,
William H. Lemmel Middle School at Woodbourne, Baltimore, MD

Robert Hagopian, History Teacher, Scotts Valley Middle School, Scotts Valley, CA

Francis N. Stites, Professor of History, Department of History, San Diego State University, San Diego, CA

Arthur Zilversmit, Distinguished Service Professor, Emeritus,
Department of History, Lake Forest College, Lake Forest, IL

PHOTO CREDITS

Credit abbreviations

Arch.   Archive Photos   NW   North Wind Picture Archive
C   Corbis   SB   Stock Boston
FPG   FPG International LLC   TSI   Tony Stone Images
GC   The Granger Collection, New York

front cover (left, right) GC; **back cover** Lambert/Arch.; **14** Jonathan Scott–TCL/Masterfile; **16** C/Macduff Everton; **17** C/Yann Arthus-Bertrand; **18** GC; **19** Simeone Huber/TSI; **20** Paul Chesley/TSI; **21** C/Michael Freeman; **23** Patrick Curtet/Point De Vue/Liaison Agency Inc.; **28** NW; **30** C/Tom Bean; **31** Kindra Clineff/TSI; **37** GC; **39** Stock Montage; **40** GC; **41** NW; **43** NW; **44** NW; **46** GC; **47** Art Wolfe/TSI; **48** Stock Montage; **49** GC; **50** Jake Rajs/TSI; **52** GC; **53** Heyward Hardy/Fine Art Photographic Library/PNI; **55** Christie's Images/Superstock; **56** John Eastcott/Yva Momatiuk/SB; **59** C; **65** Terry Farmer/TSI; **66** Dave Bartruff/SB; **67** FPG; **68** GC; **69** GC; **71** Idaho State Historical Society; **72** Arch.; **75** GC; **76** GC; **77** C/Bettmann; **78** C; **81** C; **83** GC; **84** C/Bettmann; **85** C; **87** (left) Sporting News/Arch.; **87** (right) Sy Seidman Collection/Culver Pictures, Inc.; **88** FPG; **89** GC; **91** Culver Pictures, Inc./Superstock; **92** FPG; **94** Sy Seidman Collection/Culver Pictures, Inc.; **95** C; **96** GC; **97** GC; **98** Lambert/Arch.; **99** C; **100** FPG; **102** FPG; **104** Jose L. Pelaez, Inc./The Stock Market; **106** C/Nathan Benn; **108** Philip J. Griffiths/Magnum Photos; **109** Costa Manos/Magnum Photos; **110** C/Owen Franken; **111** Jeremy Bigwood/Liaison Agency Inc.; **113** David R. Frazier/TSI; **114** Jon Feingersh/SB; **117** Robert Cameron/TSI; **118** Robert E. Daemmrich/TSI; **119** David Young Wolff/TSI

2001 Update of Names and Boundaries
Copyright © 2000 NYSTROM Division of Herff Jones, Inc.
3333 N. Elston Avenue, Chicago, Illinois 60618

Statistics and estimates are from government sources: for the date given where specified, otherwise for the most recent available date.

ISBN 0-7825-0782-4   10 9 8 7 6 5 4 3   04 03 02 01

Printed in U.S.A.
Product Code Number 9AUSH

For information about ordering this atlas, call toll-free 800-621-8086.

Contents

Using This Atlas

★ Follow the numbered steps to get the most out of your atlas.

★ The other notes explain how maps, graphs, photos, and other features help bring history to life.

Maps show the stories of history. They can help you visualize locations, events, and movements.

1 First look at the **era title** and **dates**. The title states the theme for the section, and the dates give you the time frame. The atlas is divided into 10 eras, or periods of time.

2 Read the **timeline** for a preview of major events of the era.

3 Check the **topic title** to find out what these two pages cover.

4 Read the **overview**. It will help you understand the maps, graphs, and photos on these two pages.

5 Study the **maps**, **graphs**, and **photos** in order. Think about the story each tells and how it relates to the topic title.

Locator maps show you the subject area of the map.

A **map legend** explains what the map colors and symbols mean. Always read the legend before studying the map.

What does this word mean? Check the **glossary**.

ERA **7** Emergence of Modern America 1890–1930

Late 1800s **Jim Crow laws** passed to limit rights of African Americans.

1890 **National Park Service** establishes three parks in California.

1898 **Spanish-American War** involves America in Cuba and Philippines.

Hawaii becomes a U.S. possession.

1890 1895 1900

The Spanish-American War and World Power

- The United States gained recognition as a world power during the Spanish-American War.

- The Spanish-American War was fought over the independence of Cuba, a Spanish colony for 400 years.

- After the *Maine*, a U.S. warship, exploded in Havana harbor, Americans called for U.S. intervention in Cuba.

- U.S. victories over Spain brought independence to Cuba and made the Philippines a U.S. territory.

Gulf of Mexico

Tampa
UNITED STATES

Feb. 15 *U.S.S. Maine* explodes and ignites the war.

Havana

Bahama Is. (Br.)

ATLANTIC OCEAN

Cuba (Sp.)

Jul. 1 San Juan Hill
Jul. 1 El Caney
Santiago de Cuba
Jul. 3

HAITI   DOMINICAN REPUBLIC

Caribbean Sea

Jamaica (Br.)

(from Curaçao)

Puerto Rico (Sp.)

Soon after the sinking of the *Maine*, the U.S. Navy blockaded Cuba. When a fleet from Spain tried to break through, the Americans sank all seven Spanish ships.

FIGHTING IN CUBA, 1898

- Spanish possession
- American fleet movement
- Spanish fleet movement
- U.S. blockade
- Major battle site

0   150   300 miles
0   150   300 kilometers

CHINA

Taiwan (Formosa)

Hong Kong (Br.)

1898 Philippines becomes a U.S. territory.

Philippines (Sp.)

May 1 Manila

South China Sea

Philippine Sea

1898–1902 Philippine insurrection fails to win independence from the United States.

Borneo

FIGHTING IN THE PHILIPPINES, 1898

- Spanish possession
- American fleet movement
- Major battle site
- British colony

0   250   500 miles
0   250   500 kilometers

The U.S. Navy destroyed a Spanish fleet in Manila, preventing Spain's ground forces from sailing to Cuba and helping the Spanish cause there.

80

- Bohemian
- Italian
- French
- French Canadian
- German
- Irish
- English speakers (not Irish)
- Polish
- Russian-Jewish
- Not residential

0   100   200 feet
0   50   100 meters

This neighborhood, just a home to Irish and German begun to replace them by and daughters of immigra

IMMIGRANTS 1895–1929

Largest Groups
Movement
ITALIAN Ethnicity

Other Groups
Movement
Turkish Ethnicity

More and more immigrants came from Southern and Eastern Europe. Many were culturally inferior. In 1921 and 1924, Congress set new immigration qu

1921 Peak of Polish immig follows World War I.

BRITISH IRISH

CANADIAN

Japanese

Portuguese

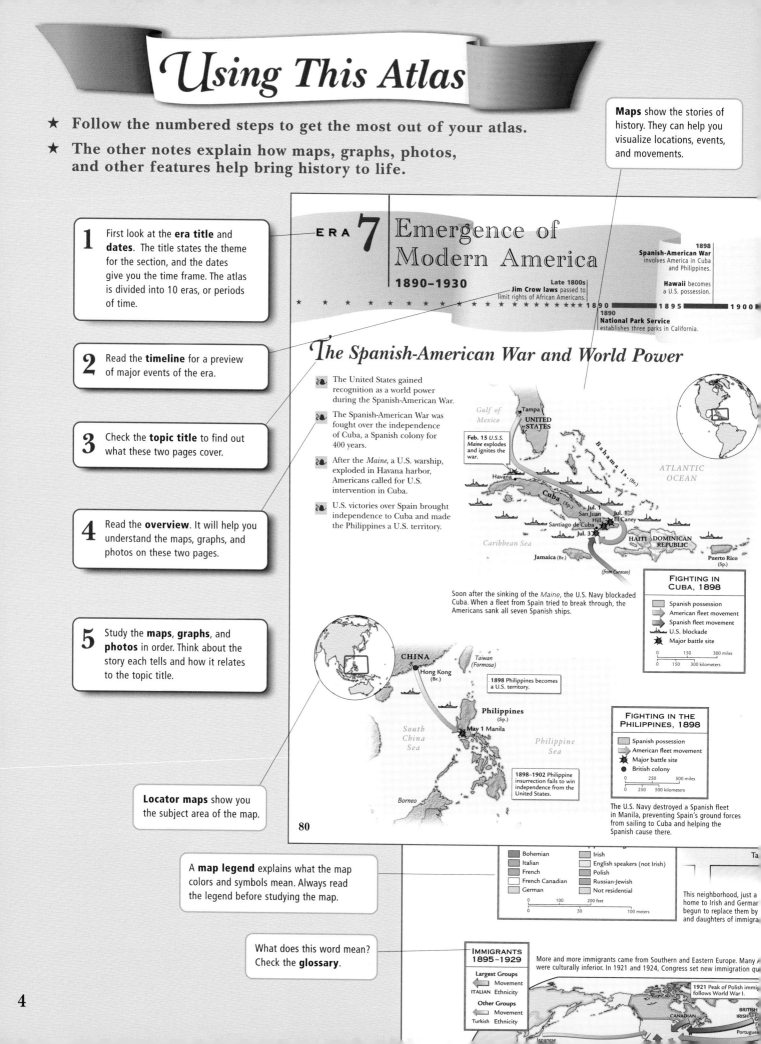

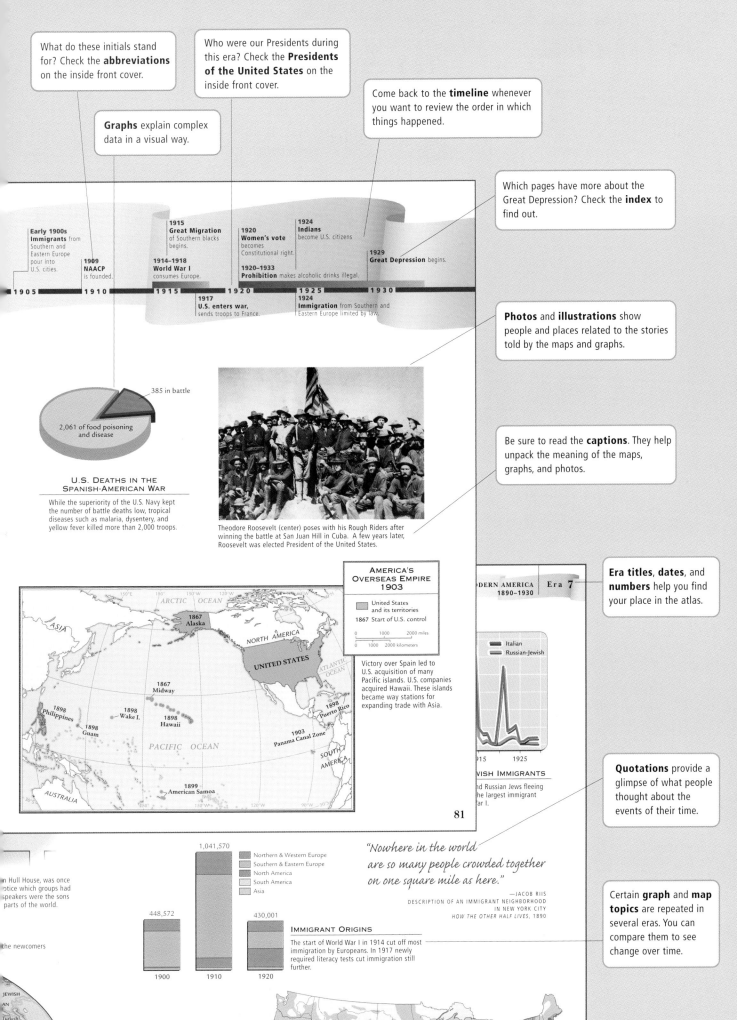

What do these initials stand for? Check the **abbreviations** on the inside front cover.

Who were our Presidents during this era? Check the **Presidents of the United States** on the inside front cover.

Graphs explain complex data in a visual way.

Come back to the **timeline** whenever you want to review the order in which things happened.

Which pages have more about the Great Depression? Check the **index** to find out.

Early 1900s
Immigrants from Southern and Eastern Europe pour into U.S. cities.

1909
NAACP is founded.

1915
Great Migration of Southern blacks begins.

1914–1918
World War I consumes Europe.

1917
U.S. enters war, sends troops to France.

1920
Women's vote becomes Constitutional right.

1920–1933
Prohibition makes alcoholic drinks illegal.

1924
Immigration from Southern and Eastern Europe limited by law.

1924
Indians become U.S. citizens

1929
Great Depression begins.

1905   1910   1915   1920   1925   1930

Photos and **illustrations** show people and places related to the stories told by the maps and graphs.

385 in battle

2,061 of food poisoning and disease

U.S. DEATHS IN THE SPANISH-AMERICAN WAR

While the superiority of the U.S. Navy kept the number of battle deaths low, tropical diseases such as malaria, dysentery, and yellow fever killed more than 2,000 troops.

Theodore Roosevelt (center) poses with his Rough Riders after winning the battle at San Juan Hill in Cuba. A few years later, Roosevelt was elected President of the United States.

Be sure to read the **captions**. They help unpack the meaning of the maps, graphs, and photos.

AMERICA'S OVERSEAS EMPIRE 1903

United States and its territories
1867 Start of U.S. control

0   1000   2000 miles
0   1000   2000 kilometers

Era titles, **dates**, and **numbers** help you find your place in the atlas.

MODERN AMERICA 1890–1930   Era **7**

ARCTIC OCEAN

1867 Alaska

ASIA

NORTH AMERICA

UNITED STATES

ATLANTIC OCEAN

1867 Midway

1898 Philippines

1898 Wake I.

1898 Hawaii

1898 Guam

1898 Puerto Rico

1903 Panama Canal Zone

SOUTH AMERICA

PACIFIC OCEAN

1899 American Samoa

AUSTRALIA

Victory over Spain led to U.S. acquisition of many Pacific islands. U.S. companies acquired Hawaii. These islands became way stations for expanding trade with Asia.

Italian
Russian-Jewish

1915   1925

...ISH IMMIGRANTS

...nd Russian Jews fleeing ...he largest immigrant ...ar I.

Quotations provide a glimpse of what people thought about the events of their time.

81

1,041,570

Northern & Western Europe
Southern & Eastern Europe
North America
South America
Asia

448,572

430,001

n Hull House, was once ...otice which groups had ...speakers were the sons ...parts of the world.

the newcomers

"Nowhere in the world are so many people crowded together on one square mile as here."

—JACOB RIIS
DESCRIPTION OF AN IMMIGRANT NEIGHBORHOOD IN NEW YORK CITY
HOW THE OTHER HALF LIVES, 1890

IMMIGRANT ORIGINS

The start of World War I in 1914 cut off most immigration by Europeans. In 1917 newly required literacy tests cut immigration still further.

1900   1910   1920

Certain **graph** and **map topics** are repeated in several eras. You can compare them to see change over time.

JEWISH
AN
Turkish

5

Reference Maps

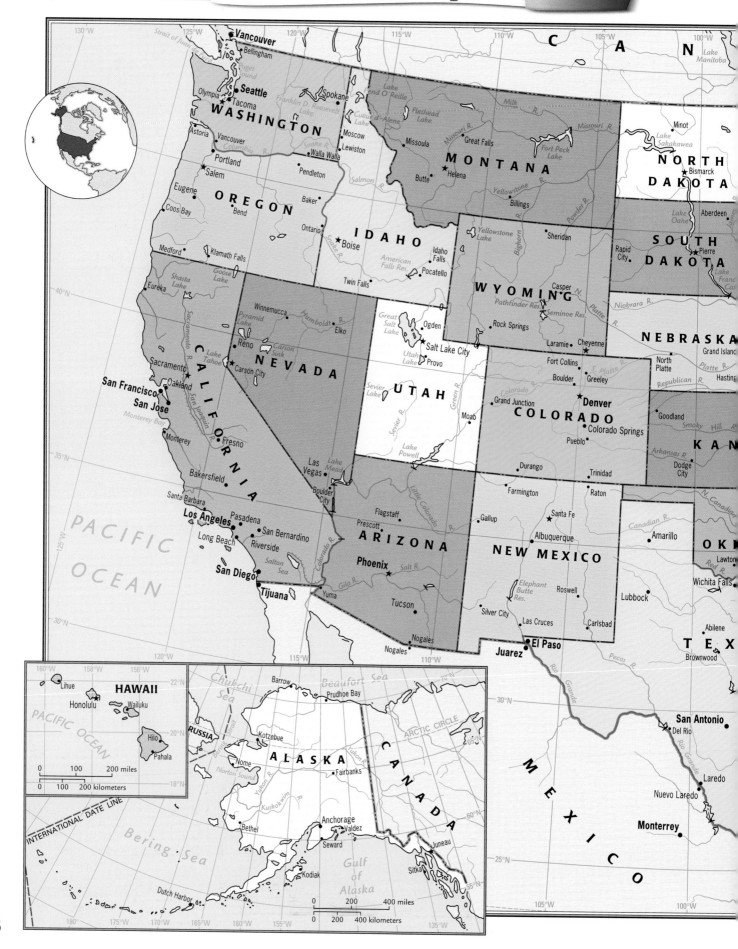

UNITED STATES
POLITICAL

Boundaries

International boundary

State boundary

Cities

● **Chicago**

▪ Anchorage

▪ Boulder

A city's relative size is shown by the size of its symbol and lettering.

⊛ **Washington, D.C.** National capital

★ Honolulu State capital

| 0 | 100 | 200 | 300 miles |
| 0 | 100 | 200 | 300 kilometers |

CANADA

Vancouver
Cape Flattery
Olympic Mts.
Seattle
WASHINGTON
Mt. Rainier 4392 m
Grand Coulee Dam
Franklin D. Roosevelt Lake
Puget Sound
Coeur d'Alene
Strait of Juan de Fuca
Columbia R.

Cape Blanco
Portland
OREGON
Cascade Range
Coast Range
Columbia Plateau
Willamette R.
Snake R.
Blue Mts.
Bitterroot Range
IDAHO
Salmon River Mts.
Salmon R.
American Falls Res.

MONTANA
Milk R.
Missouri R.
Fort Peck Lake
Yellowstone R.
Bighorn Mts.
Powder R.

NORTH DAKOTA
Lake Sakakawea
Lake Oahe
James R.

Cape Mendocino
40°N
Sacramento Valley
Coast Ranges
Sierra Nevada
CALIFORNIA
Basin and Range
NEVADA
Pyramid Lake
Carson Sink
Ruby Mts.
Great Salt Lake Desert
Great Salt Lake
Utah Lake
Wasatch Range
Uinta Mts.
Great Divide Basin
WYOMING
Great Plains
Pathfinder Res.
Seminoe Res.
Front Range
Park Range
Platte R.
SOUTH DAKOTA
Black Hills
Lake Francis Case
NEBRASKA
Sand Hills
Niobrara R.

San Francisco
35°N
Monterey Bay
San Joaquin Valley
Mt. Whitney 4418 m
Death Valley −86 m
Great Basin
UTAH
Sevier Lake
Colorado R.
Sangre de Cristo Mts.
Mt. Elbert 4399 m
COLORADO
Denver
Pikes Peak 4301 m
San Juan Mts.
Rocky Mountains
Republican R.
Smoky Hill R.
Platte R.
Arkansas R.
KAN

Pt. Conception
Los Angeles
Channel Is.
San Diego
Tijuana
Mojave Desert
Death Valley
Hoover Dam
Grand Canyon
Glen Canyon Dam
Colorado Plateau
ARIZONA
Parker Dam
Phoenix
Salt R.
Gila R.
Colorado R.
Sonoran Desert
NEW MEXICO
Elephant Butte
Sacramento Mts.
Canadian R.
N. Canadian R.
OKL
Red R.

30°N
PACIFIC OCEAN
Imperial Valley
Llano Estacado
Pecos R.
Edwards Plateau
Stockton Plateau
TEX

El Paso
Rio Grande
Rio Bravo del Norte
MEXICO
Monterrey

160°W 158°W 156°W
Kauai
Niihau
Oahu
Pearl Harbor
HAWAII
Molokai
Maui
Lanai
Kahoolawe
Hawaii
Mauna Loa 4169 m
PACIFIC OCEAN
22°N
20°N
18°N

0   100   200 miles
0 100 200 kilometers

Point Barrow
Chukchi Sea
Beaufort Sea
70°N
RUSSIA
Brooks Range
Seward Peninsula
ARCTIC CIRCLE
65°N
ALASKA
CANADA
St. Lawrence I.
Norton Sound
Yukon R.
Kuskokwim R.
Mt. McKinley 6194 m
Alaska Range
Anchorage
60°N
Nunivak I.
Kenai Peninsula
Gulf of Alaska
Bering Sea
Alaska Peninsula
Kodiak I.
Alexander Archipelago
55°N
Aleutian Islands
135°W

0   200   400 miles
0 200 400 kilometers

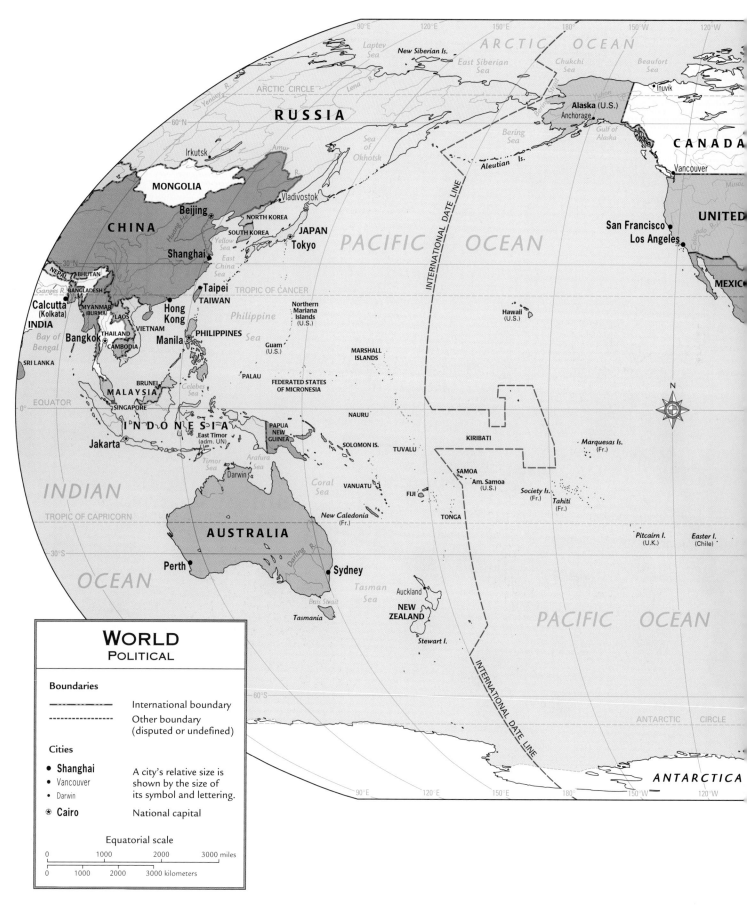

ARCTIC OCEAN

Laptev Sea
New Siberian Is.
East Siberian Sea
Chukchi Sea
Beaufort Sea

ARCTIC CIRCLE

Yenisey R.
Lena
Ob R.

RUSSIA

60°N

Irkutsk

Amur R.

Sea of Okhotsk

Vladivostok

Alaska (U.S.)
Anchorage
Gulf of Alaska
• Inuvik

CANADA

Vancouver

Bering Sea
Aleutian Is.

MONGOLIA

Beijing ⊛
NORTH KOREA

CHINA

SOUTH KOREA
JAPAN
Tokyo

PACIFIC OCEAN

San Francisco
Los Angeles

UNITED

Huang He
Shanghai

Yellow Sea
East China Sea

30°N

INTERNATIONAL DATE LINE

NEPAL BHUTAN
Ganges R. BANGLADESH
Taipei
TAIWAN

TROPIC OF CANCER

Hawaii (U.S.)

MEXICO

Calcutta (Kolkata)
MYANMAR (BURMA)
LAOS
INDIA
THAILAND VIETNAM
Bangkok ⊛ CAMBODIA
Hong Kong
Manila • PHILIPPINES

Philippine Sea

Northern Mariana Islands (U.S.)

Bay of Bengal

SRI LANKA

Guam (U.S.)

MARSHALL ISLANDS

N

BRUNEI
MALAYSIA
SINGAPORE

Celebes Sea

PALAU

FEDERATED STATES OF MICRONESIA

EQUATOR
0°

I N D O N E S I A
Jakarta ⊛
East Timor (adm. UN)

PAPUA NEW GUINEA

NAURU

KIRIBATI

Marquesas Is. (Fr.)

Timor Sea
Arafura Sea

SOLOMON IS.

TUVALU

Darwin •

Coral Sea

VANUATU

SAMOA
Am. Samoa (U.S.)

Society Is. (Fr.)

Tahiti (Fr.)

INDIAN

AUSTRALIA

New Caledonia (Fr.)

FIJI

TONGA

TROPIC OF CAPRICORN

Pitcairn I. (U.K.)

Easter I. (Chile)

30°S

Perth •

Darling R.

Sydney

OCEAN

Tasman Sea

Auckland

PACIFIC OCEAN

Bass Strait
Tasmania

NEW ZEALAND

Stewart I.

60°S

INTERNATIONAL DATE LINE

ANTARCTIC CIRCLE

90°E   120°E   150°E   180°   150°W   120°W

ANTARCTICA

WORLD
POLITICAL

Boundaries

— ·· — ·· —   International boundary

- - - - - - - -   Other boundary (disputed or undefined)

Cities

● **Shanghai**   A city's relative size is
● Vancouver   shown by the size of
• Darwin   its symbol and lettering.

⊛ **Cairo**   National capital

Equatorial scale

0   1000   2000   3000 miles

0   1000   2000   3000 kilometers

ARCTIC OCEAN

Severnaya Zemlya
New Siberian Is.
Laptev Sea
East Siberian Sea
Chukchi Sea
Banks I.
Victoria I.
Beaufort Sea

Central Siberian Plateau

Verkhoyansk Range
ARCTIC CIRCLE
Kolyma Range

Siberia

Bering Strait
Alaska Yukon (U.S.)
Mt. McKinley 6194 m

ASIA

Gobi

Amur R.

Sea of Okhotsk
Kamchatka Peninsula
Bering Sea

Kodiak I.
Gulf of Alaska

Rocky Mountains

Gr

Tien Shan
Altai Mts.

Manchurian Plain
Sakhalin
Aleutian Is.

Queen Charlotte Is.

AME

Kunlun Mts.
Plateau of Tibet

Huang He

North China Plain
Yellow Sea

Kuril Is.
Hokkaido

Honshu

Sea of Japan

PACIFIC OCEAN

Vancouver I.

Missouri R.

Mt. Everest 8850 m

Yunnan Plateau

East China Sea
Kyushu

Sierra Ma

Ganges River

Ryukyu Is.
TROPIC OF CANCER

C. San Lucas

Bay of Bengal

Taiwan

Sri Lanka

South China Sea

Philippine Is.

Philippine Sea

Mariana Is.

Hawaiian Islands

Caroline Is.

EQUATOR
Sumatra

Borneo

Celebes Sea

EQUATOR

N

Sulawesi

Java

New Guinea
Solomon Is.

INDIAN OCEAN

Timor
Timor Sea
Arafura Sea

Coral Sea

Fiji Is.

Tuamotu Archipelago

TROPIC OF CAPRICORN

Great Sandy Desert

AUSTRALIA

Great Dividing Range

New Caledonia

Pitcairn I.

Easter I.

30°S

C. Leeuwin

Mt. Kosciuszko 2228 m
Darling R.

Tasman Sea

North I.

PACIFIC

Bass Strait
Tasmania

South I.

Stewart I.

OCEAN

Auckland Is.

60°S

ANTARCTIC

ANTARCTICA

WORLD
PHYSICAL

Elevation		
Meters		Feet
Over 6000		Over 20,000
3000 to 6000		10,000 to 20,000
1500 to 3000		5,000 to 10,000
600 to 1500		2,000 to 5,000
300 to 600		1,000 to 2,000
150 to 300		500 to 1,000
0 to 150		0 to 500
Below sea level		Below sea level

Water Depth

Less than 200		Less than 600
Greater than 200		Greater than 600

International boundary
Other boundary

Equatorial scale

0   1000   2000   3000 miles

0   1000   2000   3000 kilometers

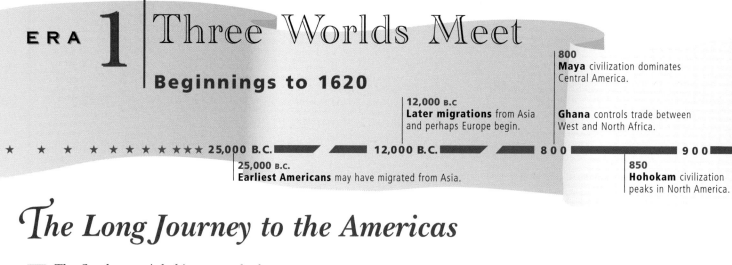

800
Maya civilization dominates Central America.

12,000 B.C
Later migrations from Asia and perhaps Europe begin.

Ghana controls trade between West and North Africa.

★ ★ ★ ★ ★ ★★★ **25,000 B.C.** ▮ **12,000 B.C.** ▮ **800** ▮ **900** ▮

25,000 B.C.
Earliest Americans may have migrated from Asia.

850
Hohokam civilization peaks in North America.

The Long Journey to the Americas

- The first human inhabitants reached North and South America long after Africa, Europe, and Asia were populated.

- During the last Ice Age, sea level dropped. People could walk from Asia to what is now Alaska.

- Some then walked to warmer parts of North America by an ice-free route east of the Rocky Mountains.

- Most people, however, probably came in boats. They followed the edge of the ice: most of them from Asia, some from Europe.

50,000 B.C. — Bering Strait

25,000–9,000 B.C. — Bering Land Bridge

Today — Bering Strait

CHANGING SEA LEVEL

Sea level dropped during the Ice Ages, exposing dry land at the Bering Strait. When the ice later melted, the seas rose.

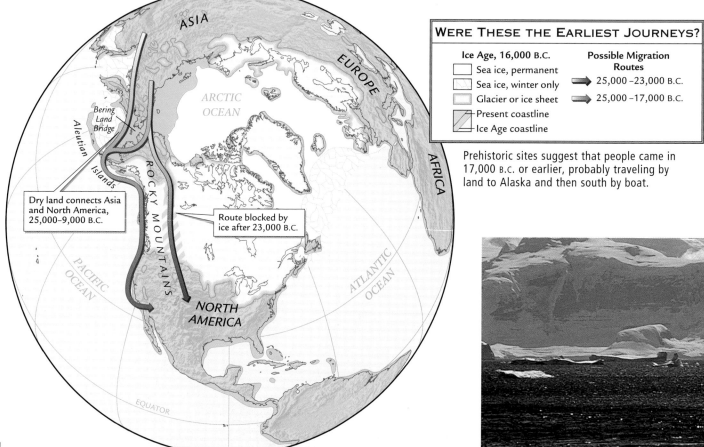

ASIA

EUROPE

ARCTIC OCEAN

AFRICA

Bering Land Bridge

Aleutian Islands

ROCKY MOUNTAINS

Dry land connects Asia and North America, 25,000–9,000 B.C.

Route blocked by ice after 23,000 B.C.

PACIFIC OCEAN

ATLANTIC OCEAN

NORTH AMERICA

EQUATOR

WERE THESE THE EARLIEST JOURNEYS?

Ice Age, 16,000 B.C.

☐ Sea ice, permanent
▨ Sea ice, winter only
▨ Glacier or ice sheet
Present coastline
Ice Age coastline

Possible Migration Routes
➡ 25,000 –23,000 B.C.
➡ 25,000 –17,000 B.C.

Prehistoric sites suggest that people came in 17,000 B.C. or earlier, probably traveling by land to Alaska and then south by boat.

14

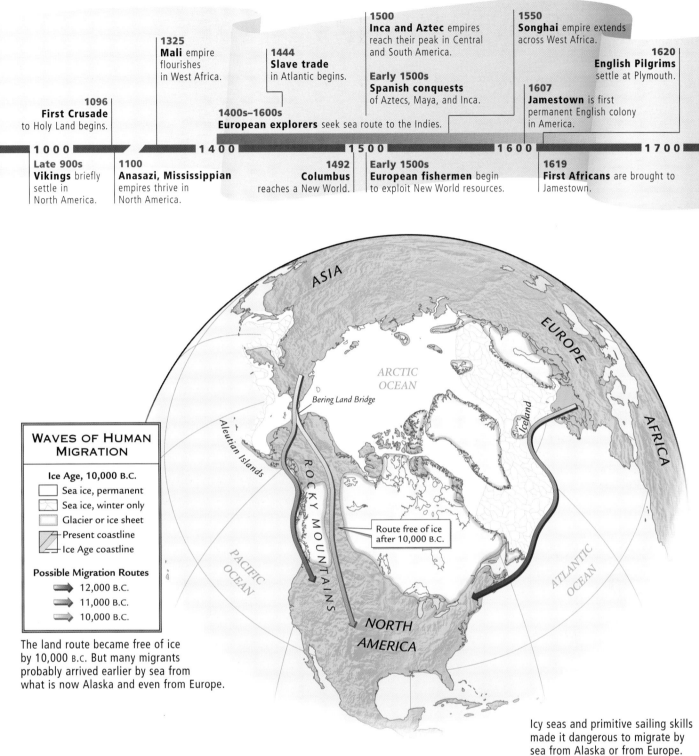

1096
First Crusade to Holy Land begins.

1325
Mali empire flourishes in West Africa.

1444
Slave trade in Atlantic begins.

1500
Inca and Aztec empires reach their peak in Central and South America.

Early 1500s
Spanish conquests of Aztecs, Maya, and Inca.

1550
Songhai empire extends across West Africa.

1620
English Pilgrims settle at Plymouth.

1607
Jamestown is first permanent English colony in America.

1400s–1600s
European explorers seek sea route to the Indies.

| 1000 | 1400 | 1500 | 1600 | 1700 |

Late 900s
Vikings briefly settle in North America.

1100
Anasazi, Mississippian empires thrive in North America.

1492
Columbus reaches a New World.

Early 1500s
European fishermen begin to exploit New World resources.

1619
First Africans are brought to Jamestown.

WAVES OF HUMAN MIGRATION

Ice Age, 10,000 B.C.

☐ Sea ice, permanent
☒ Sea ice, winter only
▨ Glacier or ice sheet
▨ Present coastline
— Ice Age coastline

Possible Migration Routes
➡ 12,000 B.C.
➡ 11,000 B.C.
➡ 10,000 B.C.

ASIA

EUROPE

AFRICA

ARCTIC OCEAN

Bering Land Bridge

Aleutian Islands

Iceland

R O C K Y   M O U N T A I N S

PACIFIC OCEAN

Route free of ice after 10,000 B.C.

ATLANTIC OCEAN

NORTH AMERICA

The land route became free of ice by 10,000 B.C. But many migrants probably arrived earlier by sea from what is now Alaska and even from Europe.

Icy seas and primitive sailing skills made it dangerous to migrate by sea from Alaska or from Europe.

The World of the First Americans

- Thousands of years after migration ended, most people in the Americas lived in small hunting or farming villages. But complex empires emerged too.

- The Maya flourished from 250 to about 900. They built pyramids and developed an accurate calendar.

- The Aztecs ruled their region from the early 1400s to 1521. They built canals, aqueducts, and large cities.

- The Incas expanded along the Andes Mountains from 1438 to 1532. They devised bookkeeping, a road network, even brain surgery.

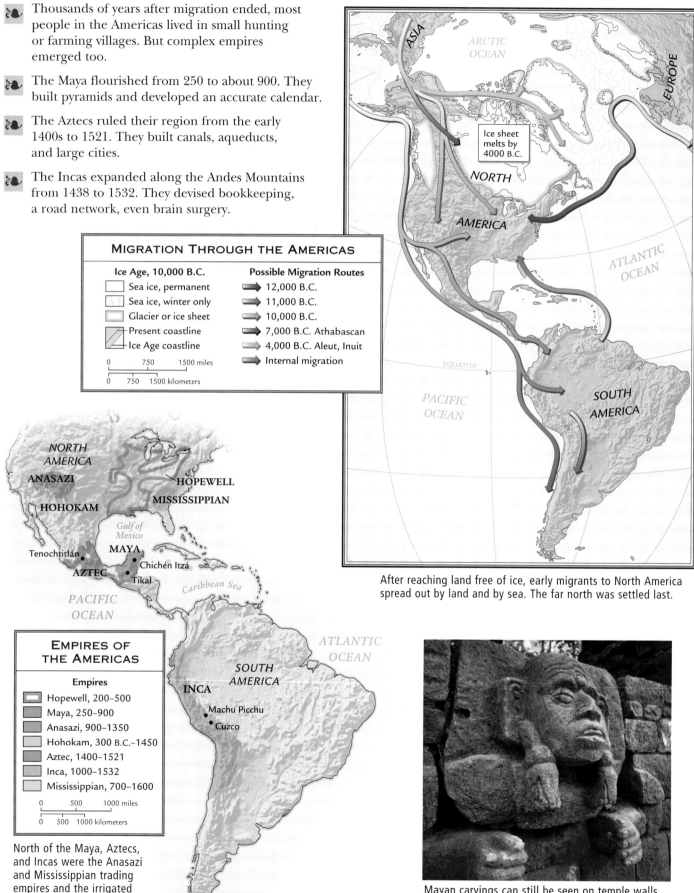

MIGRATION THROUGH THE AMERICAS

Ice Age, 10,000 B.C.
- Sea ice, permanent
- Sea ice, winter only
- Glacier or ice sheet
- Present coastline
- Ice Age coastline

0   750   1500 miles
0   750   1500 kilometers

Possible Migration Routes
- 12,000 B.C.
- 11,000 B.C.
- 10,000 B.C.
- 7,000 B.C. Athabascan
- 4,000 B.C. Aleut, Inuit
- Internal migration

Ice sheet melts by 4000 B.C.

ASIA   ARCTIC OCEAN   EUROPE
NORTH AMERICA   ATLANTIC OCEAN
EQUATOR
PACIFIC OCEAN   SOUTH AMERICA

After reaching land free of ice, early migrants to North America spread out by land and by sea. The far north was settled last.

NORTH AMERICA
ANASAZI   HOPEWELL
HOHOKAM   MISSISSIPPIAN
Gulf of Mexico
Tenochtitlán   MAYA
AZTEC   Chichén Itzá
Tikal
PACIFIC OCEAN   Caribbean Sea
ATLANTIC OCEAN
SOUTH AMERICA
INCA
Machu Picchu
Cuzco

EMPIRES OF THE AMERICAS

Empires
- Hopewell, 200–500
- Maya, 250–900
- Anasazi, 900–1350
- Hohokam, 300 B.C.–1450
- Aztec, 1400–1521
- Inca, 1000–1532
- Mississippian, 700–1600

0   500   1000 miles
0   500   1000 kilometers

North of the Maya, Aztecs, and Incas were the Anasazi and Mississippian trading empires and the irrigated lands of the Hohokam.

Mayan carvings can still be seen on temple walls in Mexico, Guatemala, and Belize.

16

The World of West Africa

- Trade with Mediterranean ports linked West Africa to Europe and Asia 1700 years ago.

- Empires and smaller kingdoms developed along the southern edge of the Sahara, connected to the north by trade routes.

- The most powerful empires controlled the north bend of the Niger River, gateway to the shortest routes to Europe.

- Ghana, then Mali, and finally Songhai each dominated West Africa in turn.

- Timbuktu, the capital of Mali, and Gao, capital of Songhai, were important centers of learning.

Arab traders carried goods by camel caravan between Mediterranean ports and West African empires. They traded luxury goods from Europe and salt from the Sahara for gold, leather, and slaves from West Africa.

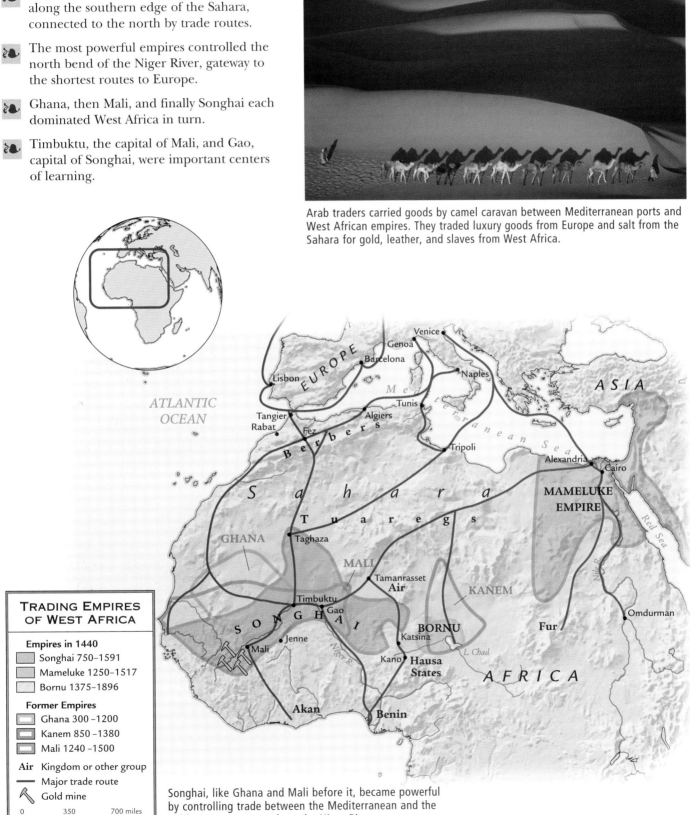

TRADING EMPIRES OF WEST AFRICA

Empires in 1440
- Songhai 750–1591
- Mameluke 1250–1517
- Bornu 1375–1896

Former Empires
- Ghana 300–1200
- Kanem 850–1380
- Mali 1240–1500

Air Kingdom or other group
— Major trade route
⚒ Gold mine

0   350   700 miles
0   350   700 kilometers

Songhai, like Ghana and Mali before it, became powerful by controlling trade between the Mediterranean and the gold mines upstream along the Niger River.

17

The World of Europe

- The period from about 1350 to 1600 in Europe is known as the *Renaissance*.

- The Renaissance was marked by a revival of learning, as Europeans studied both the ancient world and what was known of their own world.

- The new printing press, invented in the 1450s, let knowledge spread quickly and inexpensively. Art, science, and exploration flourished.

- Seafaring nations used newly acquired knowledge to broaden trade, increase wealth, and gain power.

"The world is small and six parts of it are land, the seventh part being entirely covered by water."

—CHRISTOPHER COLUMBUS

Explorers sailing from Lisbon and other European ports knew that the earth was a sphere. What surprised them was how big it was.

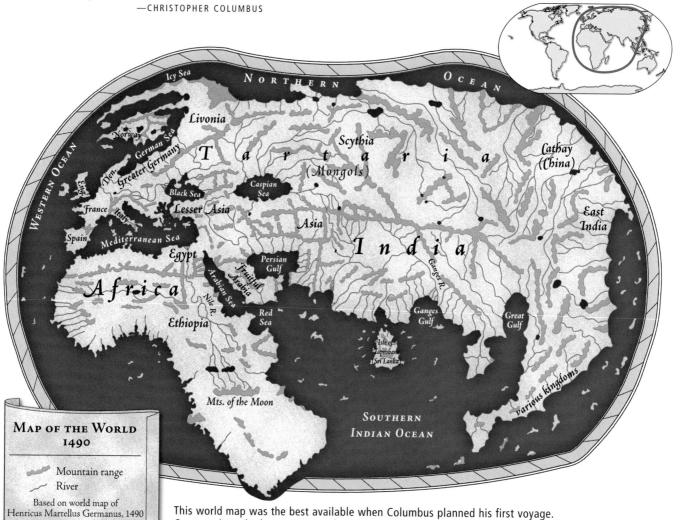

MAP OF THE WORLD
1490

〜 Mountain range
／ River

Based on world map of
Henricus Martellus Germanus, 1490

This world map was the best available when Columbus planned his first voyage. Compare it to the locator map and to the world maps on pages 10–13.

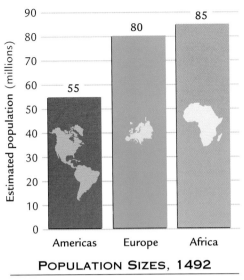

POPULATION SIZES, 1492

Europe was smaller and more crowded than Africa and the Americas, and far more of its people lived in cities.

The modern city of Venice is part of Italy, but 500 years ago it was the heart of a powerful seafaring and trading nation of its own.

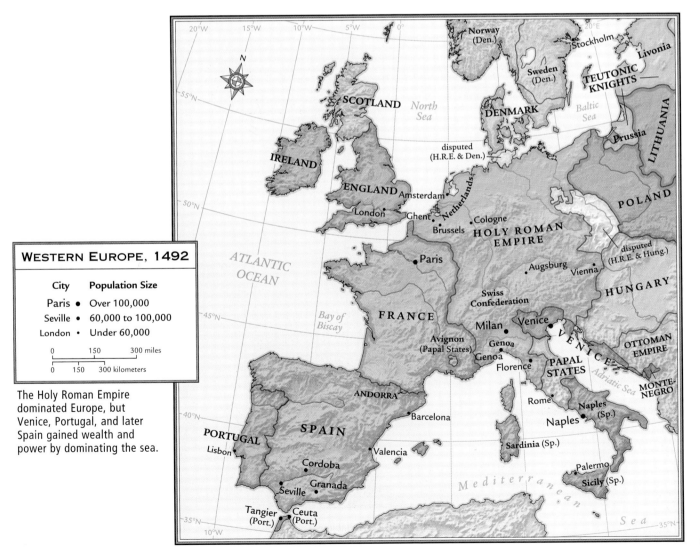

WESTERN EUROPE, 1492

City	Population Size
Paris ●	Over 100,000
Seville ●	60,000 to 100,000
London ●	Under 60,000

0   150   300 miles
0   150   300 kilometers

The Holy Roman Empire dominated Europe, but Venice, Portugal, and later Spain gained wealth and power by dominating the sea.

Trade With the Indies Spurs Exploration

- From the 1000s through the 1200s, European soldiers returned from the Crusades in the Middle East carrying treasures from Asia as souvenirs.

- Soon Europeans were trading for spices, perfume, precious stones, and other goods from the region they knew as the Indies.

- During the 1400s, the Ottoman Empire gained control of routes to the Indies and blocked trade.

- Portugal and Spain sought trade routes that they could control. Portugal looked for an eastern route; Spain looked for a western one.

Smooth, colorful, and lightweight, silk has been valued for thousands of years. Its origin in China established the Indies as a source of prized goods even after silk production had spread to western Asia and Europe.

The Ottoman Empire sought power and converts to Islam, not trade. During the 1400s and early 1500s, it cut off European access to trade routes to the Indies, including the famous Silk Road.

CUTTING OFF EURASIAN TRADE

- Ottoman Empire, 1481
- Ottoman conquests, 1481–1520
- Trade route

0   500   1000 miles
0   500   1000 kilometers

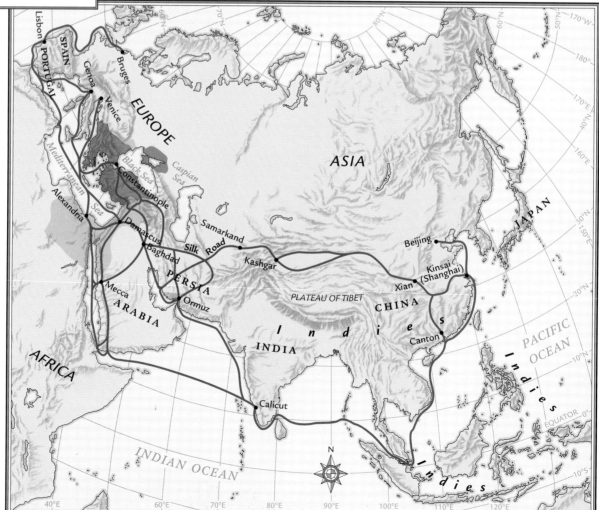

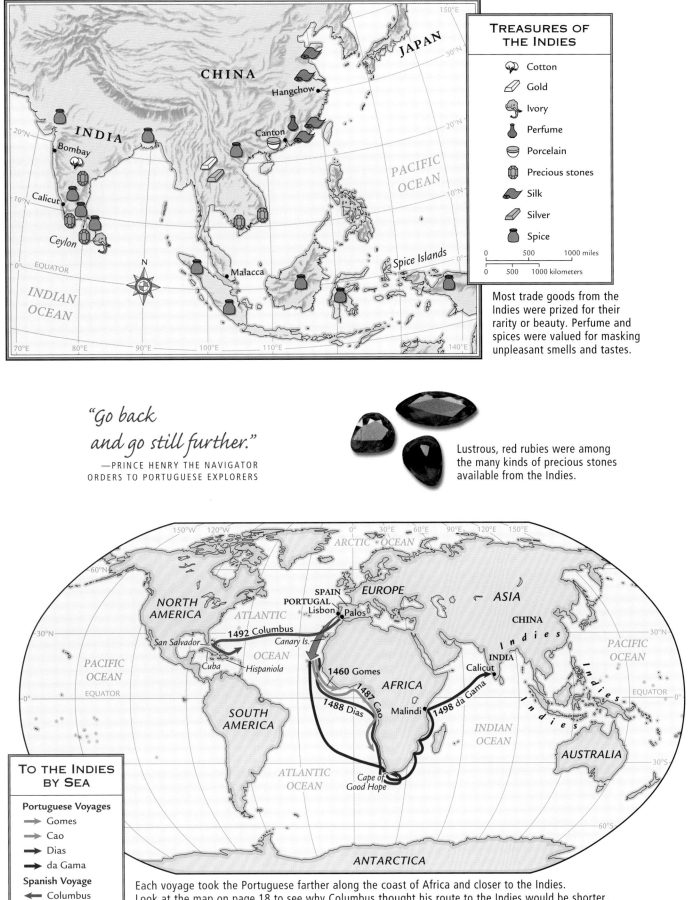

TREASURES OF THE INDIES

- 🌿 Cotton
- Gold
- Ivory
- Perfume
- Porcelain
- Precious stones
- Silk
- Silver
- Spice

0   500   1000 miles
0   500   1000 kilometers

Most trade goods from the Indies were prized for their rarity or beauty. Perfume and spices were valued for masking unpleasant smells and tastes.

"Go back and go still further."
—PRINCE HENRY THE NAVIGATOR
ORDERS TO PORTUGUESE EXPLORERS

Lustrous, red rubies were among the many kinds of precious stones available from the Indies.

TO THE INDIES BY SEA

Portuguese Voyages
→ Gomes
→ Cao
→ Dias
→ da Gama

Spanish Voyage
← Columbus

Each voyage took the Portuguese farther along the coast of Africa and closer to the Indies. Look at the map on page 18 to see why Columbus thought his route to the Indies would be shorter.

Europeans Explore the New World

In the 900s Vikings from Scandinavia sailed to North America. But word of this unfamiliar land did not reach the rest of Europe.

Five hundred years later, Columbus believed he had reached the islands of the Indies and referred to their inhabitants as Indians.

After finding no sign of the cities and treasures of the Indies, other European explorers began calling the Americas the *New World*.

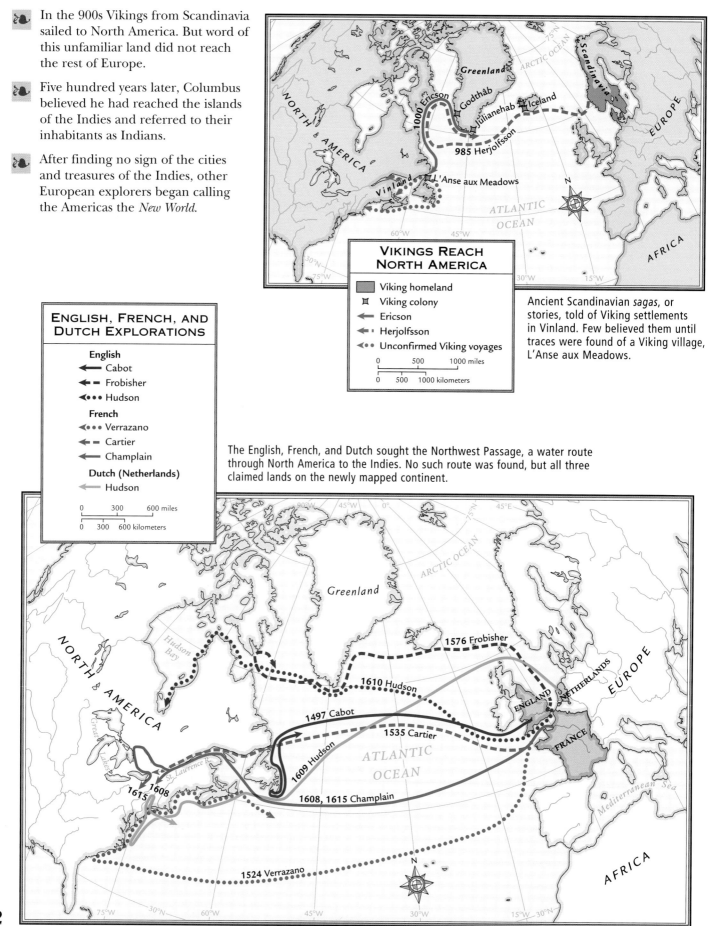

VIKINGS REACH NORTH AMERICA

- Viking homeland
- Viking colony
- Ericson
- Herjolfsson
- Unconfirmed Viking voyages

0   500   1000 miles
0   500   1000 kilometers

Ancient Scandinavian *sagas*, or stories, told of Viking settlements in Vinland. Few believed them until traces were found of a Viking village, L'Anse aux Meadows.

ENGLISH, FRENCH, AND DUTCH EXPLORATIONS

English
- Cabot
- Frobisher
- Hudson

French
- Verrazano
- Cartier
- Champlain

Dutch (Netherlands)
- Hudson

0   300   600 miles
0   300   600 kilometers

The English, French, and Dutch sought the Northwest Passage, a water route through North America to the Indies. No such route was found, but all three claimed lands on the newly mapped continent.

Treasures of the Incas and the Aztecs fueled Spain's quest for gold.

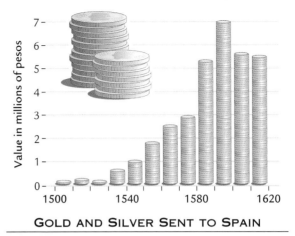

GOLD AND SILVER SENT TO SPAIN

Spanish explorers soon stopped looking for the Indies and started looking for gold. They mined silver and seized gold objects made by Aztecs and other Native Americans.

The Spanish explored coasts and traveled inland searching for gold. They based their land claims on their explorations and their conquests of native empires.

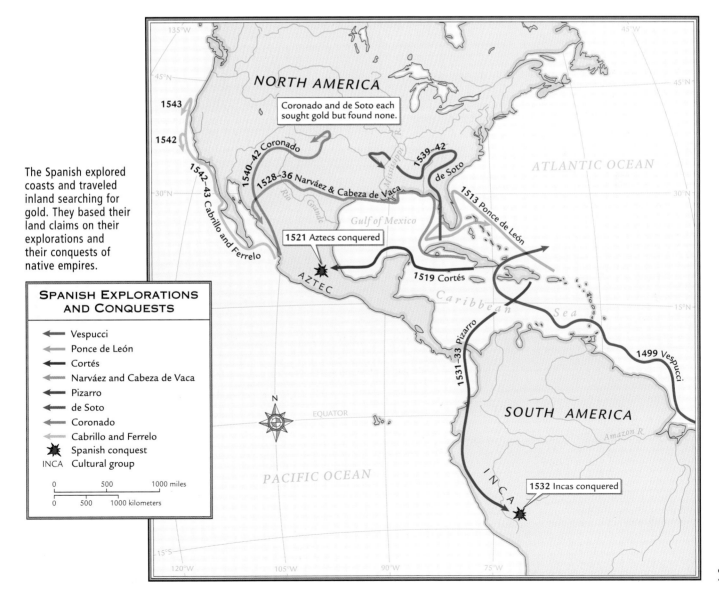

Coronado and de Soto each sought gold but found none.

1521 Aztecs conquered

1519 Cortés

1532 Incas conquered

SPANISH EXPLORATIONS AND CONQUESTS

- Vespucci
- Ponce de León
- Cortés
- Narváez and Cabeza de Vaca
- Pizarro
- de Soto
- Coronado
- Cabrillo and Ferrelo
- ✸ Spanish conquest
- INCA Cultural group

Exploitation and Settlement Begin

- People of the Americas, West Africa, and Europe came together in the New World.

- By the mid-1400s, Portuguese ships reached the African homeland of people long prized in Europe as slaves. The Atlantic slave trade was born.

- In the early 1500s, the Spanish enslaved the Caribbean Indians. When the Indians died, slave ships brought Africans to replace them.

- Soon European fishing captains and landlords made fortunes in the Americas. Indians and Africans died there of disease and overwork.

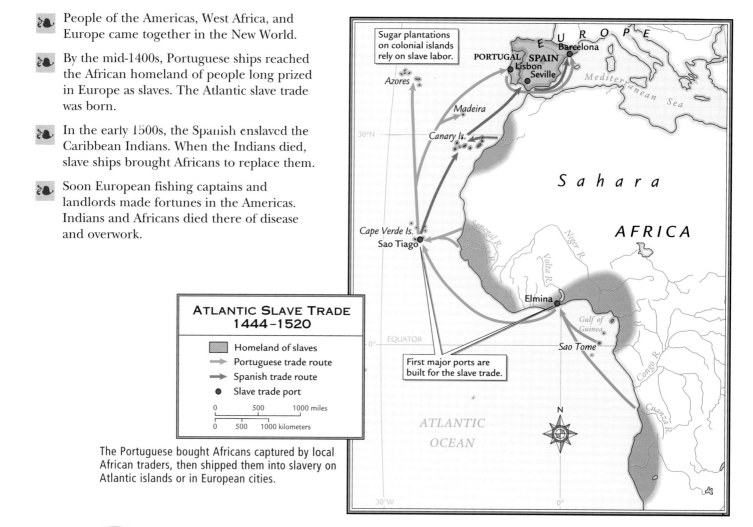

Sugar plantations on colonial islands rely on slave labor.

First major ports are built for the slave trade.

ATLANTIC SLAVE TRADE 1444–1520

- Homeland of slaves
- Portuguese trade route
- Spanish trade route
- Slave trade port

The Portuguese bought Africans captured by local African traders, then shipped them into slavery on Atlantic islands or in European cities.

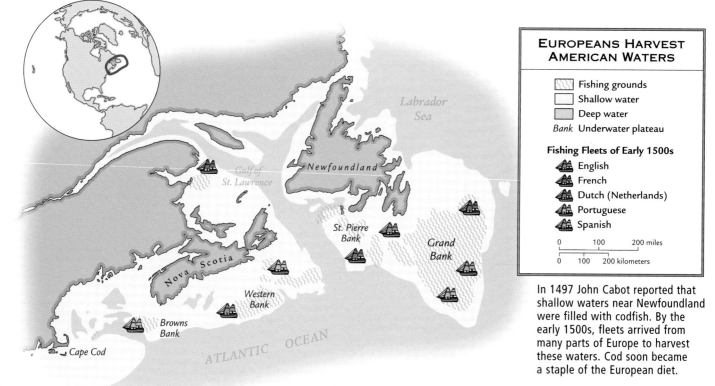

EUROPEANS HARVEST AMERICAN WATERS

- Fishing grounds
- Shallow water
- Deep water
- *Bank* Underwater plateau

Fishing Fleets of Early 1500s
- English
- French
- Dutch (Netherlands)
- Portuguese
- Spanish

In 1497 John Cabot reported that shallow waters near Newfoundland were filled with codfish. By the early 1500s, fleets arrived from many parts of Europe to harvest these waters. Cod soon became a staple of the European diet.

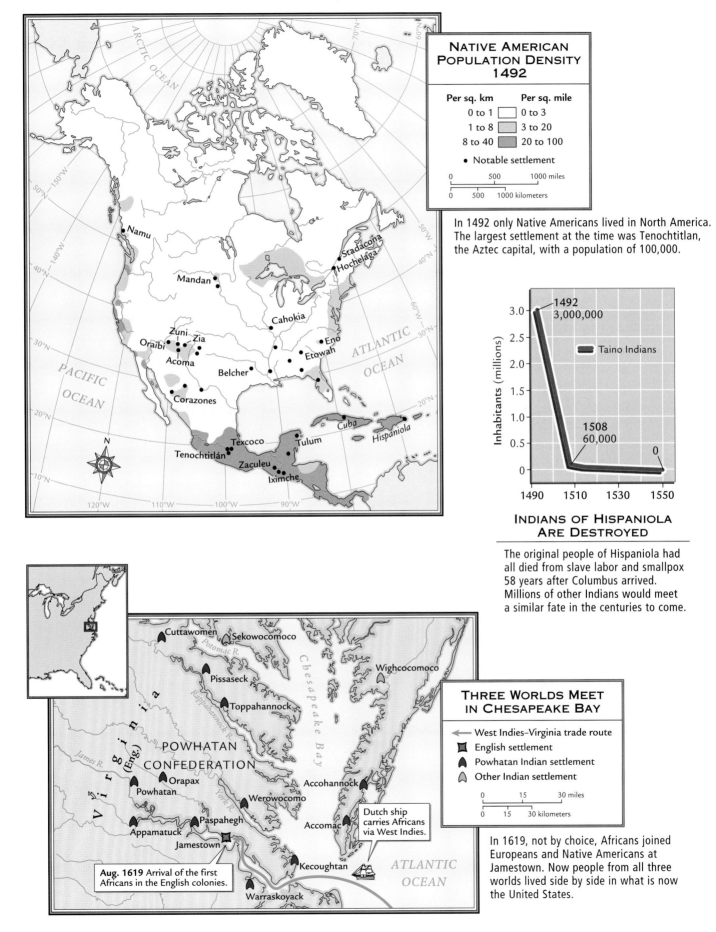

NATIVE AMERICAN POPULATION DENSITY 1492

Per sq. km	Per sq. mile
0 to 1	0 to 3
1 to 8	3 to 20
8 to 40	20 to 100

• Notable settlement

In 1492 only Native Americans lived in North America. The largest settlement at the time was Tenochtitlan, the Aztec capital, with a population of 100,000.

INDIANS OF HISPANIOLA ARE DESTROYED

The original people of Hispaniola had all died from slave labor and smallpox 58 years after Columbus arrived. Millions of other Indians would meet a similar fate in the centuries to come.

THREE WORLDS MEET IN CHESAPEAKE BAY

← West Indies–Virginia trade route
◆ English settlement
◣ Powhatan Indian settlement
◺ Other Indian settlement

Dutch ship carries Africans via West Indies.

Aug. 1619 Arrival of the first Africans in the English colonies.

In 1619, not by choice, Africans joined Europeans and Native Americans at Jamestown. Now people from all three worlds lived side by side in what is now the United States.

25

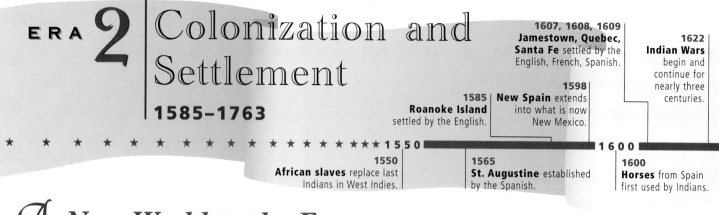

1607, 1608, 1609
Jamestown, Quebec, Santa Fe settled by the English, French, Spanish.

1622
Indian Wars begin and continue for nearly three centuries.

1598
New Spain extends into what is now New Mexico.

1585
Roanoke Island settled by the English.

1550

1600

1550
African slaves replace last Indians in West Indies.

1565
St. Augustine established by the Spanish.

1600
Horses from Spain first used by Indians.

A New World to the Europeans

- Europeans thought the natural resources of the New World—as they called the Americas—were unlimited, to be used as they pleased.

- Long before Europeans arrived, Native Americans had developed many different cultures and ways of life based on the same resources.

- The meeting of the Old World with the New had a cultural impact that began with Columbus.

- As explorers crisscrossed the Atlantic, they introduced new plants, animals, and even germs to both areas of the world.

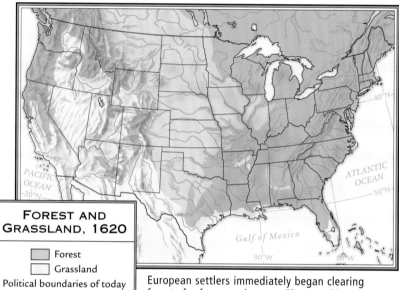

FOREST AND GRASSLAND, 1620

- Forest
- Grassland

Political boundaries of today

European settlers immediately began clearing forests for farms and towns. They used large amounts of wood for lumber and fuel.

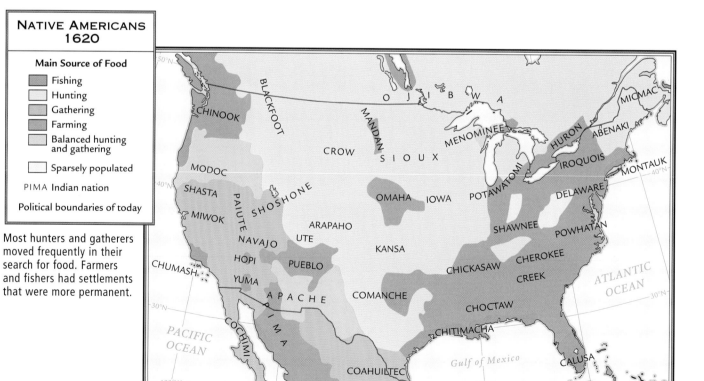

NATIVE AMERICANS 1620

Main Source of Food

- Fishing
- Hunting
- Gathering
- Farming
- Balanced hunting and gathering
- Sparsely populated

PIMA Indian nation

Political boundaries of today

Most hunters and gatherers moved frequently in their search for food. Farmers and fishers had settlements that were more permanent.

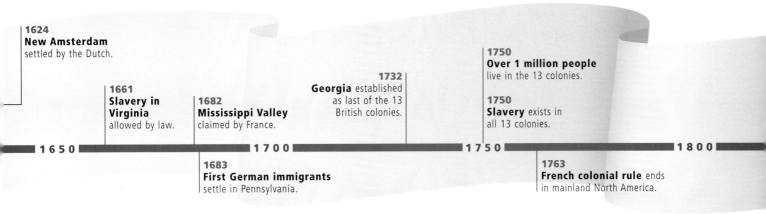

1624
New Amsterdam
settled by the Dutch.

1661
Slavery in Virginia
allowed by law.

1682
Mississippi Valley
claimed by France.

1732
Georgia established as last of the 13 British colonies.

1750
Over 1 million people live in the 13 colonies.

1750
Slavery exists in all 13 colonies.

1650   1700   1750   1800

1683
First German immigrants settle in Pennsylvania.

1763
French colonial rule ends in mainland North America.

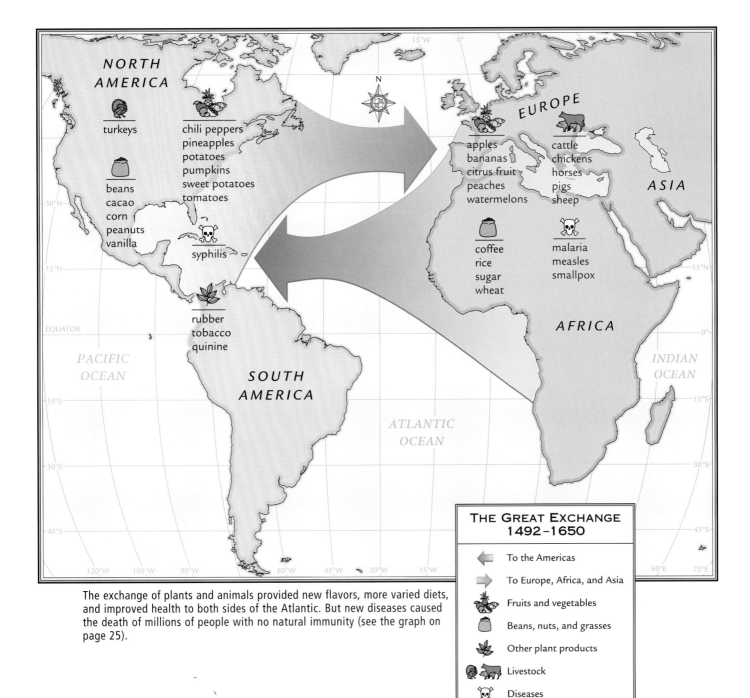

The exchange of plants and animals provided new flavors, more varied diets, and improved health to both sides of the Atlantic. But new diseases caused the death of millions of people with no natural immunity (see the graph on page 25).

Early Claims, Early Conflicts

🐚 European explorers claimed vast areas of the Americas for the countries that sponsored their expeditions.

🐚 The largest land claims were made by Spain, France, and England.

🐚 The European powers were confident of their right to claim the Americas as their own.

🐚 European claims quickly caused violent conflict with Native Americans throughout the hemisphere.

The first horses in the Americas were brought by Spanish explorers, such as this one drawn by Frederic Remington (color added). When Plains Indians captured and learned to ride horses, their lives were transformed.

SPAIN'S EMPIRE IN THE NEW WORLD

Viceroyalties

New Spain
New Castile
New Andalusia

Political boundaries of 1625

0   500   1000 miles
0 500 1000 kilometers

Spain gained much of its territory by conquering the Aztecs in Mexico and the Incas in South America. See the map on page 23.

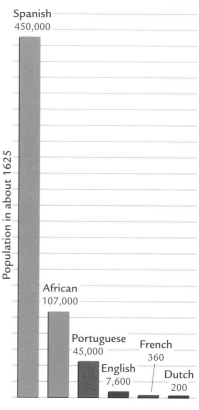

Population in about 1625

- Spanish 450,000
- African 107,000
- Portuguese 45,000
- English 7,600
- French 360
- Dutch 200

NEWCOMERS TO THE AMERICAS

In the early 1600s, most Africans in the Americas were slaves in the West Indies and Brazil.

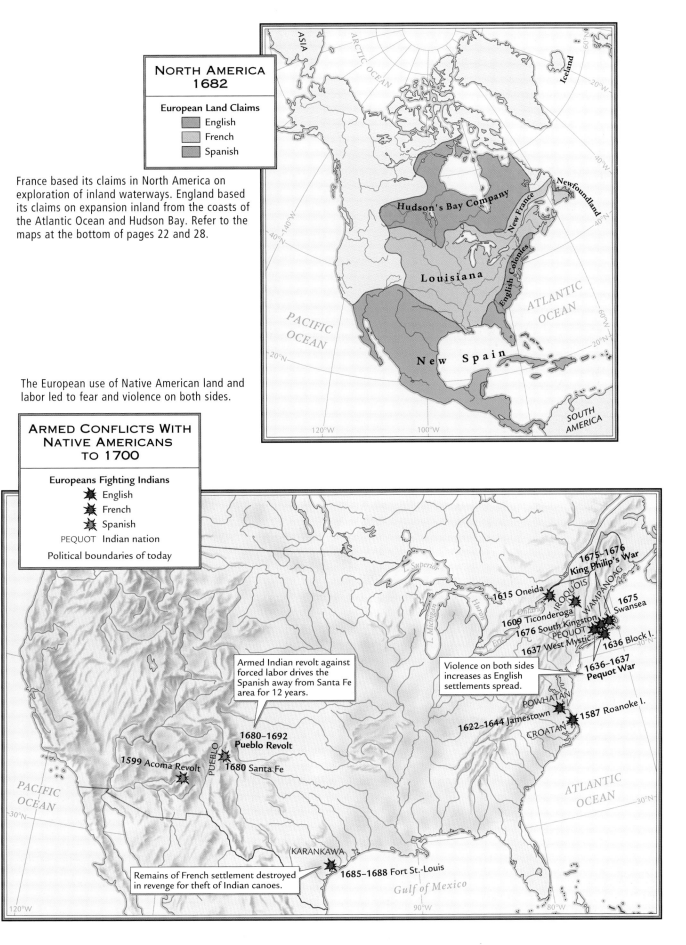

NORTH AMERICA 1682

European Land Claims

- English
- French
- Spanish

France based its claims in North America on exploration of inland waterways. England based its claims on expansion inland from the coasts of the Atlantic Ocean and Hudson Bay. Refer to the maps at the bottom of pages 22 and 28.

The European use of Native American land and labor led to fear and violence on both sides.

ARMED CONFLICTS WITH NATIVE AMERICANS TO 1700

Europeans Fighting Indians

- English
- French
- Spanish

PEQUOT   Indian nation

Political boundaries of today

Armed Indian revolt against forced labor drives the Spanish away from Santa Fe area for 12 years.

Violence on both sides increases as English settlements spread.

Remains of French settlement destroyed in revenge for theft of Indian canoes.

1680–1692 Pueblo Revolt

1599 Acoma Revolt

1680 Santa Fe

1685–1688 Fort St.-Louis

KARANKAWA

1675–1676 King Philip's War

1615 Oneida

1675 Swansea

1609 Ticonderoga

1676 South Kingston

1637 West Mystic

1636 Block I.

1636–1637 Pequot War

1622–1644 Jamestown

1587 Roanoke I.

POWHATAN

CROATAN

29

European Settlements in North America

- The Spanish settled in areas originally claimed by Columbus, Ponce de León, de Soto, and Coronado.

- The French and Dutch settled farther north in areas first explored by Cartier and Hudson.

- English and Swedish colonists settled in previously unclaimed lands along the Atlantic coast.

- Some colonists sought freedom in a new land. Others were committed to long terms of hard labor. Still others came to make their fortunes and return to Europe.

"...to give light to those who were in darkness, and to procure wealth which all men desire."

—BERNAL DIAZ DEL CASTILLO
ON THE GOALS OF THE SPANISH CONQUERORS
OF INDIAN CIVILIZATIONS

Taos Pueblo is more than 200 years older than nearby Santa Fe, the oldest Spanish settlement in the area. It survives as home to descendants of its Pueblo Indian builders.

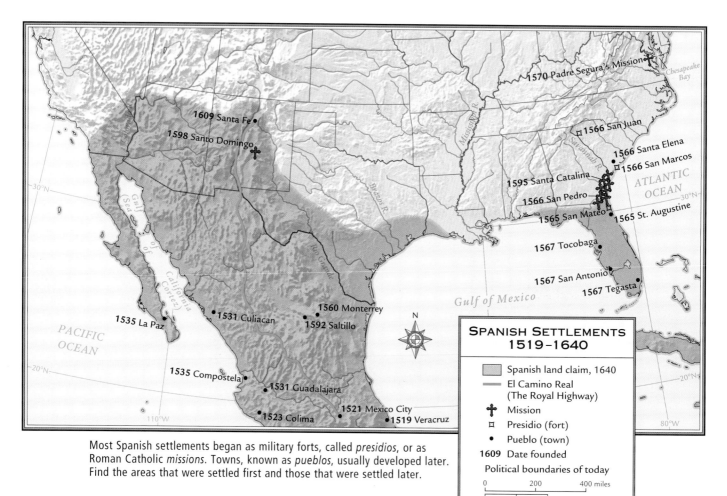

SPANISH SETTLEMENTS 1519–1640

- ▨ Spanish land claim, 1640
- ─── El Camino Real (The Royal Highway)
- ✝ Mission
- ⚑ Presidio (fort)
- • Pueblo (town)
- **1609** Date founded

Political boundaries of today

| 0 | 200 | 400 miles |
| 0 | 200 | 400 kilometers |

Most Spanish settlements began as military forts, called *presidios*, or as Roman Catholic *missions*. Towns, known as *pueblos*, usually developed later. Find the areas that were settled first and those that were settled later.

30

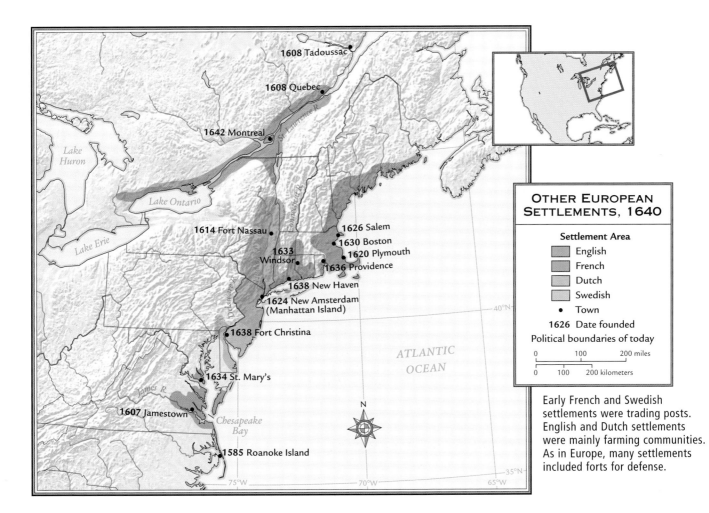

OTHER EUROPEAN SETTLEMENTS, 1640

Settlement Area
- English
- French
- Dutch
- Swedish
- • Town
- **1626** Date founded
- Political boundaries of today

0   100   200 miles
0   100   200 kilometers

Early French and Swedish settlements were trading posts. English and Dutch settlements were mainly farming communities. As in Europe, many settlements included forts for defense.

Map labels:
- **1608** Tadoussac
- **1608** Quebec
- **1642** Montreal
- **1614** Fort Nassau
- **1626** Salem
- **1630** Boston
- **1633** Windsor
- **1620** Plymouth
- **1636** Providence
- **1638** New Haven
- **1624** New Amsterdam (Manhattan Island)
- **1638** Fort Christina
- **1634** St. Mary's
- **1607** Jamestown
- **1585** Roanoke Island

Lake Huron, Lake Ontario, Lake Erie, St. Lawrence R., Connecticut R., Delaware R., James R., Chesapeake Bay, ATLANTIC OCEAN

40°N, 35°N, 75°W, 70°W, 65°W

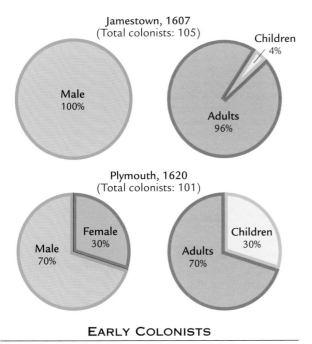

Jamestown, 1607
(Total colonists: 105)

Male 100%

Children 4%
Adults 96%

Plymouth, 1620
(Total colonists: 101)

Male 70%
Female 30%

Adults 70%
Children 30%

EARLY COLONISTS

Some colonies, such as Jamestown, were founded with the goal of gaining wealth. In others, such as Plymouth, the main goal was to start a new life in a new land. Compare these distinct groups of original settlers.

Just as they had in England, the colonists at Plymouth planted gardens and built board houses—some with thatched roofs—like those at the reconstructed historical site above. Log cabins were introduced by Swedish settlers.

The Thirteen British Colonies

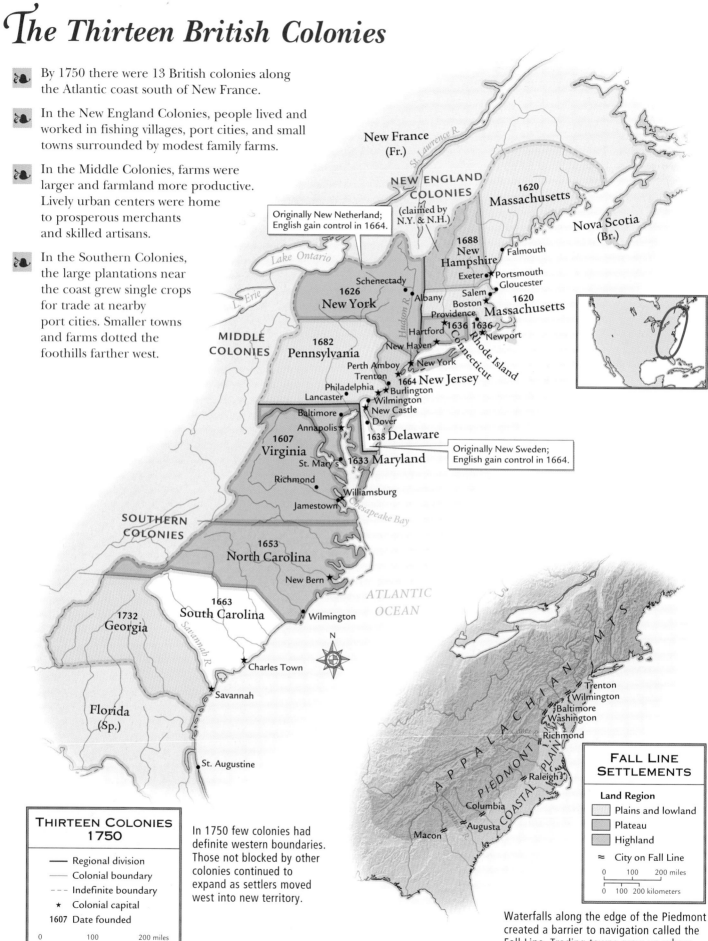

- By 1750 there were 13 British colonies along the Atlantic coast south of New France.

- In the New England Colonies, people lived and worked in fishing villages, port cities, and small towns surrounded by modest family farms.

- In the Middle Colonies, farms were larger and farmland more productive. Lively urban centers were home to prosperous merchants and skilled artisans.

- In the Southern Colonies, the large plantations near the coast grew single crops for trade at nearby port cities. Smaller towns and farms dotted the foothills farther west.

New France (Fr.)

St. Lawrence R.

NEW ENGLAND COLONIES (claimed by N.Y. & N.H.)

1620 Massachusetts

Nova Scotia (Br.)

Originally New Netherland; English gain control in 1664.

Lake Ontario

L. Erie

1626 New York

1688 New Hampshire

Falmouth

Exeter • Portsmouth
Gloucester

Salem

Schenectady

Albany • Boston ★

Providence

1620 Massachusetts

MIDDLE COLONIES

1682 Pennsylvania

Hudson R.

Hartford ★

1636 1636

New Haven ★

Newport ★

Connecticut

Rhode Island

Perth Amboy ★
Trenton ★

1664 New Jersey

Philadelphia ★ ★ Burlington

Lancaster •

Wilmington ★

Baltimore •

New Castle •

Annapolis ★

Dover •

1638 Delaware

1607 Virginia

St. Mary's ★

1633 Maryland

Originally New Sweden; English gain control in 1664.

Richmond •

Williamsburg ★

Jamestown ★

Chesapeake Bay

SOUTHERN COLONIES

1653 North Carolina

New Bern ★

ATLANTIC OCEAN

1663 South Carolina

Wilmington •

1732 Georgia

Savannah R.

Charles Town ★

Florida (Sp.)

Savannah ★

St. Augustine •

N

In 1750 few colonies had definite western boundaries. Those not blocked by other colonies continued to expand as settlers moved west into new territory.

THIRTEEN COLONIES 1750

— Regional division
— Colonial boundary
--- Indefinite boundary
★ Colonial capital
1607 Date founded

0 — 100 — 200 miles
0 — 100 — 200 kilometers

FALL LINE SETTLEMENTS

APPALACHIAN MTS.

Trenton
Wilmington
Baltimore
Washington
Richmond

PIEDMONT

COASTAL PLAIN

Raleigh

Columbia

Augusta

Macon

Land Region
☐ Plains and lowland
☐ Plateau
☐ Highland
≈ City on Fall Line

0 — 100 — 200 miles
0 — 100 — 200 kilometers

Waterfalls along the edge of the Piedmont created a barrier to navigation called the Fall Line. Trading towns grew up where goods to be carried past the falls were unloaded from boats.

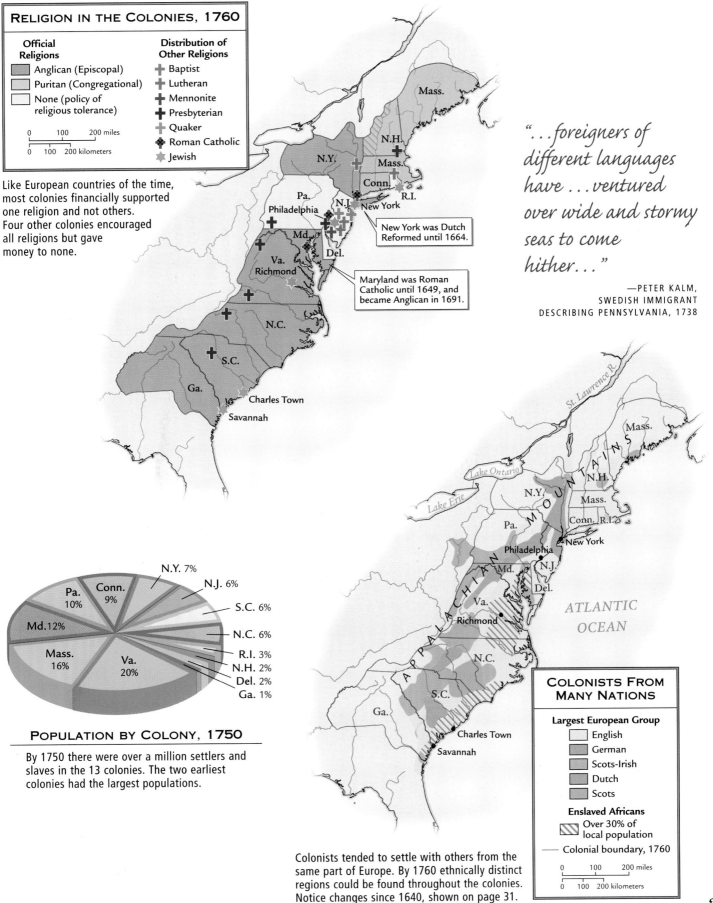

RELIGION IN THE COLONIES, 1760

Official Religions
- Anglican (Episcopal)
- Puritan (Congregational)
- None (policy of religious tolerance)

0   100   200 miles
0   100   200 kilometers

Distribution of Other Religions
- ✚ Baptist
- ✚ Lutheran
- ✚ Mennonite
- ✚ Presbyterian
- ✚ Quaker
- ✦ Roman Catholic
- ★ Jewish

Like European countries of the time, most colonies financially supported one religion and not others. Four other colonies encouraged all religions but gave money to none.

New York was Dutch Reformed until 1664.

Maryland was Roman Catholic until 1649, and became Anglican in 1691.

"...foreigners of different languages have ...ventured over wide and stormy seas to come hither..."

—PETER KALM, SWEDISH IMMIGRANT DESCRIBING PENNSYLVANIA, 1738

POPULATION BY COLONY, 1750

N.Y. 7%
Conn. 9%
Pa. 10%
Md. 12%
Mass. 16%
Va. 20%
N.J. 6%
S.C. 6%
N.C. 6%
R.I. 3%
N.H. 2%
Del. 2%
Ga. 1%

By 1750 there were over a million settlers and slaves in the 13 colonies. The two earliest colonies had the largest populations.

COLONISTS FROM MANY NATIONS

Largest European Group
- English
- German
- Scots-Irish
- Dutch
- Scots

Enslaved Africans
- Over 30% of local population
- — Colonial boundary, 1760

0   100   200 miles
0   100   200 kilometers

Colonists tended to settle with others from the same part of Europe. By 1760 ethnically distinct regions could be found throughout the colonies. Notice changes since 1640, shown on page 31.

Slavery in the Americas

- More than 11 million Africans were sold into slavery in the Americas. Most were put to work on plantations in the West Indies and Brazil.

- In North America, the Southern Colonies copied the plantation system, which relied on slave labor.

- By 1760 slaves were held in all 13 colonies, but slavery remained concentrated on plantations and in large cities.

- Although far outnumbered by slaves, many people of African descent gained their freedom and continued to live in the colonies.

TRIANGLES OF TRADE

→ Trade route

Ships sailed to Africa or the West Indies to trade manufactured goods for enslaved Africans. Next the slaves were taken to ports near plantations. Then ships completed their routes by carrying plantation crops to their home ports.

Slaves on plantations dug pits for planting sugar cane and later harvested it with large knives. Then they crushed and boiled the cane in mills where temperatures reached 140°F. Millions died after leading short lives of brutal labor.

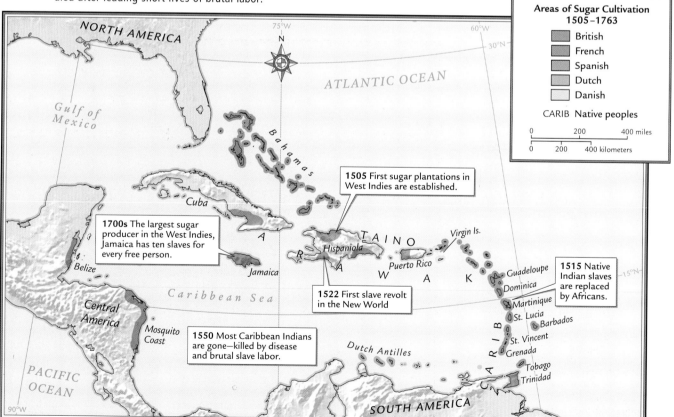

SUGAR AND SLAVERY

Areas of Sugar Cultivation 1505–1763

- British
- French
- Spanish
- Dutch
- Danish

CARIB Native peoples

1505 First sugar plantations in West Indies are established.

1700s The largest sugar producer in the West Indies, Jamaica has ten slaves for every free person.

1515 Native Indian slaves are replaced by Africans.

1522 First slave revolt in the New World

1550 Most Caribbean Indians are gone—killed by disease and brutal slave labor.

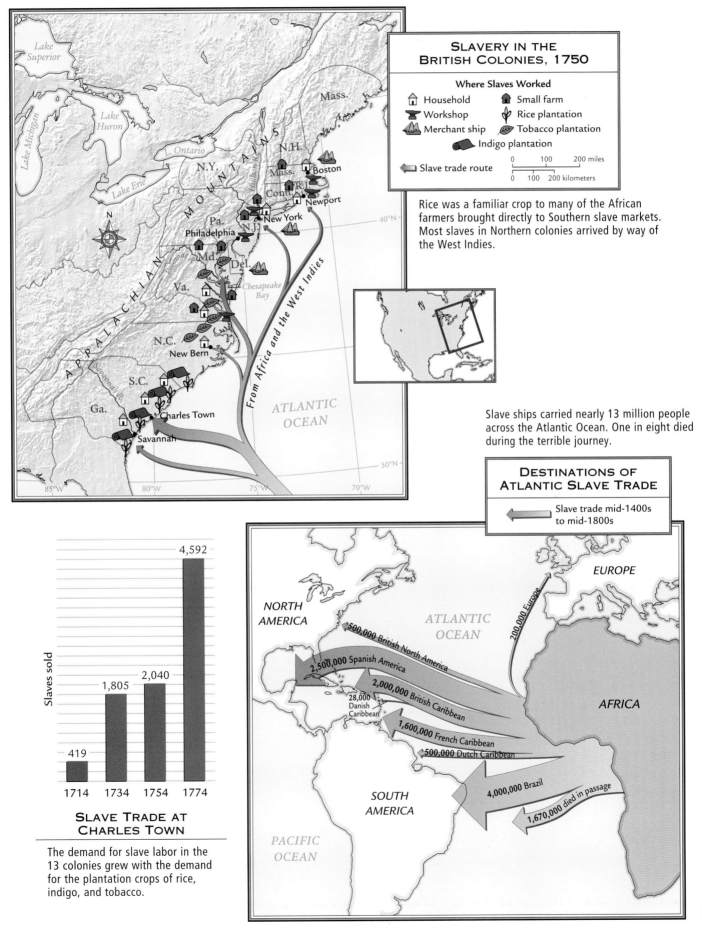

SLAVERY IN THE BRITISH COLONIES, 1750

Where Slaves Worked

- 🏠 Household
- 🏚 Small farm
- ⚒ Workshop
- 🌱 Rice plantation
- ⛵ Merchant ship
- 🍃 Tobacco plantation
- Indigo plantation

⬅ Slave trade route

| 0 | 100 | 200 miles |
| 0 | 100 | 200 kilometers |

Rice was a familiar crop to many of the African farmers brought directly to Southern slave markets. Most slaves in Northern colonies arrived by way of the West Indies.

Slave ships carried nearly 13 million people across the Atlantic Ocean. One in eight died during the terrible journey.

DESTINATIONS OF ATLANTIC SLAVE TRADE

⬅ Slave trade mid-1400s to mid-1800s

200,000 Europe
500,000 British North America
2,500,000 Spanish America
2,000,000 British Caribbean
28,000 Danish Caribbean
1,600,000 French Caribbean
500,000 Dutch Caribbean
4,000,000 Brazil
1,670,000 died in passage

Slave Trade at Charles Town

Slaves sold:
- 1714: 419
- 1734: 1,805
- 1754: 2,040
- 1774: 4,592

The demand for slave labor in the 13 colonies grew with the demand for the plantation crops of rice, indigo, and tobacco.

1754–1763
French and Indian War ends in victory for Britain.

1764
Sugar Act is first of new taxes imposed on colonists.

★ ★ ★ ★ ★ ★ ★ ★ ★ ★ ★ ★ ★ ★ ★★★**1750** | **1760** | **1770**

The French and Indian War Changes America

- The bitter rivalry between France and Britain led to war over their competing claims in North America.

- Huron and Algonkin Indians fought with the French. Colonists and Iroquois Indians fought with the British.

- Britain won the war and took control of French territory east of the Mississippi River.

- In the Proclamation of 1763, Britain reserved all lands west of the Appalachians for Native Americans.

- Colonists faced new British taxes and tighter British control after the war. Many colonists grew rebellious.

NORTH AMERICA 1754

European Land Claims

	British
	French
	Spanish

Bands of color show conflicting claims.

Britain challenged the French land claims west of the Appalachians. Compare this with the upper map on page 29.

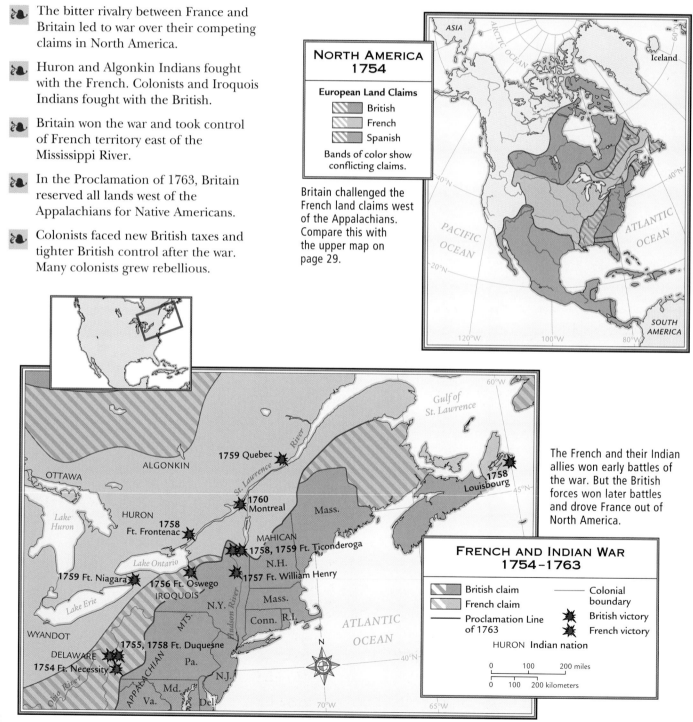

The French and their Indian allies won early battles of the war. But the British forces won later battles and drove France out of North America.

FRENCH AND INDIAN WAR 1754–1763

British claim	—— Colonial boundary
French claim	
— Proclamation Line of 1763	✸ British victory
	✸ French victory

HURON Indian nation

0   100   200 miles
0   100   200 kilometers

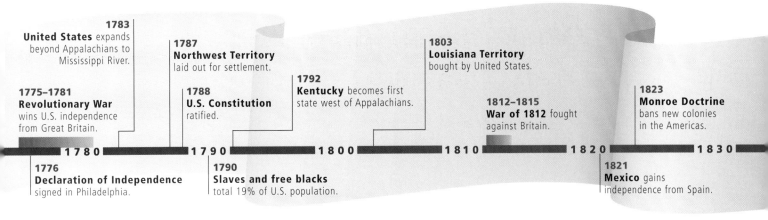

1783
United States expands beyond Appalachians to Mississippi River.

1775–1781
Revolutionary War wins U.S. independence from Great Britain.

1787
Northwest Territory laid out for settlement.

1788
U.S. Constitution ratified.

1792
Kentucky becomes first state west of Appalachians.

1803
Louisiana Territory bought by United States.

1812–1815
War of 1812 fought against Britain.

1823
Monroe Doctrine bans new colonies in the Americas.

1780 **1790** **1800** **1810** **1820** **1830**

1776
Declaration of Independence signed in Philadelphia.

1790
Slaves and free blacks total 19% of U.S. population.

1821
Mexico gains independence from Spain.

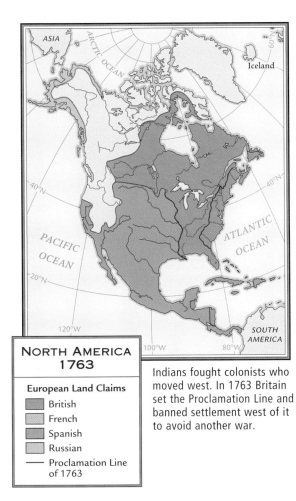

Indians fought colonists who moved west. In 1763 Britain set the Proclamation Line and banned settlement west of it to avoid another war.

Year	Tax Law	Items Taxed
1764	Sugar Act	Molasses
1765	Stamp Act	Newspapers, dice, playing cards, legal documents
1767	Townshend Act	Imported paint, lead, glass, paper, tea
1773	Tea Act	Tea

BRITISH TAXES ON COLONISTS

After the French and Indian War, Britain taxed colonists for the first time. Taxes were meant to pay for defense of the colonies and to assert British control over colonists and colonial trade.

The Tea Act was despised throughout the colonies, but especially in Boston. In 1773 colonists, some dressed as Indians, boarded British ships and dumped tea into Boston Harbor. Their protest became known as the Boston Tea Party.

1773

739,221 lbs.

TEA IMPORTED FROM BRITAIN

To avoid paying taxes, some colonists chose to boycott British imports. The demand for tea and other British goods quickly dropped.

1774

73,274 lbs.

1775

22,198 lbs.

Patriots Fight the Revolutionary War

- Colonial rebellion grew into the American Revolution, the war for independence from Great Britain.

- French, Spanish, and Dutch forces helped the Patriots fight Britain.

- On the British side were American Loyalists, Hessian (German) troops, and Indians west of the colonies.

- Slaves fought in both the Patriot and British armies in exchange for offers of freedom.

- After six years of fighting on land and at sea, the Patriots won the war and Great Britain lost its 13 colonies.

At first the Revolutionary War was fought mostly in New England and the Middle Colonies. Later the war shifted to the Southern Colonies. The British surrendered after losing battles on sea at Virginia Capes and on land at Yorktown.

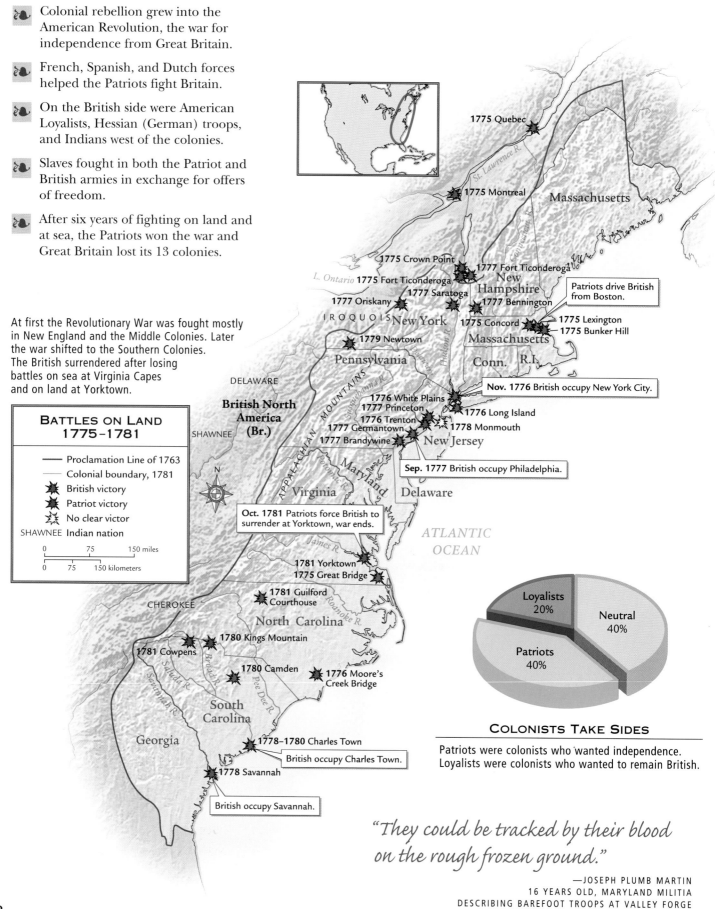

BATTLES ON LAND 1775–1781

— Proclamation Line of 1763
— Colonial boundary, 1781
✶ British victory
✶ Patriot victory
✶ No clear victor
SHAWNEE Indian nation

0   75   150 miles
0   75   150 kilometers

1775 Quebec
1775 Montreal
Massachusetts
1775 Crown Point
1775 Fort Ticonderoga
1777 Fort Ticonderoga
New Hampshire
1777 Saratoga
1777 Oriskany
1777 Bennington
L. Ontario 1775 Fort Ticonderoga
Patriots drive British from Boston.
IROQUOIS New York
1775 Concord 1775 Lexington
1775 Bunker Hill
1779 Newtown
Massachusetts
Pennsylvania
Conn.   R.I.
DELAWARE
Nov. 1776 British occupy New York City.
1776 White Plains
1777 Princeton 1776 Long Island
British North America (Br.)
1776 Trenton 1778 Monmouth
SHAWNEE
1777 Germantown
1777 Brandywine New Jersey
Sep. 1777 British occupy Philadelphia.
APPALACHIAN MOUNTAINS
Maryland
Virginia Delaware
Oct. 1781 Patriots force British to surrender at Yorktown, war ends.
ATLANTIC OCEAN
1781 Yorktown
1775 Great Bridge
1781 Guilford Courthouse
North Carolina
CHEROKEE
1780 Kings Mountain
1781 Cowpens
1780 Camden
1780 Savannah
1776 Moore's Creek Bridge
South Carolina
Georgia
1778–1780 Charles Town
British occupy Charles Town.
1778 Savannah
British occupy Savannah.

COLONISTS TAKE SIDES

Loyalists 20%
Neutral 40%
Patriots 40%

Patriots were colonists who wanted independence. Loyalists were colonists who wanted to remain British.

"They could be tracked by their blood on the rough frozen ground."

—JOSEPH PLUMB MARTIN
16 YEARS OLD, MARYLAND MILITIA
DESCRIBING BAREFOOT TROOPS AT VALLEY FORGE

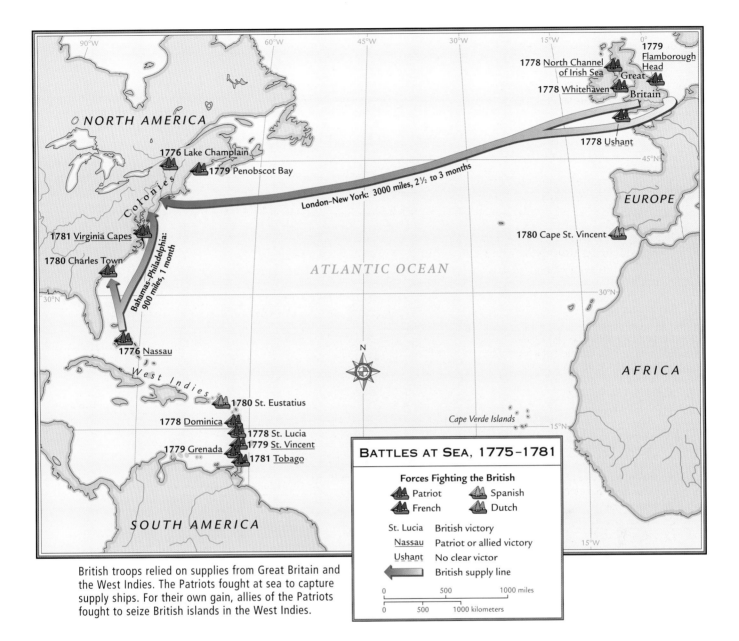

BATTLES AT SEA, 1775–1781

90°W 60°W 45°W 30°W 15°W 0°

NORTH AMERICA

1778 North Channel
of Irish Sea

1779 Flamborough
Head

Great

1778 Whitehaven

Britain

1778 Ushant

1776 Lake Champlain

1779 Penobscot Bay

45°N

Colonies

EUROPE

London–New York: 3000 miles, 2½ to 3 months

1781 Virginia Capes

1780 Cape St. Vincent

1780 Charles Town

30°N

Bahamas–Philadelphia: 900 miles, 1 month

ATLANTIC OCEAN

1776 Nassau

West Indies

AFRICA

1780 St. Eustatius

1778 Dominica

1778 St. Lucia

1779 Grenada

1779 St. Vincent

1781 Tobago

Cape Verde Islands

15°N

SOUTH AMERICA

15°W

Forces Fighting the British

| Patriot | Spanish |
| French | Dutch |

St. Lucia — British victory
Nassau — Patriot or allied victory
Ushant — No clear victor
← — British supply line

0   500   1000 miles
0   500   1000 kilometers

British troops relied on supplies from Great Britain and the West Indies. The Patriots fought at sea to capture supply ships. For their own gain, allies of the Patriots fought to seize British islands in the West Indies.

At Flamborough Head and elsewhere, warships fought with cannon at close range.

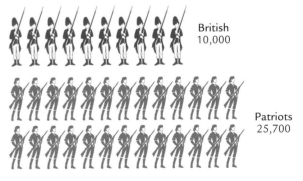

British
10,000

Patriots
25,700

SOLDIERS' DEATHS

Patriot troops outnumbered the British but were poorly fed and clothed. Only 28 percent of those who died were killed in battle. The rest died from disease, of exposure, or as prisoners.

A New Nation: The United States of America

- In 1783 the Treaty of Paris officially recognized the United States as an independent country.

- The new nation gained all British land west of the Appalachians, east of the Mississippi River, and south of the Great Lakes.

- In 1781 the states were loosely organized under the Articles of Confederation. The new country could not collect taxes, so it could not afford to carry out its responsibilities.

- In 1788 the Constitution replaced the Articles of Confederation, uniting the states under a stronger federal government.

NORTH AMERICA 1783

U.S. and European Land Claims

- United States
- British
- Spanish
- Russian
- French

Compare this map with the one on page 37 to see who gained and who lost after the American Revolution.

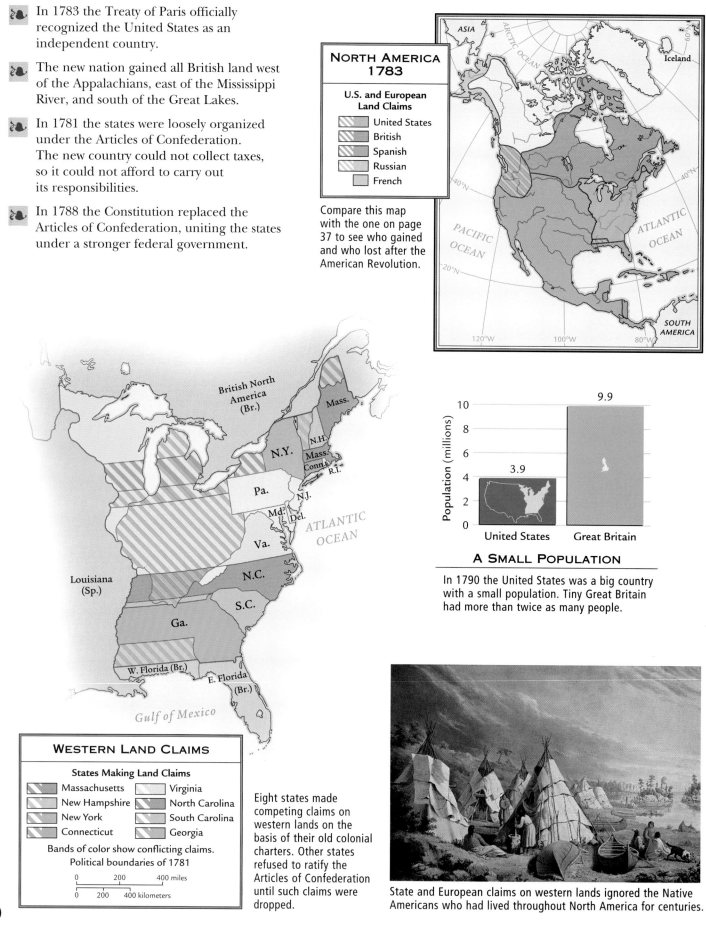

A SMALL POPULATION

In 1790 the United States was a big country with a small population. Tiny Great Britain had more than twice as many people.

WESTERN LAND CLAIMS

States Making Land Claims

- Massachusetts
- New Hampshire
- New York
- Connecticut
- Virginia
- North Carolina
- South Carolina
- Georgia

Bands of color show conflicting claims.
Political boundaries of 1781

0   200   400 miles
0   200   400 kilometers

Eight states made competing claims on western lands on the basis of their old colonial charters. Other states refused to ratify the Articles of Confederation until such claims were dropped.

State and European claims on western lands ignored the Native Americans who had lived throughout North America for centuries.

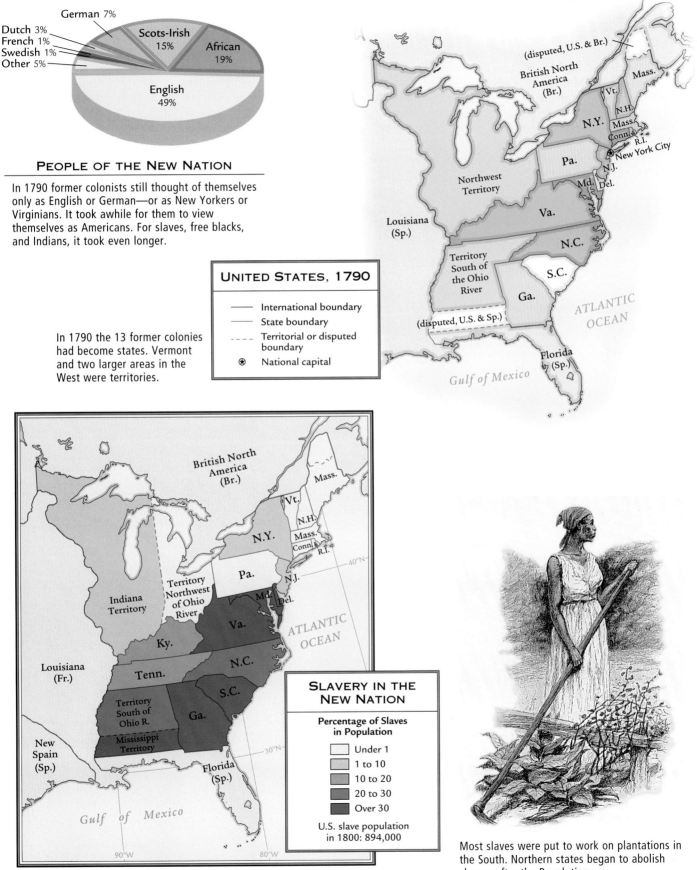

PEOPLE OF THE NEW NATION

In 1790 former colonists still thought of themselves only as English or German—or as New Yorkers or Virginians. It took awhile for them to view themselves as Americans. For slaves, free blacks, and Indians, it took even longer.

German 7%
Dutch 3%
French 1%
Swedish 1%
Other 5%
Scots-Irish 15%
African 19%
English 49%

UNITED STATES, 1790

——— International boundary
——— State boundary
- - - Territorial or disputed boundary
⊛ National capital

In 1790 the 13 former colonies had become states. Vermont and two larger areas in the West were territories.

SLAVERY IN THE NEW NATION

Percentage of Slaves in Population

Under 1
1 to 10
10 to 20
20 to 30
Over 30

U.S. slave population in 1800: 894,000

Most slaves were put to work on plantations in the South. Northern states began to abolish slavery after the Revolution.

The new Constitution based representation in Congress on population. The South wanted to count slaves, but the North did not. The compromise, which lasted more than 75 years, counted each slave as three-fifths of a person. (The map above counts each slave as an entire person.)

A Growing Population Spreads West

- In 1775 Daniel Boone helped build the Wilderness Road, the first wagon road across the Appalachians. Other wagon roads leading west soon followed.

- After the Revolution, people headed west across the mountains, looking for affordable land to settle.

- Despite Indian resistance to American claims, newly surveyed land was soon dotted with farms, schools, and towns.

- By road and river, growing numbers of settlers pushed the frontier westward to the Mississippi River.

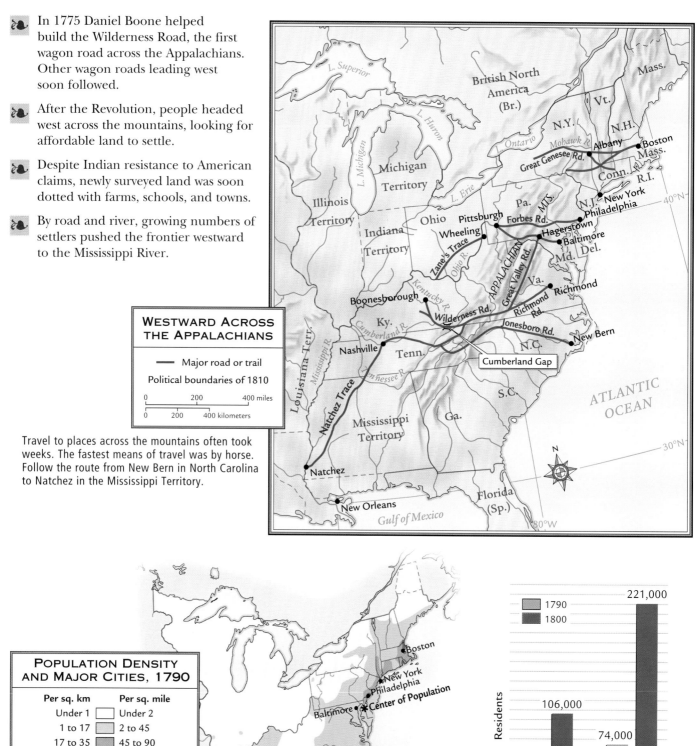

WESTWARD ACROSS THE APPALACHIANS

— Major road or trail
Political boundaries of 1810

| 0 | 200 | 400 miles |
| 0 | 200 | 400 kilometers |

Travel to places across the mountains often took weeks. The fastest means of travel was by horse. Follow the route from New Bern in North Carolina to Natchez in the Mississippi Territory.

POPULATION DENSITY AND MAJOR CITIES, 1790

Per sq. km	Per sq. mile
Under 1	Under 2
1 to 17	2 to 45
17 to 35	45 to 90
Over 35	Over 90

By 1790 about 200,000 people had crossed the Appalachians. Even so, 95 percent of the population still lived east of the mountains.

POPULATION BOOM

Tennessee: 1790: 36,000 — 1800: 106,000
Kentucky: 1790: 74,000 — 1800: 221,000

Once an area in the territories had 60,000 settlers, it could apply for statehood. Kentucky became a state in 1792, Tennessee in 1796.

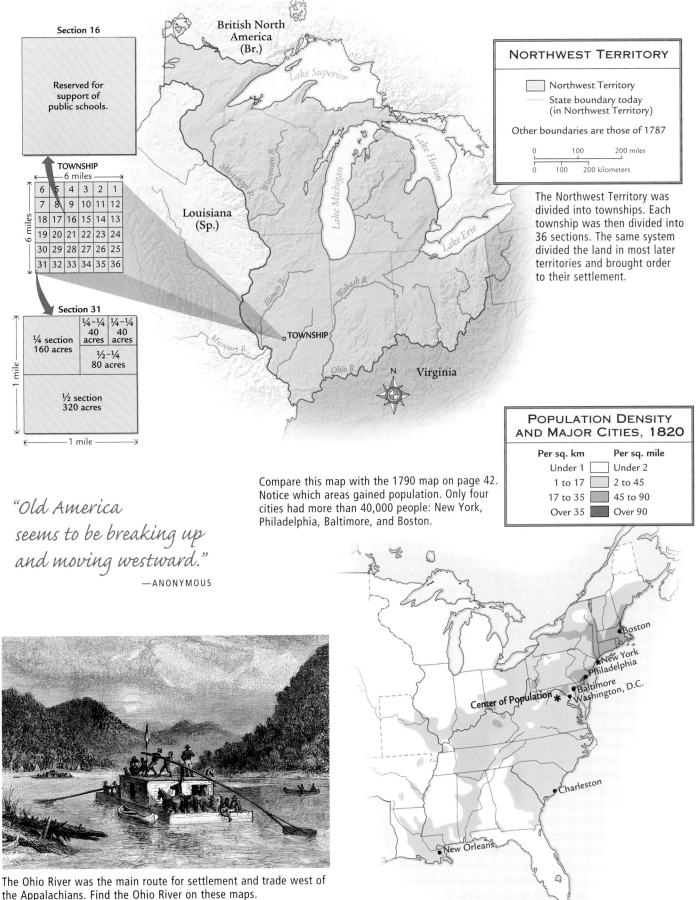

Section 16

Reserved for support of public schools.

TOWNSHIP
6 miles

6	5	4	3	2	1
7	8	9	10	11	12
18	17	16	15	14	13
19	20	21	22	23	24
30	29	28	27	26	25
31	32	33	34	35	36

6 miles

Section 31

¼ section 160 acres	¼-¼ 40 acres	¼-¼ 40 acres
	½-¼ 80 acres	
½ section 320 acres		

1 mile

1 mile

British North America (Br.)

Lake Superior

Louisiana (Sp.)

Mississippi R.

Wisconsin R.

Lake Michigan

Lake Huron

Lake Erie

Illinois R.

Wabash R.

Missouri R.

TOWNSHIP

Ohio R.

N

Virginia

NORTHWEST TERRITORY

☐ Northwest Territory
— State boundary today (in Northwest Territory)

Other boundaries are those of 1787

0   100   200 miles
0   100   200 kilometers

The Northwest Territory was divided into townships. Each township was then divided into 36 sections. The same system divided the land in most later territories and brought order to their settlement.

"Old America seems to be breaking up and moving westward."
—ANONYMOUS

Compare this map with the 1790 map on page 42. Notice which areas gained population. Only four cities had more than 40,000 people: New York, Philadelphia, Baltimore, and Boston.

POPULATION DENSITY AND MAJOR CITIES, 1820

Per sq. km	Per sq. mile
Under 1	Under 2
1 to 17	2 to 45
17 to 35	45 to 90
Over 35	Over 90

Boston
New York
Philadelphia
Center of Population ✶ Baltimore
Washington, D.C.
Charleston
New Orleans

The Ohio River was the main route for settlement and trade west of the Appalachians. Find the Ohio River on these maps.

Neighbors Gain Their Independence

- In the early 1800s, the spirit of revolution swept from the United States through the rest of the Americas.

- Mexico and several other colonies broke away from Spain. Haiti won independence from France.

- Russia, Austria, and Prussia feared revolution and offered to help Spain and France regain their colonies.

- President James Monroe warned Europe that the Americas were off-limits to future colonization.

- His policy, known as the Monroe Doctrine, established the United States as the dominant country of the Americas.

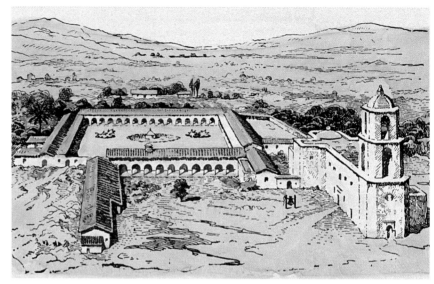

New Spain's last missions were built in California. Most missions had not only a church but a courtyard lined with workshops, storerooms, and places to cook, eat, and sleep. Fields, stables, and water were usually nearby.

New Spain expanded until 1795. Then it broke apart under pressure from Mexican desires for independence and U.S. desires for new territory. Compare this with the map on page 30.

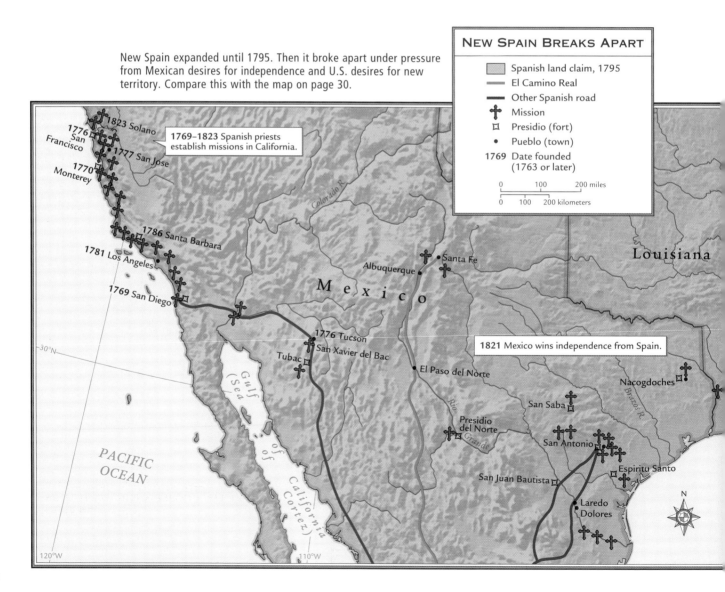

NEW SPAIN BREAKS APART

- Spanish land claim, 1795
- El Camino Real
- Other Spanish road
- ✝ Mission
- ⌂ Presidio (fort)
- • Pueblo (town)
- 1769 Date founded (1763 or later)

0   100   200 miles
0   100   200 kilometers

1769–1823 Spanish priests establish missions in California.

1823 Solano
1776 San Francisco
1777 San Jose
1770 Monterey
1786 Santa Barbara
1781 Los Angeles
1769 San Diego
1776 Tucson
San Xavier del Bac
Tubac
Albuquerque · Santa Fe
El Paso del Norte
Mexico
Colorado R.
Louisiana
1821 Mexico wins independence from Spain.
Nacogdoches
San Saba
Presidio del Norte
Rio Grande
Brazos R.
San Antonio
Espiritu Santo
San Juan Bautista
Laredo Dolores
PACIFIC OCEAN
Gulf of California (Sea of Cortez)
30°N
120°W   110°W

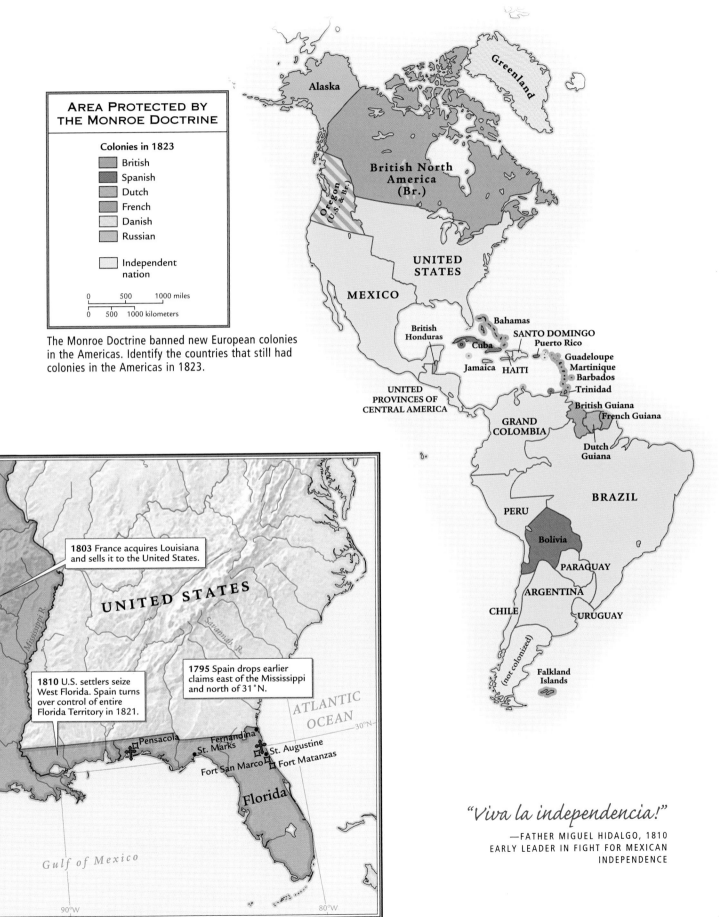

AREA PROTECTED BY THE MONROE DOCTRINE

Colonies in 1823

- British
- Spanish
- Dutch
- French
- Danish
- Russian

- Independent nation

0   500   1000 miles
0   500   1000 kilometers

The Monroe Doctrine banned new European colonies in the Americas. Identify the countries that still had colonies in the Americas in 1823.

Alaska

Greenland

British North America (Br.)

Oregon (U.S. & Br.)

UNITED STATES

MEXICO

British Honduras

Bahamas
Cuba
Jamaica
SANTO DOMINGO
Puerto Rico
HAITI
Guadeloupe
Martinique
Barbados
Trinidad

UNITED PROVINCES OF CENTRAL AMERICA

British Guiana
French Guiana
Dutch Guiana

GRAND COLOMBIA

PERU

BRAZIL

Bolivia

PARAGUAY

CHILE

ARGENTINA

URUGUAY

(not colonized)

Falkland Islands

1803 France acquires Louisiana and sells it to the United States.

UNITED STATES

Mississippi R.

Savannah R.

1795 Spain drops earlier claims east of the Mississippi and north of 31°N.

1810 U.S. settlers seize West Florida. Spain turns over control of entire Florida Territory in 1821.

ATLANTIC OCEAN

30°N

Pensacola
Fernandina
St. Marks
St. Augustine
Fort San Marco
Fort Matanzas

Florida

Gulf of Mexico

90°W   80°W

"Viva la independencia!"

—FATHER MIGUEL HIDALGO, 1810
EARLY LEADER IN FIGHT FOR MEXICAN
INDEPENDENCE

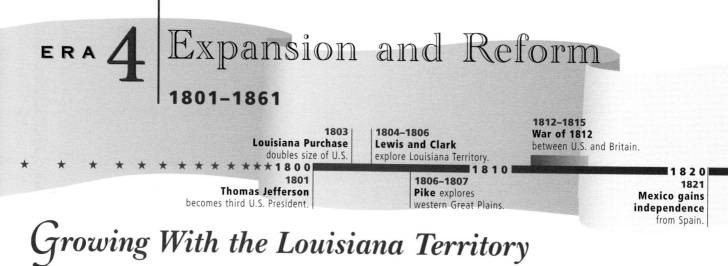

1803
Louisiana Purchase
doubles size of U.S.

1804–1806
Lewis and Clark
explore Louisiana Territory.

1812–1815
War of 1812
between U.S. and Britain.

1800

1810

1820

1801
Thomas Jefferson
becomes third U.S. President.

1806–1807
Pike explores
western Great Plains.

1821
**Mexico gains
independence**
from Spain.

Growing With the Louisiana Territory

- The Louisiana Purchase was the first step in the expansion of the country during the 1800s.

- When the United States bought the Louisiana Territory from France in 1803, the size of the country doubled.

- In 1804–1806, an expedition led by Meriwether Lewis and William Clark explored the new territory.

- Information they gathered about the route and its people, terrain, plants, and wildlife guided later exploration and settlement.

Much of the Louisiana Territory consisted of the Great Plains. In 1803 they were inhabited by Native Americans such as these hunters painted by George Catlin.

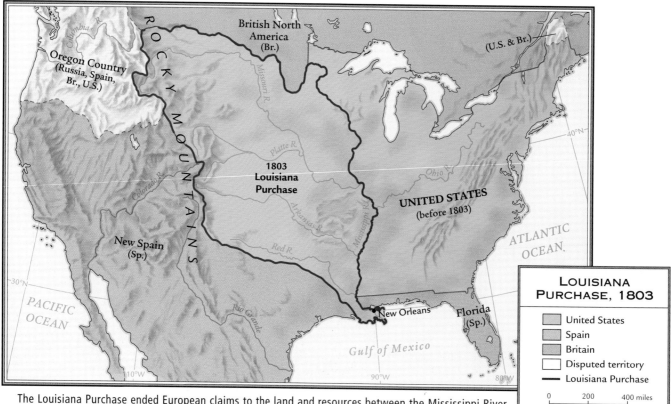

**LOUISIANA
PURCHASE, 1803**

- United States
- Spain
- Britain
- Disputed territory
- — Louisiana Purchase

0   200   400 miles

0   200   400 kilometers

The Louisiana Purchase ended European claims to the land and resources between the Mississippi River and the Rocky Mountains. It did not end older claims by Native Americans.

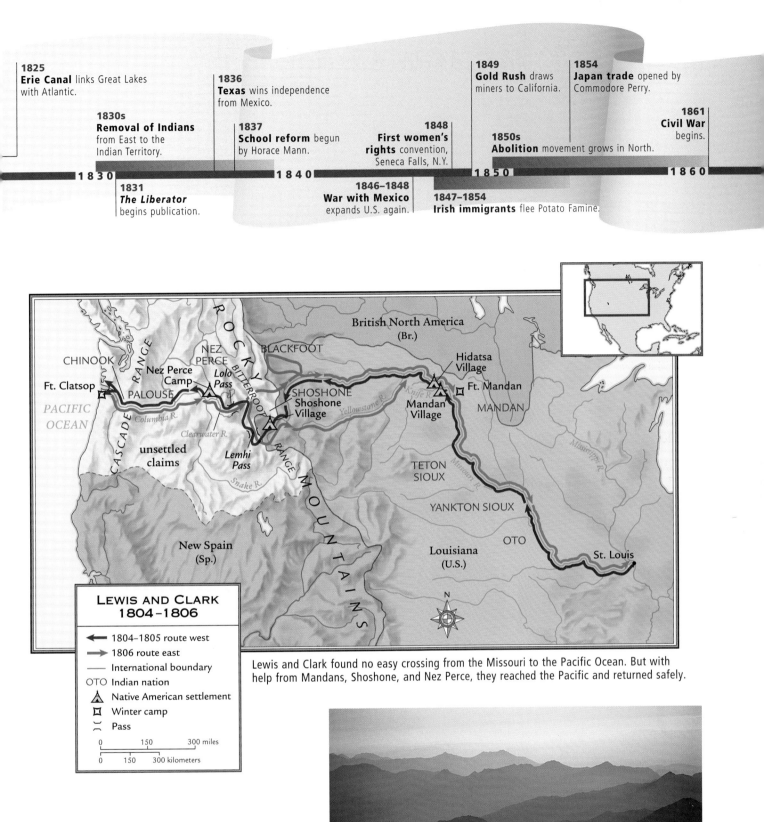

1825
Erie Canal links Great Lakes with Atlantic.

1830s
Removal of Indians from East to the Indian Territory.

1831
The Liberator begins publication.

1836
Texas wins independence from Mexico.

1837
School reform begun by Horace Mann.

1846–1848
War with Mexico expands U.S. again.

1848
First women's rights convention, Seneca Falls, N.Y.

1847–1854
Irish immigrants flee Potato Famine.

1849
Gold Rush draws miners to California.

1850s
Abolition movement grows in North.

1854
Japan trade opened by Commodore Perry.

1861
Civil War begins.

1830   1840   1850   1860

LEWIS AND CLARK 1804–1806

- **◄—** 1804–1805 route west
- **—►** 1806 route east
- — International boundary
- OTO Indian nation
- ▲ Native American settlement
- ⌂ Winter camp
- ⌣ Pass

0   150   300 miles
0   150   300 kilometers

Lewis and Clark found no easy crossing from the Missouri to the Pacific Ocean. But with help from Mandans, Shoshone, and Nez Perce, they reached the Pacific and returned safely.

"I discovered immense ranges of high mountains still to the West..."

—CAPTAIN MERIWETHER LEWIS, AUGUST 12, 1805 DESCRIBING THE VIEW FROM LEMHI PASS ON THE CONTINENTAL DIVIDE

When the Lewis and Clark expedition began to climb the Rockies, they hoped to see an easy route to the Pacific Coast once they reached the top. All they saw were more mountains.

47

War of 1812 and Indian Resettlement

- In 1812 the United States went to war with Great Britain over the seizure of American ships trading in Europe.

- Organized by the Shawnee leader Tecumseh, a confederation of eastern American Indian tribes had been fighting U.S. expansion. Now they joined forces with the British.

- In 1814 the Treaty of Ghent officially ended the war. Neither country lost or gained territory, but the British gave up attempts to stop U.S. expansion.

- Indians lost the most. By 1840 the United States gained control of more than 100 million acres of Indian land.

The Battle of New Orleans, the most famous American victory of the War of 1812, was fought after the war was officially over. Neither side knew that a peace treaty had been signed weeks before.

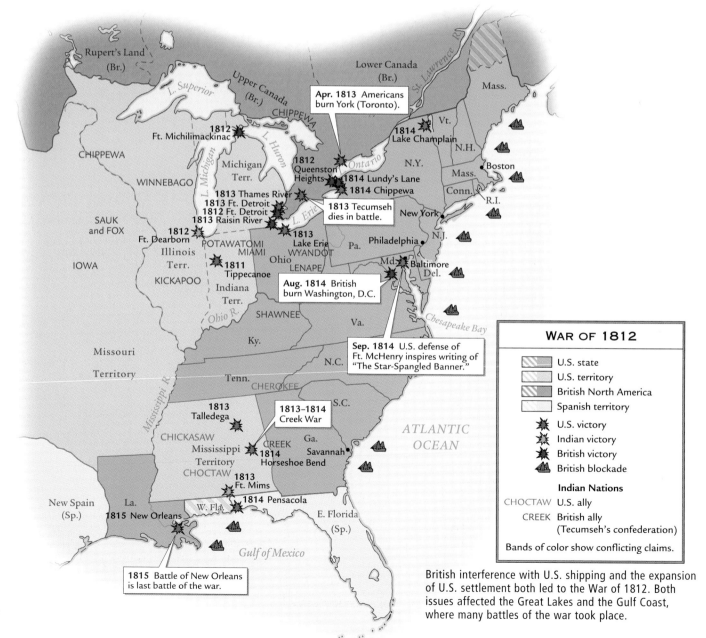

Apr. 1813 Americans burn York (Toronto).

Aug. 1814 British burn Washington, D.C.

Sep. 1814 U.S. defense of Ft. McHenry inspires writing of "The Star-Spangled Banner."

1813 Tecumseh dies in battle.

1813–1814 Creek War

1815 Battle of New Orleans is last battle of the war.

1812 Ft. Michilimackinac
1812 Queenston Heights
1814 Lundy's Lane
1814 Chippewa
1814 Lake Champlain
1813 Thames River
1813 Ft. Detroit
1812 Ft. Detroit
1813 Raisin River
1813 Lake Erie
1812 Ft. Dearborn
1811 Tippecanoe
1813 Talledega
1814 Horseshoe Bend
1813 Ft. Mims
1814 Pensacola
1815 New Orleans

Rupert's Land (Br.)
Upper Canada (Br.)
Lower Canada (Br.)
Mass.
Vt.
N.H.
N.Y.
Mass.
Conn.
R.I.
Boston
New York
N.J.
Philadelphia
Pa.
Md.
Del.
Baltimore
Va.
Ky.
N.C.
Tenn.
S.C.
Ga.
Savannah
E. Florida (Sp.)
W. Fla.
La.
New Spain (Sp.)
Missouri Territory
Iowa
Illinois Terr.
Indiana Terr.
Ohio
Michigan Terr.
Mississippi Territory

CHIPPEWA
CHIPPEWA
WINNEBAGO
SAUK and FOX
KICKAPOO
POTAWATOMI
MIAMI
WYANDOT
LENAPE
SHAWNEE
CHEROKEE
CHICKASAW
CHOCTAW
CREEK

L. Superior
L. Michigan
L. Huron
L. Erie
L. Ontario
St. Lawrence R.
Ohio R.
Mississippi R.
Chesapeake Bay
ATLANTIC OCEAN
Gulf of Mexico

WAR OF 1812

▨	U.S. state
▨	U.S. territory
▨	British North America
▨	Spanish territory
✹	U.S. victory
✹	Indian victory
✹	British victory
⛴	British blockade

Indian Nations

CHOCTAW U.S. ally
CREEK British ally (Tecumseh's confederation)

Bands of color show conflicting claims.

British interference with U.S. shipping and the expansion of U.S. settlement both led to the War of 1812. Both issues affected the Great Lakes and the Gulf Coast, where many battles of the war took place.

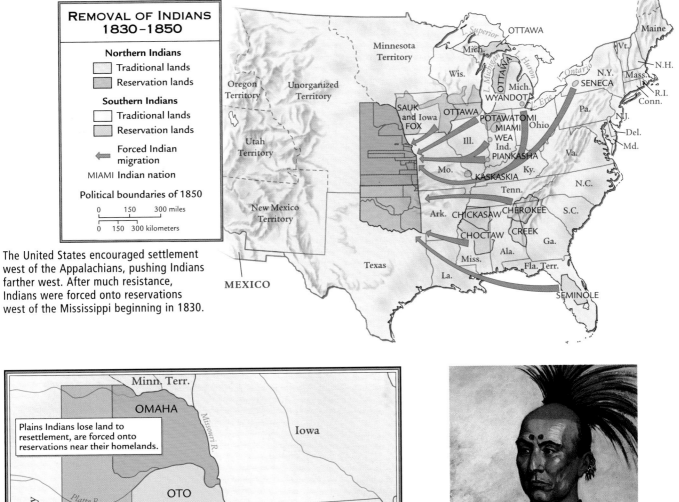

REMOVAL OF INDIANS 1830–1850

Northern Indians
- Traditional lands
- Reservation lands

Southern Indians
- Traditional lands
- Reservation lands

← Forced Indian migration

MIAMI Indian nation

Political boundaries of 1850

0   150   300 miles
0   150   300 kilometers

The United States encouraged settlement west of the Appalachians, pushing Indians farther west. After much resistance, Indians were forced onto reservations west of the Mississippi beginning in 1830.

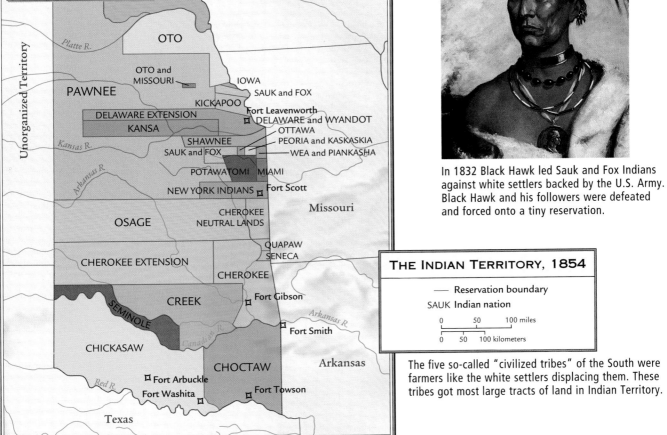

Plains Indians lose land to resettlement, are forced onto reservations near their homelands.

In 1832 Black Hawk led Sauk and Fox Indians against white settlers backed by the U.S. Army. Black Hawk and his followers were defeated and forced onto a tiny reservation.

THE INDIAN TERRITORY, 1854

— Reservation boundary
SAUK Indian nation

0   50   100 miles
0   50   100 kilometers

The five so-called "civilized tribes" of the South were farmers like the white settlers displacing them. These tribes got most large tracts of land in Indian Territory.

Exploration Opens the West

🐂 Between 1790 and 1820, the United States doubled its size and added ten new states.

🐂 The larger country offered new opportunities to the white settlers who replaced the Indians.

🐂 During the first half of the 1800s, Americans blazed new trails, gathered information, and scouted the West for places to settle.

🐂 By 1860 older territories were settled by farmers who grew crops where forests and prairies had been.

🐂 Few settlers moved farther west onto the vast, treeless Great Plains.

In 1820 Captain Stephen Long described the western plains as the "Great American Desert." Few settlers disturbed the people and wildlife of the plains for years afterward.

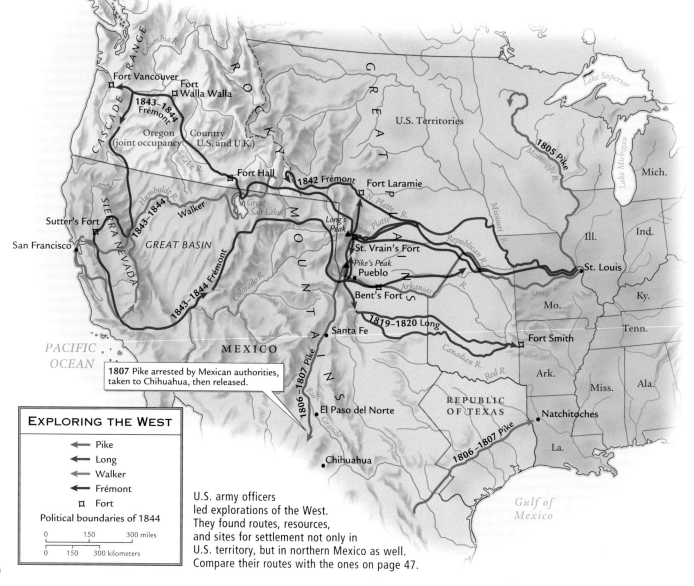

1807 Pike arrested by Mexican authorities, taken to Chihuahua, then released.

EXPLORING THE WEST

⬅ Pike
⬅ Long
⬅ Walker
⬅ Frémont
⌑ Fort
Political boundaries of 1844

0   150   300 miles
0   150   300 kilometers

U.S. army officers led explorations of the West. They found routes, resources, and sites for settlement not only in U.S. territory, but in northern Mexico as well. Compare their routes with the ones on page 47.

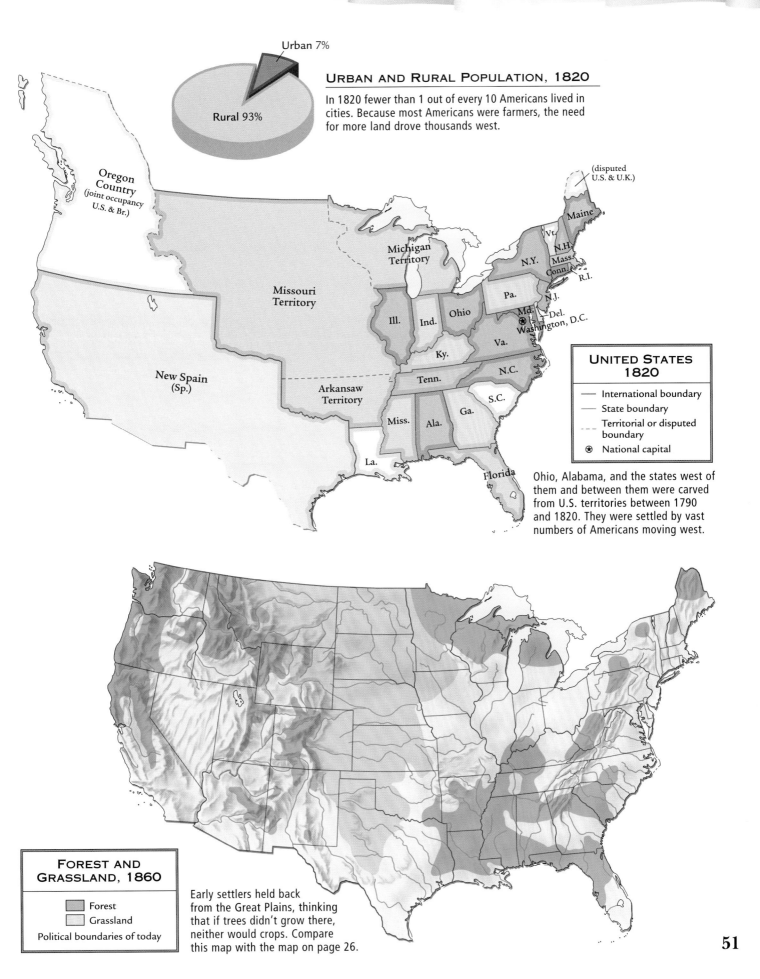

URBAN AND RURAL POPULATION, 1820

Urban 7%

Rural 93%

In 1820 fewer than 1 out of every 10 Americans lived in cities. Because most Americans were farmers, the need for more land drove thousands west.

Oregon Country (joint occupancy U.S. & Br.)

(disputed U.S. & U.K.)

Maine

Vt.

N.H.

Michigan Territory

N.Y.

Mass.

Conn.

R.I.

Missouri Territory

Pa.

N.J.

Ill.

Ind.

Ohio

Md.

Del.

Washington, D.C.

Va.

Ky.

New Spain (Sp.)

Tenn.

N.C.

Arkansaw Territory

S.C.

Miss.

Ala.

Ga.

La.

Florida

UNITED STATES 1820

— International boundary

— State boundary

--- Territorial or disputed boundary

⊛ National capital

Ohio, Alabama, and the states west of them and between them were carved from U.S. territories between 1790 and 1820. They were settled by vast numbers of Americans moving west.

FOREST AND GRASSLAND, 1860

■ Forest

□ Grassland

Political boundaries of today

Early settlers held back from the Great Plains, thinking that if trees didn't grow there, neither would crops. Compare this map with the map on page 26.

Travel in a Growing Nation

- The great size of the growing United States made overland transportation difficult and expensive.

- In the early 1800s, travel by steamboat was the fastest and least expensive way to get around.

- During the 1820s and 1830s, canals were built to link eastern cities to the Great Lakes and western rivers.

- In the 1840s, railroads improved travel again, and by 1860 railroad lines ran through most of the eastern United States.

NATURAL WATERWAYS

☐ United States, 1825
— Inland boat service
— Coastal steamboat service

0   200   400 miles
0 200 400 kilometers

Because there were few passable roads in the young nation, heavy goods going long distances usually were transported on waterways. Compare this map with the Fall Line map on page 32.

Robert Fulton invented the first successful steamboat, the *Clermont*, in 1807. Steamboats soon dominated eastern waterways. By 1860 they also were the primary mode of travel on western rivers.

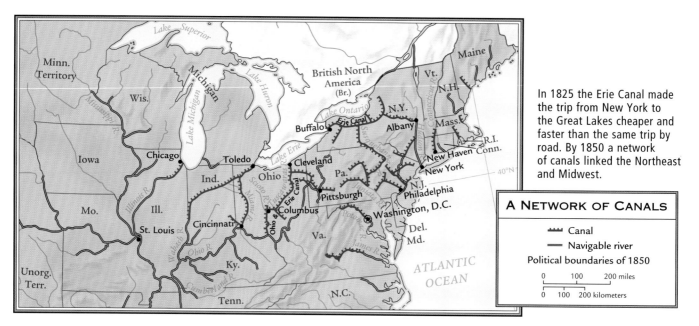

In 1825 the Erie Canal made the trip from New York to the Great Lakes cheaper and faster than the same trip by road. By 1850 a network of canals linked the Northeast and Midwest.

A NETWORK OF CANALS

⚏ Canal
— Navigable river
Political boundaries of 1850

0   100   200 miles
0 100 200 kilometers

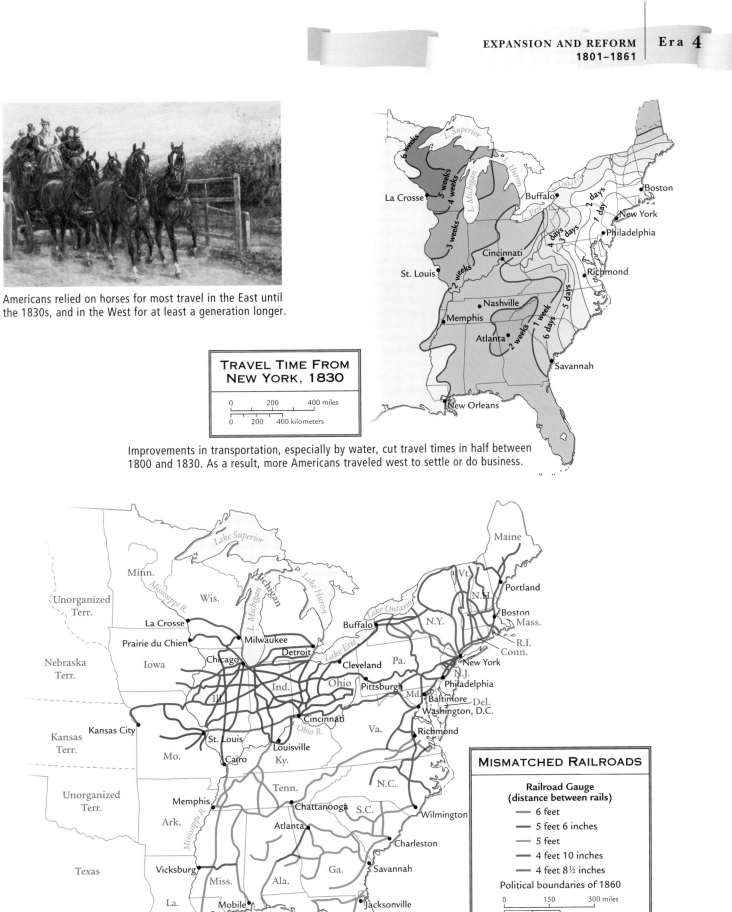

Americans relied on horses for most travel in the East until the 1830s, and in the West for at least a generation longer.

TRAVEL TIME FROM NEW YORK, 1830

0   200   400 miles

0   200   400 kilometers

Improvements in transportation, especially by water, cut travel times in half between 1800 and 1830. As a result, more Americans traveled west to settle or do business.

MISMATCHED RAILROADS

Railroad Gauge (distance between rails)

- 6 feet
- 5 feet 6 inches
- 5 feet
- 4 feet 10 inches
- 4 feet 8½ inches

Political boundaries of 1860

0   150   300 miles

0   150   300 kilometers

Train cars could run only on rails of a certain *gauge*, or distance apart. In the mid-1800s, several changes of train might be necessary on a long trip.

America Expands to the Pacific

- In the 1840s, the United States sought land from Texas, Mexico, and Britain so that it could expand to the Pacific.

- Texas had won independence from Mexico in 1836. The United States annexed it in 1845.

- In 1848, victory in the War with Mexico gave the northern third of Mexico to the United States.

- Farther north, the United States gained the southern half of Oregon Country in an 1846 agreement with Britain.

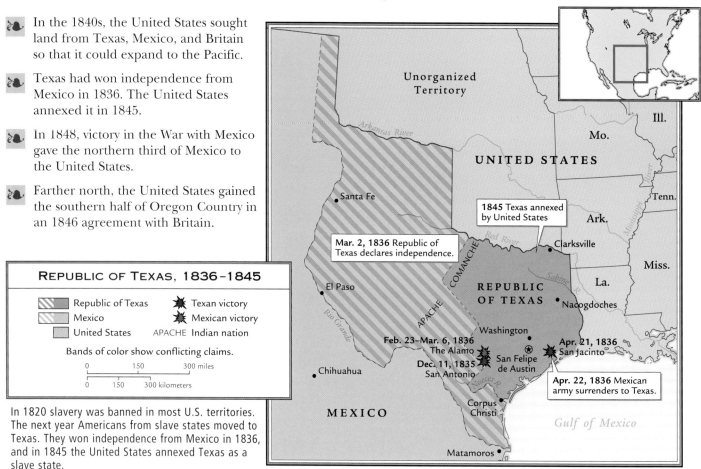

REPUBLIC OF TEXAS, 1836–1845

- Republic of Texas
- Mexico
- United States
- Texan victory
- Mexican victory
- APACHE Indian nation

Bands of color show conflicting claims.

0   150   300 miles
0   150   300 kilometers

1845 Texas annexed by United States

Mar. 2, 1836 Republic of Texas declares independence.

Feb. 23–Mar. 6, 1836 The Alamo

Dec. 11, 1835 San Antonio

Apr. 21, 1836 San Jacinto

Apr. 22, 1836 Mexican army surrenders to Texas.

In 1820 slavery was banned in most U.S. territories. The next year Americans from slave states moved to Texas. They won independence from Mexico in 1836, and in 1845 the United States annexed Texas as a slave state.

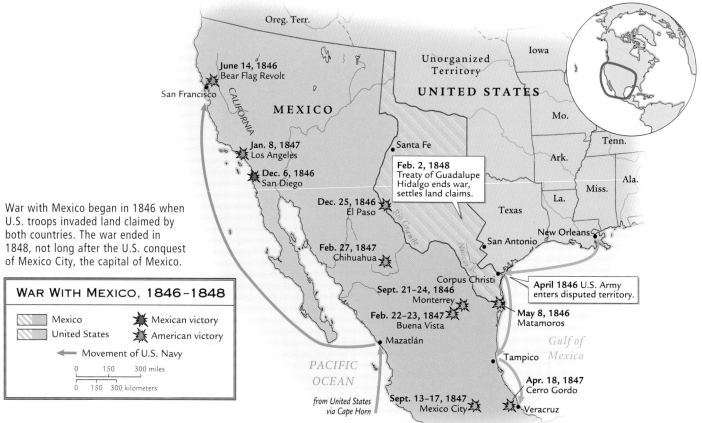

War with Mexico began in 1846 when U.S. troops invaded land claimed by both countries. The war ended in 1848, not long after the U.S. conquest of Mexico City, the capital of Mexico.

WAR WITH MEXICO, 1846–1848

- Mexico
- United States
- Movement of U.S. Navy
- Mexican victory
- American victory

0   150   300 miles
0   150   300 kilometers

June 14, 1846 Bear Flag Revolt

Jan. 8, 1847 Los Angeles

Dec. 6, 1846 San Diego

Dec. 25, 1846 El Paso

Feb. 27, 1847 Chihuahua

Feb. 2, 1848 Treaty of Guadalupe Hidalgo ends war, settles land claims.

April 1846 U.S. Army enters disputed territory.

Sept. 21–24, 1846 Monterrey

Feb. 22–23, 1847 Buena Vista

May 8, 1846 Matamoros

Apr. 18, 1847 Cerro Gordo

Sept. 13–17, 1847 Mexico City

Veracruz

Tampico

from United States via Cape Horn

With the Texas Annexation and the Mexican Cession, more than 75,000 Mexicans living in the Southwest came under the authority of the United States.

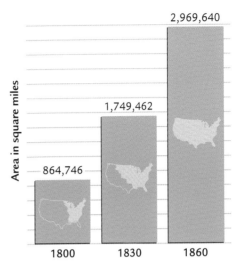

LAND AREA OF THE UNITED STATES

The United States tripled in size between 1800 and 1860. Many Americans believed it fulfilled their "Manifest Destiny" to inhabit the continent from the Atlantic to the Pacific.

The United States gained most of its western land in four steps between 1845 and 1853. Each acquisition was different: an annexation, a peaceful treaty, a treaty ending a war, and a purchase.

AMERICAN EXPANSION 1818–1853

State boundaries of today

0   250   500 miles
0   250   500 kilometers

1846 Split by Oregon Treaty; Britain gets northern part

1842 Webster-Ashburton Treaty with Britain.

1818 Ceded to Britain, Convention of 1818

1818 From Britain, Convention of 1818

1819 Adams-Onis Treaty with Spain

1845 Annexed by Act of U.S. Congress

1848 Ceded by Treaty of Guadalupe Hidalgo

1853 From Mexico

1819 Adams-Onis Treaty with Spain

Oregon Country

Mexican Cession

Gadsden Purchase

Texas Annexation

Red River Basin

Florida Cession

Great Salt Lake

PACIFIC OCEAN

ATLANTIC OCEAN

L. Superior

L. Michigan

L. Huron

L. Erie

L. Ontario

55

West Across the Rockies

- Until the 1860s, trails provided the only routes for settlers, traders, soldiers, freight, and mail bound for the West.

- Westward journeys covered great distances at walking speed. Water was scarce, help far away.

- During the 1840s, wagon trails saw heavy use from farmers seeking land, miners seeking gold, and Mormons seeking religious freedom.

- Increasing western settlement soon demanded better trails for freight and, briefly, for the Pony Express.

Emigrants on the Oregon Trail traveled nearly half a year before they reached their destination. In this reenactment, a wagon train crosses the vast plains.

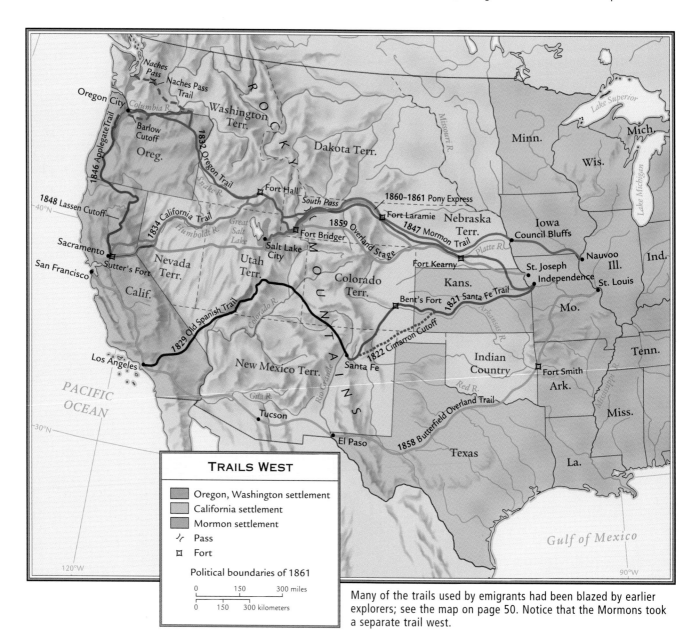

TRAILS WEST

- ▮ Oregon, Washington settlement
- ▮ California settlement
- ▮ Mormon settlement
- ⅄ Pass
- ⌑ Fort

Political boundaries of 1861

| 0 | 150 | 300 miles |
| 0 | 150 | 300 kilometers |

Many of the trails used by emigrants had been blazed by earlier explorers; see the map on page 50. Notice that the Mormons took a separate trail west.

> "One night my oldest sister and I were going from one wagon to another and a big wolf came up. We didn't stay to see what he wanted."
>
> —10 YEAR OLD SARAH SPRENGER, REMINISCENCE: OHIO TO OREGON, 1852

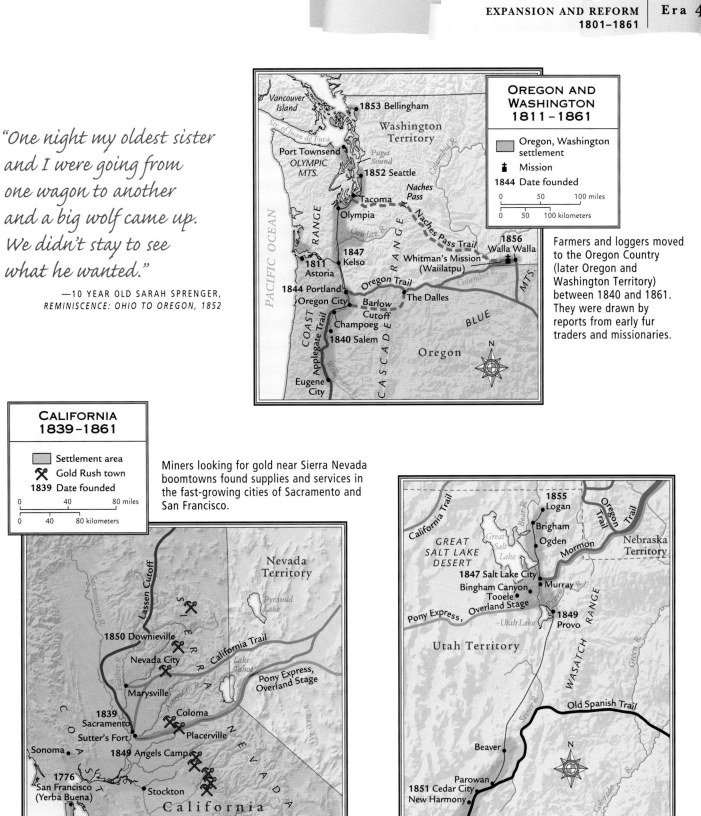

OREGON AND WASHINGTON 1811–1861

- Oregon, Washington settlement
- Mission
- **1844** Date founded

0   50   100 miles
0   50   100 kilometers

Farmers and loggers moved to the Oregon Country (later Oregon and Washington Territory) between 1840 and 1861. They were drawn by reports from early fur traders and missionaries.

CALIFORNIA 1839–1861

- Settlement area
- Gold Rush town
- **1839** Date founded

0   40   80 miles
0   40   80 kilometers

Miners looking for gold near Sierra Nevada boomtowns found supplies and services in the fast-growing cities of Sacramento and San Francisco.

UTAH, 1847–1861

- Mormon settlement area
- **1851** Date founded

0   40   80 miles
0   40   80 kilometers

The Mormons escaped religious persecution by moving to the harsh Utah desert, hoping that isolation would enable them to practice their religion in peace.

Immigrants and Runaway Slaves

- Opportunity in the growing United States was a beacon that drew people from other parts of the world.

- Between 1820 and 1860, about 5.1 million immigrants came to the United States, most from Northern and Western Europe.

- Freedom in the North and in Canada drew African American slaves escaping the South.

- By the 1830s, reformers were supporting the abolition movement to abolish slavery and the Underground Railroad to aid escaped slaves.

IMMIGRANT ORIGINS

Most immigrants were from the same places as the original colonists (see the graph at the top of page 41). Others often faced bigotry and discrimination. For example, in many U.S. cities Irish immigrants were denied jobs.

Legend:
- Northern & Western Europe
- Southern & Eastern Europe
- North America
- South America
- Asia
- All other

Bar values: 8,385 (1820), 23,322 (1830), 84,066 (1840), 369,980 (1850), 153,640 (1860)

Irish and British Immigrants graph

- Irish
- British

221,253

Immigrants (thousands): 0, 50, 100, 150, 200, 250
Years: 1820, 1830, 1840, 1850, 1860

IRISH AND BRITISH IMMIGRANTS

Immigrants from rural Ireland came to America to escape poverty. Their numbers soared to unprecedented levels in the 1840s and 1850s after the Irish potato crop failed.

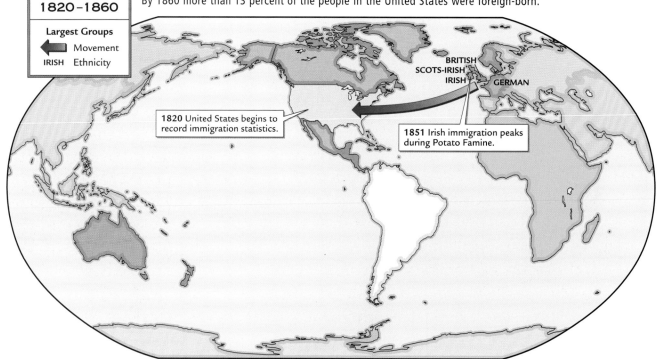

IMMIGRANTS 1820–1860

Largest Groups
- Movement
- IRISH Ethnicity

In 1820 less than 1 percent of the total population had been born in another country. By 1860 more than 13 percent of the people in the United States were foreign-born.

BRITISH
SCOTS-IRISH
IRISH
GERMAN

1820 United States begins to record immigration statistics.

1851 Irish immigration peaks during Potato Famine.

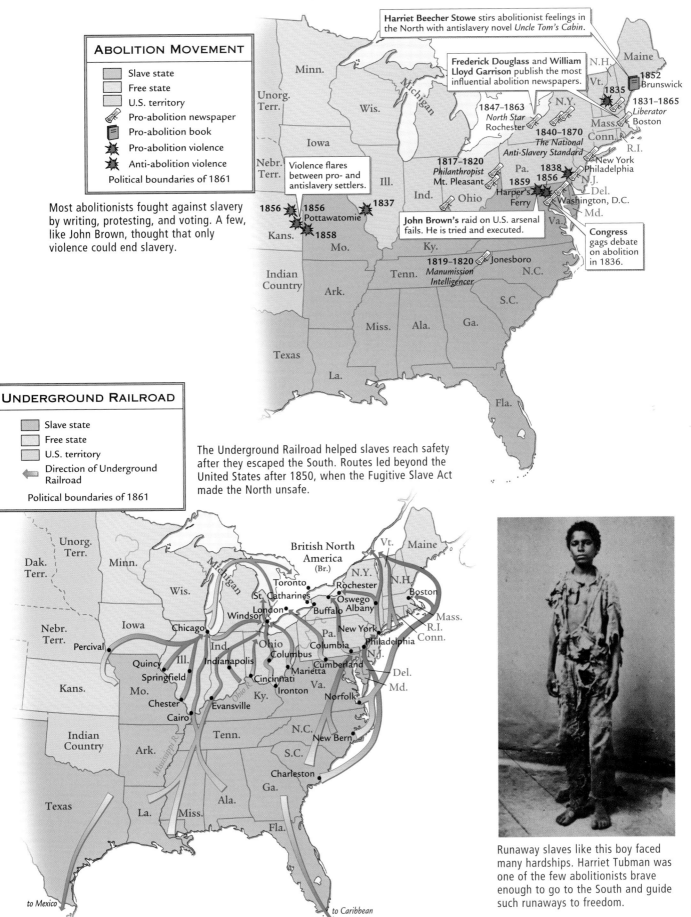

ABOLITION MOVEMENT

- Slave state
- Free state
- U.S. territory
- Pro-abolition newspaper
- Pro-abolition book
- Pro-abolition violence
- Anti-abolition violence

Political boundaries of 1861

Most abolitionists fought against slavery by writing, protesting, and voting. A few, like John Brown, thought that only violence could end slavery.

Harriet Beecher Stowe stirs abolitionist feelings in the North with antislavery novel *Uncle Tom's Cabin*.

Frederick Douglass and **William Lloyd Garrison** publish the most influential abolition newspapers.

1852 Brunswick

1835

1831–1865 *Liberator* Boston

1847–1863 *North Star* Rochester

1840–1870 *The National Anti-Slavery Standard*

New York

Philadelphia

1817–1820 *Philanthropist* Mt. Pleasant

Violence flares between pro- and antislavery settlers.

1856 1856 Pottawatomie
1837
1858

Kans.

Mo.

Ill.

Ind. Ohio

Pa.

1838
1859 1856
Harper's Ferry

Washington, D.C.

John Brown's raid on U.S. arsenal fails. He is tried and executed.

Congress gags debate on abolition in 1836.

1819–1820 *Manumission Intelligencer*

Jonesboro

Va.

Md.

N.C.

Minn.

Unorg. Terr.

Wis.

Michigan

N.Y.

N.H. Maine

Vt.

Mass.

Conn.

R.I.

N.J.

Del.

Iowa

Nebr. Terr.

Indian Country

Ark.

Tenn.

S.C.

Texas

Miss. Ala. Ga.

La.

Fla.

UNDERGROUND RAILROAD

- Slave state
- Free state
- U.S. territory
- Direction of Underground Railroad

Political boundaries of 1861

The Underground Railroad helped slaves reach safety after they escaped the South. Routes led beyond the United States after 1850, when the Fugitive Slave Act made the North unsafe.

Unorg. Terr.

Dak. Terr.

Minn.

Michigan

British North America (Br.)

Vt. Maine

Toronto
St. Catharines
London
Windsor

Rochester
Oswego
Buffalo Albany

N.Y.

N.H

Boston

Mass.

R.I.
Conn.

Wis.

Iowa

Chicago

Ind.

Ohio

Columbus

Columbia

Pa.

New York

Philadelphia

N.J.

Del.
Md.

Nebr. Terr.

Percival

Quincy
Springfield

Ill.
Indianapolis

Cincinnati

Marietta
Cumberland

Ironton

Va.

Kans.

Mo.

Chester

Evansville

Cairo

Ohio R.

Ky.

Norfolk

Indian Country

Ark.

Tenn.

N.C.

New Bern

Mississippi R.

S.C.

Charleston

Ga.

Texas

La. Miss. Ala.

Fla.

to Mexico

to Caribbean

Runaway slaves like this boy faced many hardships. Harriet Tubman was one of the few abolitionists brave enough to go to the South and guide such runaways to freedom.

ERA 5 | Civil War and Reconstruction
1820–1877

1854
Republican Party founded to oppose slavery in the territories.

1860
Democratic Party divides into antislavery and proslavery factions.

Republican candidate Abraham Lincoln elected U.S. President.

South Carolina secedes from the Union, first of 11 states to do so.

1820

1855

1820
Missouri Compromise prohibits slavery north of 36°30′N.

1857
Dred Scott decision declares blacks are not U.S. citizens.

Slavery Divides the Nation

The issue of slavery affected national decisions for decades. Congress twice compromised to satisfy both North and South, but without lasting success.

The Missouri Compromise divided new territories at 36°30′N. Slavery was banned north of this line and allowed south of it.

The Compromise of 1850 allowed territory gained from Mexico to decide on slavery by a vote of the residents, or *popular sovereignty.*

The Kansas-Nebraska Act allowed slavery in those two territories, even though they were north of 36°30′N.

In the Dred Scott case, the Supreme Court ruled that Congress had no power to prohibit slavery. This opened *all* territories to slavery.

The Missouri Compromise was designed to maintain the balance of power between North and South. It admitted Maine as a free state and Missouri as a slave state, giving each region 24 Senate seats.

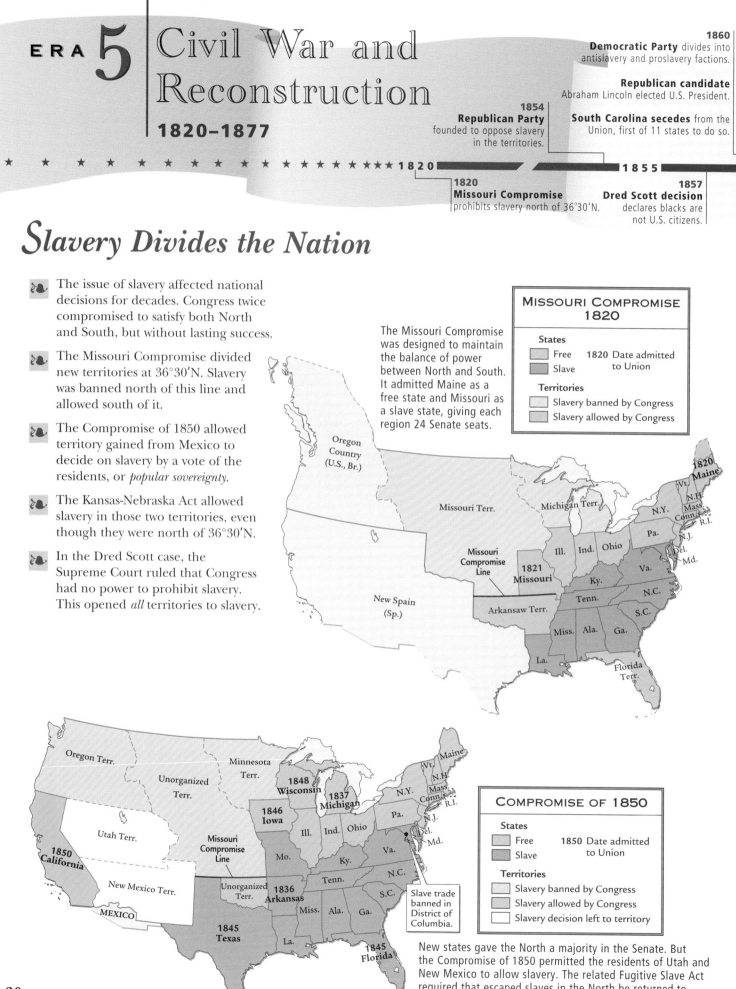

MISSOURI COMPROMISE 1820

States
- Free   1820 Date admitted to Union
- Slave

Territories
- Slavery banned by Congress
- Slavery allowed by Congress

COMPROMISE OF 1850

States
- Free   1850 Date admitted to Union
- Slave

Territories
- Slavery banned by Congress
- Slavery allowed by Congress
- Slavery decision left to territory

New states gave the North a majority in the Senate. But the Compromise of 1850 permitted the residents of Utah and New Mexico to allow slavery. The related Fugitive Slave Act required that escaped slaves in the North be returned to their Southern owners.

60

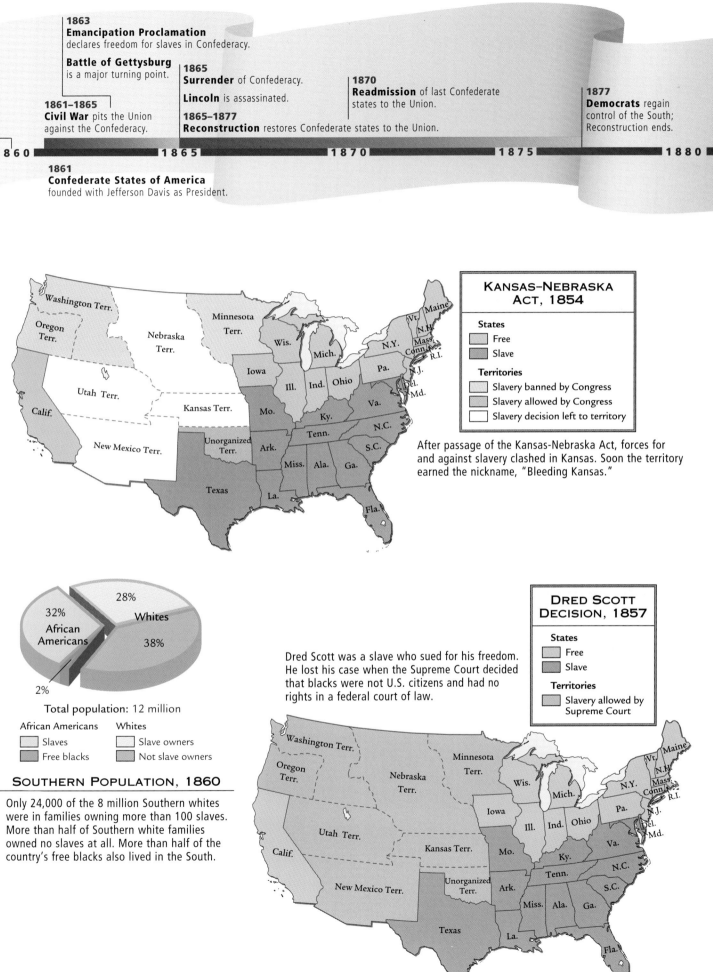

1863
Emancipation Proclamation declares freedom for slaves in Confederacy.

Battle of Gettysburg is a major turning point.

1861–1865
Civil War pits the Union against the Confederacy.

1865
Surrender of Confederacy.

Lincoln is assassinated.

1865–1877
Reconstruction restores Confederate states to the Union.

1870
Readmission of last Confederate states to the Union.

1877
Democrats regain control of the South; Reconstruction ends.

1860   **1865**   **1870**   **1875**   **1880**

1861
Confederate States of America founded with Jefferson Davis as President.

KANSAS–NEBRASKA ACT, 1854

States
- Free
- Slave

Territories
- Slavery banned by Congress
- Slavery allowed by Congress
- Slavery decision left to territory

After passage of the Kansas-Nebraska Act, forces for and against slavery clashed in Kansas. Soon the territory earned the nickname, "Bleeding Kansas."

28% Whites

32% African Americans

38%

2%

Total population: 12 million

African Americans
- Slaves
- Free blacks

Whites
- Slave owners
- Not slave owners

SOUTHERN POPULATION, 1860

Only 24,000 of the 8 million Southern whites were in families owning more than 100 slaves. More than half of Southern white families owned no slaves at all. More than half of the country's free blacks also lived in the South.

DRED SCOTT DECISION, 1857

States
- Free
- Slave

Territories
- Slavery allowed by Supreme Court

Dred Scott was a slave who sued for his freedom. He lost his case when the Supreme Court decided that blacks were not U.S. citizens and had no rights in a federal court of law.

61

The United States Before the Civil War

- By 1861 the United States stretched to the Pacific and consisted of 34 states and 8 organized territories.

- The South covered a larger area, but the North was more populous and had more cities.

- The North had a mixed economy based on a variety of crops and on manufacturing of many kinds.

- The Southern economy relied on *cash crops* (crops grown for sale), especially cotton. Its plantations, in turn, relied on slaves.

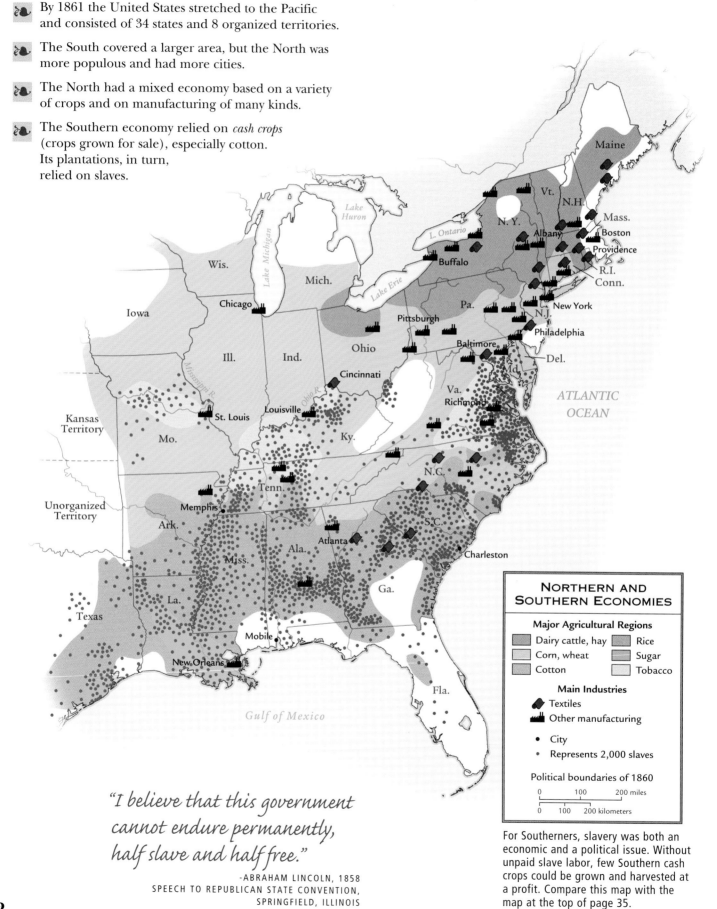

NORTHERN AND SOUTHERN ECONOMIES

Major Agricultural Regions

- Dairy cattle, hay
- Corn, wheat
- Cotton
- Rice
- Sugar
- Tobacco

Main Industries

- Textiles
- Other manufacturing
- City
- Represents 2,000 slaves

Political boundaries of 1860

| 0 | 100 | 200 miles |
| 0 | 100 | 200 kilometers |

"I believe that this government cannot endure permanently, half slave and half free."

—ABRAHAM LINCOLN, 1858
SPEECH TO REPUBLICAN STATE CONVENTION,
SPRINGFIELD, ILLINOIS

For Southerners, slavery was both an economic and a political issue. Without unpaid slave labor, few Southern cash crops could be grown and harvested at a profit. Compare this map with the map at the top of page 35.

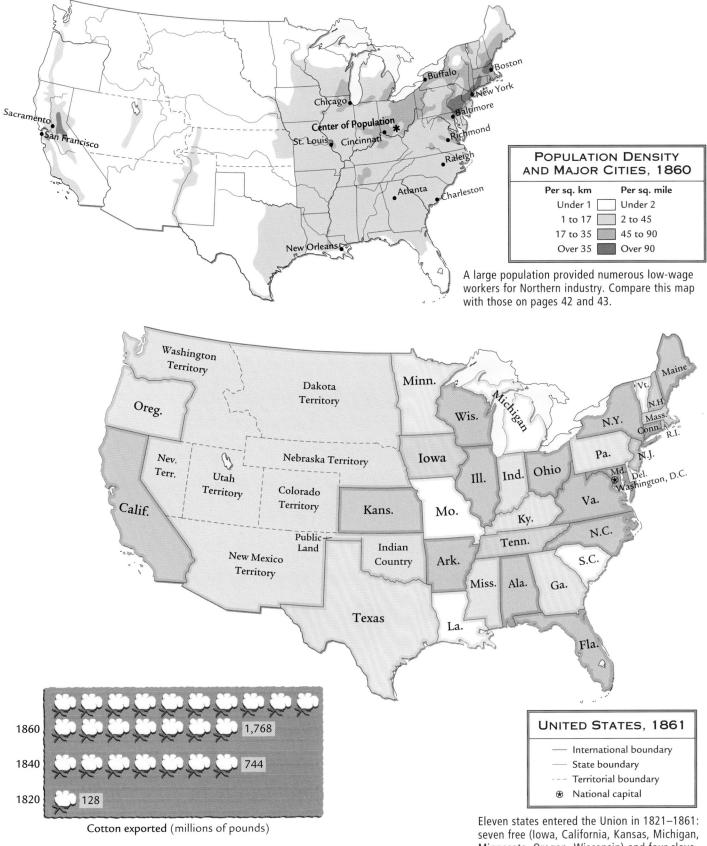

POPULATION DENSITY AND MAJOR CITIES, 1860

Per sq. km	Per sq. mile
Under 1	Under 2
1 to 17	2 to 45
17 to 35	45 to 90
Over 35	Over 90

A large population provided numerous low-wage workers for Northern industry. Compare this map with those on pages 42 and 43.

UNITED STATES, 1861

— International boundary
— State boundary
--- Territorial boundary
⊛ National capital

Eleven states entered the Union in 1821–1861: seven free (Iowa, California, Kansas, Michigan, Minnesota, Oregon, Wisconsin) and four slave (Arkansas, Florida, Missouri, Texas). Compare this map with the map on page 51.

1860   1,768
1840   744
1820   128

Cotton exported (millions of pounds)

SOUTHERN COTTON EXPORTS

Between 1820 and 1860, textile mills both in the North and in Europe came to rely on Southern cotton. The more cotton it grew, the more the South came to rely on slavery.

The Civil War Begins

- The Civil War broke out in 1861 over the right of states to *secede*, or withdraw, from the United States.

- Soon after Abraham Lincoln was elected President in 1860, 11 slave states seceded to form the Confederate States of America.

- Lincoln believed that individual states could not leave the nation. The North fought to preserve the Union—the United States of America.

- The Confederate army fought with skill and determination. It dealt the Union army many early defeats.

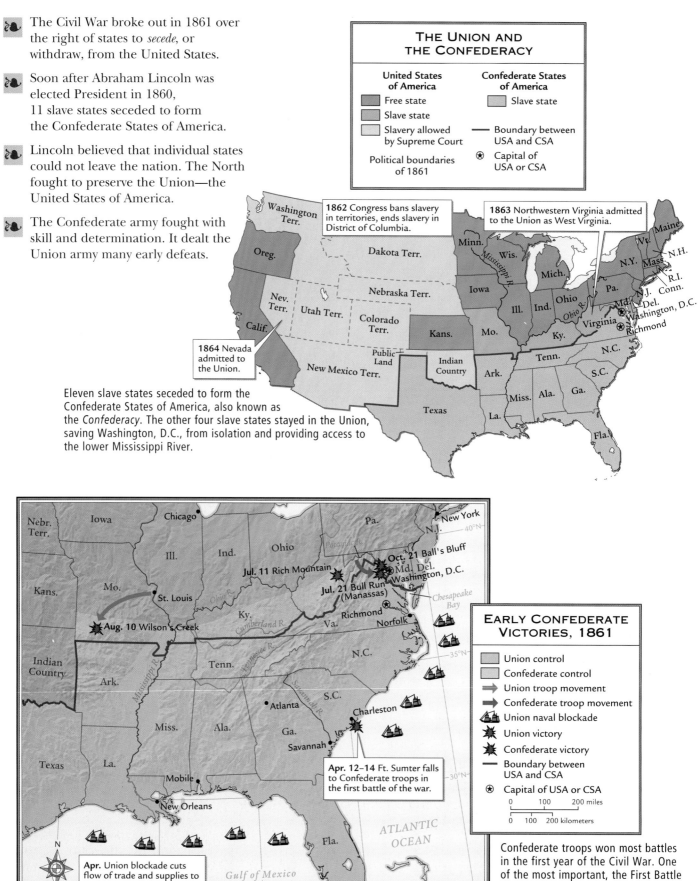

THE UNION AND THE CONFEDERACY

United States of America
- Free state
- Slave state
- Slavery allowed by Supreme Court
- Political boundaries of 1861

Confederate States of America
- Slave state
- ——— Boundary between USA and CSA
- ⊛ Capital of USA or CSA

1862 Congress bans slavery in territories, ends slavery in District of Columbia.

1863 Northwestern Virginia admitted to the Union as West Virginia.

1864 Nevada admitted to the Union.

Eleven slave states seceded to form the Confederate States of America, also known as the *Confederacy*. The other four slave states stayed in the Union, saving Washington, D.C., from isolation and providing access to the lower Mississippi River.

EARLY CONFEDERATE VICTORIES, 1861
- Union control
- Confederate control
- → Union troop movement
- → Confederate troop movement
- Union naval blockade
- Union victory
- Confederate victory
- ——— Boundary between USA and CSA
- ⊛ Capital of USA or CSA

0   100   200 miles
0   100   200 kilometers

Jul. 11 Rich Mountain
Oct. 21 Ball's Bluff
Jul. 21 Bull Run (Manassas)
Aug. 10 Wilson's Creek
Apr. 12–14 Ft. Sumter falls to Confederate troops in the first battle of the war.
Apr. Union blockade cuts flow of trade and supplies to and from Confederate ports.

Confederate troops won most battles in the first year of the Civil War. One of the most important, the First Battle of Bull Run, or Manassas, was fought 30 miles from Washington, D.C.

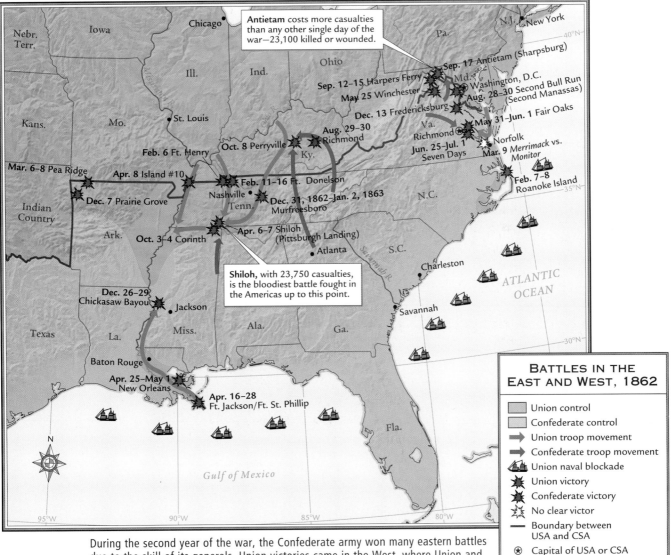

Antietam costs more casualties than any other single day of the war—23,100 killed or wounded.

Sep. 17 Antietam (Sharpsburg)
Sep. 12–15 Harpers Ferry
May 25 Winchester
Aug. 28–30 Second Bull Run (Second Manassas)
Washington, D.C.
Dec. 13 Fredericksburg
Aug. 29–30 Richmond
Oct. 8 Perryville
May 31–Jun. 1 Fair Oaks
Richmond
Jun. 25–Jul. 1 Seven Days
Norfolk
Mar. 9 Merrimack vs. Monitor
Mar. 6–8 Pea Ridge
Apr. 8 Island #10
Feb. 11–16 Ft. Donelson
Feb. 6 Ft. Henry
Dec. 7 Prairie Grove
Nashville
Dec. 31, 1862–Jan. 2, 1863 Murfreesboro
Feb. 7–8 Roanoke Island
Oct. 3–4 Corinth
Apr. 6–7 Shiloh (Pittsburgh Landing)
Atlanta
Dec. 26–29 Chickasaw Bayou
Jackson
Charleston

Shiloh, with 23,750 casualties, is the bloodiest battle fought in the Americas up to this point.

Savannah
Texas
La.
Miss.
Ala.
Ga.
Baton Rouge
Apr. 25–May 1 New Orleans
Apr. 16–28 Ft. Jackson/Ft. St. Phillip
Fla.
Gulf of Mexico

ATLANTIC OCEAN

BATTLES IN THE EAST AND WEST, 1862

- Union control
- Confederate control
- → Union troop movement
- → Confederate troop movement
- Union naval blockade
- Union victory
- Confederate victory
- No clear victor
- — Boundary between USA and CSA
- ⊛ Capital of USA or CSA

0   100   200 miles
0 100 200 kilometers

During the second year of the war, the Confederate army won many eastern battles due to the skill of its generals. Union victories came in the West, where Union and Confederate forces fought for control of the Mississippi River.

	Union		Confederate
Land in farms	58%		42%
Population	71%		29%
Railroad track	71%		29%
Factories	86%		14%

UNION AND CONFEDERATE RESOURCES

The resources of the Union made it better able to withstand a long, destructive conflict than the Confederacy, which had more troops with prior training and experience.

Confederate troops, called "rebels" by Northerners, wore gray uniforms, such as the ones in this battle reenactment. Union troops, called "Yankees" by Southerners, wore blue.

The Civil War Continues

- In 1863 decisive Union victories at Vicksburg and Gettysburg marked the turning point of the Civil War.

- The Union strategy of cutting off Confederate supplies and trade was also having an effect.

- The Confederacy had expected support from England and France, but help did not come.

- After the Emancipation Proclamation, Europe saw the war as a conflict over slavery. It honored the Union blockade.

- By 1864 the Confederate army was short of men and supplies, but it continued to fight.

Many Civil War battles were fought in farm fields, and most soldiers, like the Union troops in this reenactment, arrived on foot.

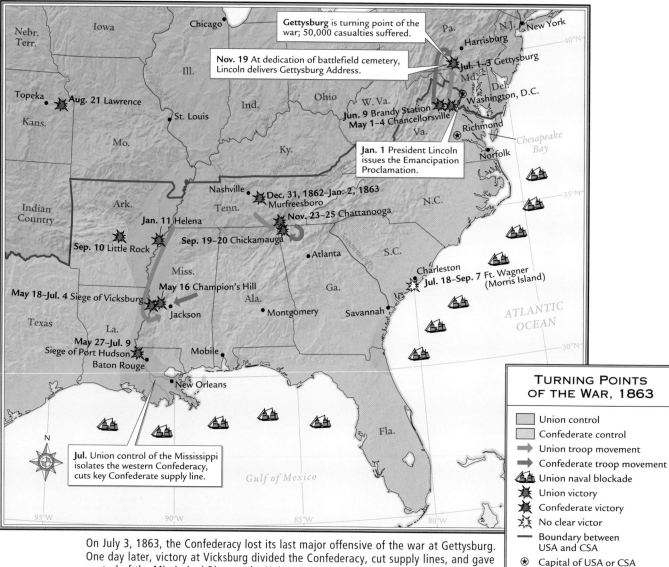

Gettysburg is turning point of the war; 50,000 casualties suffered.

Nov. 19 At dedication of battlefield cemetery, Lincoln delivers Gettysburg Address.

Jul. 1-3 Gettysburg

Jun. 9 Brandy Station
May 1-4 Chancellorsville

Jan. 1 President Lincoln issues the Emancipation Proclamation.

Aug. 21 Lawrence

Dec. 31, 1862–Jan. 2, 1863 Murfreesboro

Nov. 23-25 Chattanooga

Jan. 11 Helena

Sep. 19-20 Chickamauga

Sep. 10 Little Rock

May 16 Champion's Hill

May 18-Jul. 4 Siege of Vicksburg

Jul. 18-Sep. 7 Ft. Wagner (Morris Island)

May 27-Jul. 9 Siege of Port Hudson
Baton Rouge

Jul. Union control of the Mississippi isolates the western Confederacy, cuts key Confederate supply line.

TURNING POINTS OF THE WAR, 1863

- Union control
- Confederate control
- → Union troop movement
- → Confederate troop movement
- Union naval blockade
- Union victory
- Confederate victory
- No clear victor
- Boundary between USA and CSA
- ✳ Capital of USA or CSA

0   100   200 miles

0   100   200 kilometers

On July 3, 1863, the Confederacy lost its last major offensive of the war at Gettysburg. One day later, victory at Vicksburg divided the Confederacy, cut supply lines, and gave control of the Mississippi River to the Union.

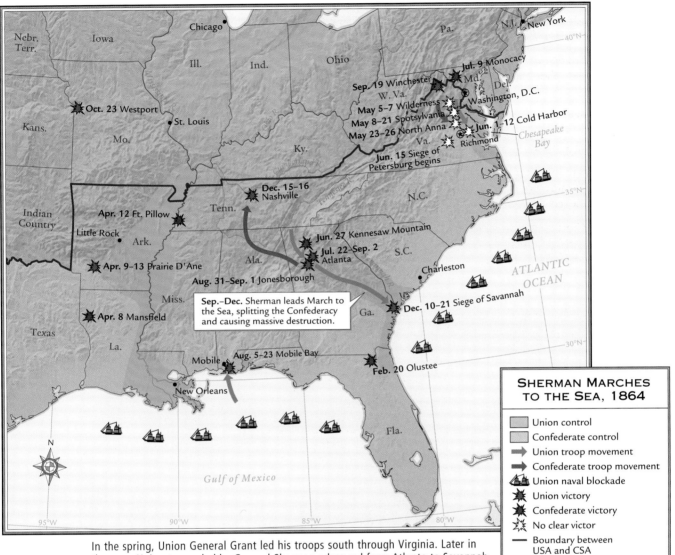

Nebr. Terr.
Iowa
Chicago
Ill.
Ind.
Ohio
Pa.
N.J.
New York
40°N

Jul. 9 Monocacy
Md.
Del.
Sep. 19 Winchester
W. Va.
Washington, D.C.
May 5–7 Wilderness
May 8–21 Spotsylvania
Jun. 1–12 Cold Harbor
May 23–26 North Anna
Chesapeake Bay
Va.
Richmond
Jun. 15 Siege of Petersburg begins

Kans.
Oct. 23 Westport
St. Louis
Mo.
Ky.
35°N

Tenn.
Dec. 15–16 Nashville
N.C.

Indian Country
Apr. 12 Ft. Pillow
Little Rock
Ark.
Jun. 27 Kennesaw Mountain
S.C.
ATLANTIC OCEAN

Apr. 9–13 Prairie D'Ane
Ala.
Jul. 22–Sep. 2 Atlanta
Charleston
Aug. 31–Sep. 1 Jonesborough
Miss.
Sep.–Dec. Sherman leads March to the Sea, splitting the Confederacy and causing massive destruction.
Ga.
Dec. 10–21 Siege of Savannah

Apr. 8 Mansfield
Texas
La.
Aug. 5–23 Mobile Bay
Mobile
Feb. 20 Olustee

New Orleans
Fla.
30°N

N
Gulf of Mexico

95°W
90°W
85°W
80°W

SHERMAN MARCHES TO THE SEA, 1864

- Union control
- Confederate control
- → Union troop movement
- → Confederate troop movement
- Union naval blockade
- Union victory
- Confederate victory
- No clear victor
- — Boundary between USA and CSA
- ✱ Capital of USA or CSA

0   100   200 miles
0   100   200 kilometers

In the spring, Union General Grant led his troops south through Virginia. Later in the year, Union troops led by General Sherman advanced from Atlanta to Savannah. They destroyed roads, bridges, and buildings in a path 60 miles wide.

Charleston, South Carolina, was one of many Southern cities damaged during the war. Most Northern cities were far from the fighting and suffered no physical damage.

World War II 407,000
World War I 116,500
Civil War 620,000
Vietnam War 58,000
Korean War 37,000
Revolutionary War 25,700
Mexican War 13,000
Other major wars 5,000

AMERICAN WAR DEATHS

Medical practices of the 1800s were overwhelmed by the deadly tactics and weapons of the Civil War. Loss of blood, shock, and infection cost thousands of lives. Disease cost many more.

The War Ends, Reconstruction Follows

- In April 1865 General Lee surrendered his Confederate army to Grant. Other Confederate generals soon surrendered too, and the Civil War ended.

- During *Reconstruction*, former Confederate states had to accept new constitutional amendments before they could re-enter the Union.

- The 13th, 14th, and 15th Amendments ended slavery and extended the vote and other rights of citizenship to all men regardless of "race, color, or condition of previous servitude."

- By 1877 all Union forces had left the South. Former Confederates had regained power, and soon afterward blacks were denied their newly won rights.

The 13th Amendment to the Constitution ended slavery in the United States. Having few alternatives, most former slaves, like the sharecropper family in this hand-painted photo, continued to work on Southern farms.

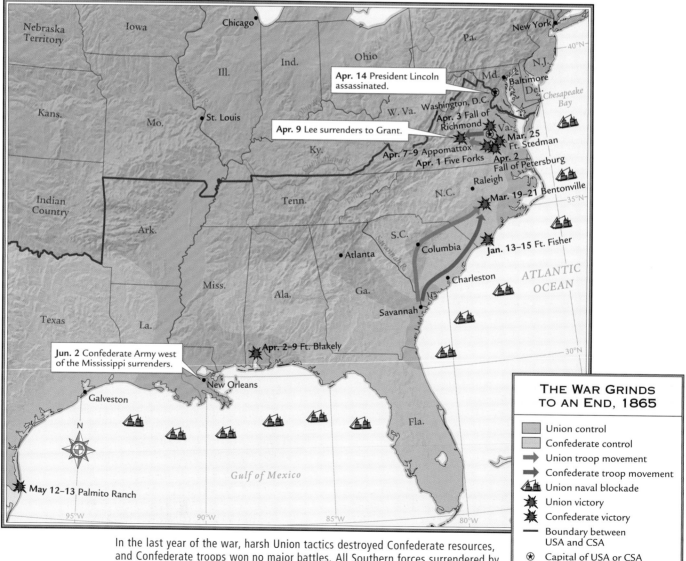

Apr. 14 President Lincoln assassinated.

Apr. 9 Lee surrenders to Grant.

Apr. 3 Fall of Richmond

Mar. 25 Ft. Stedman

Apr. 7–9 Appomattox

Apr. 1 Five Forks

Apr. 2 Fall of Petersburg

Mar. 19–21 Bentonville

Jan. 13–15 Ft. Fisher

Jun. 2 Confederate Army west of the Mississippi surrenders.

Apr. 2–9 Ft. Blakely

May 12–13 Palmito Ranch

THE WAR GRINDS TO AN END, 1865

- Union control
- Confederate control
- Union troop movement
- Confederate troop movement
- Union naval blockade
- Union victory
- Confederate victory
- Boundary between USA and CSA
- Capital of USA or CSA

0   100   200 miles
0   100   200 kilometers

In the last year of the war, harsh Union tactics destroyed Confederate resources, and Confederate troops won no major battles. All Southern forces surrendered by the middle of the year.

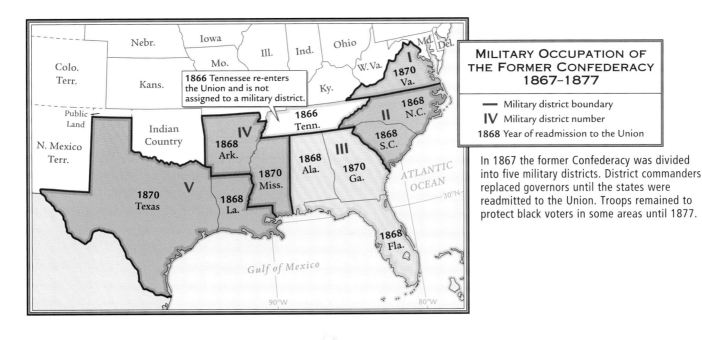

1866 Tennessee re-enters the Union and is not assigned to a military district.

1866 Tenn.

MILITARY OCCUPATION OF THE FORMER CONFEDERACY 1867–1877

— Military district boundary
IV Military district number
1868 Year of readmission to the Union

In 1867 the former Confederacy was divided into five military districts. District commanders replaced governors until the states were readmitted to the Union. Troops remained to protect black voters in some areas until 1877.

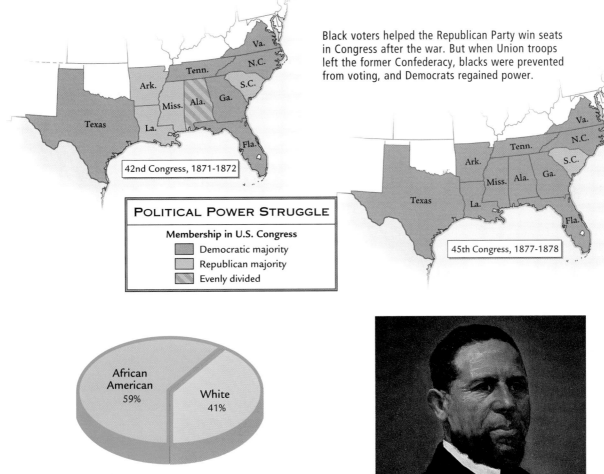

Black voters helped the Republican Party win seats in Congress after the war. But when Union troops left the former Confederacy, blacks were prevented from voting, and Democrats regained power.

42nd Congress, 1871-1872

45th Congress, 1877-1878

POLITICAL POWER STRUGGLE

Membership in U.S. Congress

- Democratic majority
- Republican majority
- Evenly divided

SOUTH CAROLINA POPULATION, 1870

African American 59%

White 41%

Southern whites feared loss of political power if blacks had the chance to vote. Blacks outnumbered whites in three former Confederate states, and nearly equaled their numbers in three others.

Hiram Revels of Mississippi was the first African American elected to the U.S. Senate. During Reconstruction many blacks were elected to state and federal offices.

69

1869
Union Pacific and Central Pacific
link East and West.

1866
Sedalia Trail
brings Texas cattle to Missouri railhead.

1865
Civil War ends.

1860 ▮ 1865 ▮ 1870

Early 1860s
Chinese immigrants in California begin work on Central Pacific Railroad.

1867
Alaska purchased from Russia.

Immigration Swells the Work Force

- After the Civil War, immigration increased so much that total U.S. population rose despite wartime losses.

- Immigrants provided a vast new pool of labor for the rapidly industrializing nation. They built railroads, worked in mines and factories, and farmed the Great Plains.

- By 1890 almost one out of every seven people in the United States was foreign-born.

387,203 — 1870
457,257 — 1880
455,302 — 1890

- Northern & Western Europe
- Southern & Eastern Europe
- North America
- Asia

IMMIGRANT ORIGINS

Most immigrants still came from Northern and Western Europe, but the numbers from Southern and Eastern Europe were increasing. Compare this graph to the one on page 58.

"Give me your tired, your poor, your huddled masses yearning to breathe free . . ."

—INSCRIPTION AT THE BASE OF THE STATUE OF LIBERTY FROM THE POEM, "NEW WORLD COLOSSUS," BY EMMA LAZARUS, 1883

Some immigrants fled political or religious persecution. Others came seeking land or jobs.

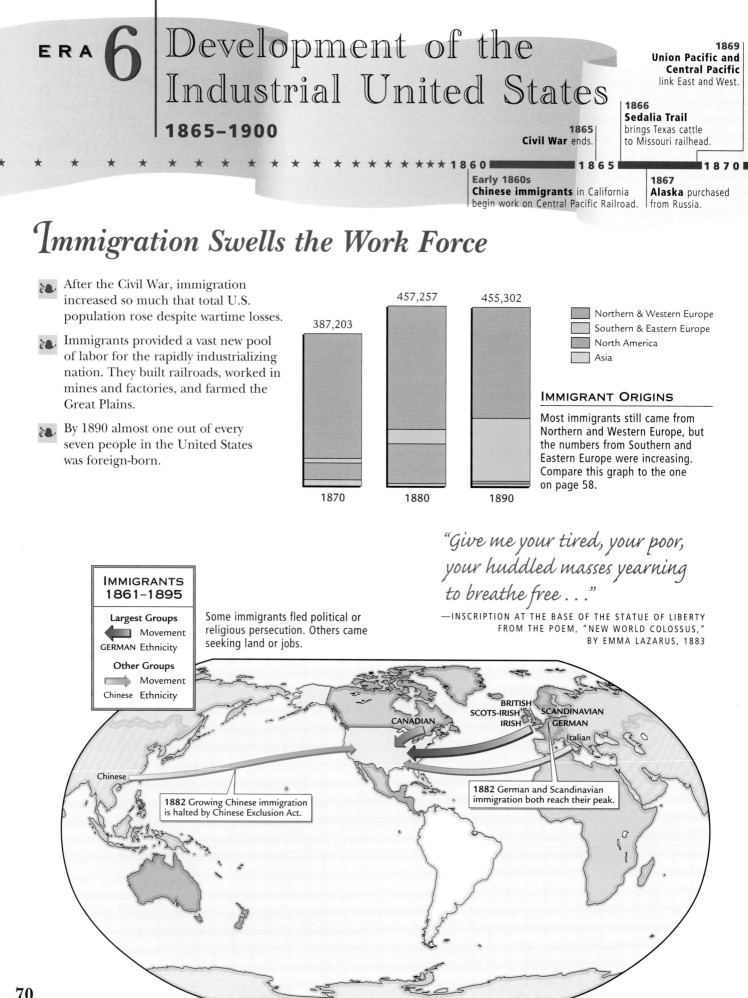

IMMIGRANTS 1861–1895

Largest Groups
← Movement
GERMAN Ethnicity

Other Groups
→ Movement
Chinese Ethnicity

CANADIAN

BRITISH
SCOTS-IRISH
IRISH

SCANDINAVIAN
GERMAN

Italian

Chinese

1882 Growing Chinese immigration is halted by Chinese Exclusion Act.

1882 German and Scandinavian immigration both reach their peak.

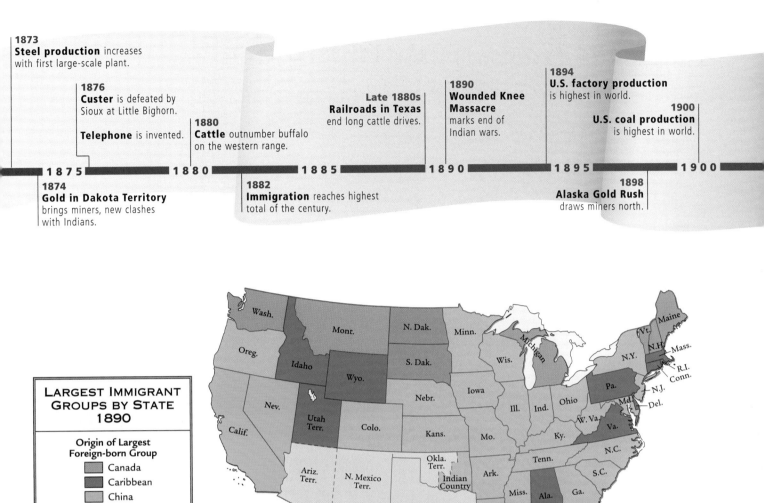

1873
Steel production increases with first large-scale plant.

1876
Custer is defeated by Sioux at Little Bighorn.

Telephone is invented.

1880
Cattle outnumber buffalo on the western range.

Late 1880s
Railroads in Texas end long cattle drives.

1890
Wounded Knee Massacre marks end of Indian wars.

1894
U.S. factory production is highest in world.

1900
U.S. coal production is highest in world.

1875   **1880**   **1885**   **1890**   **1895**   **1900**

1874
Gold in Dakota Territory brings miners, new clashes with Indians.

1882
Immigration reaches highest total of the century.

1898
Alaska Gold Rush draws miners north.

LARGEST IMMIGRANT GROUPS BY STATE 1890

Origin of Largest Foreign-born Group

- Canada
- Caribbean
- China
- England
- Germany
- Ireland
- Mexico
- Norway

Foreign-born residents often settled in the same states as others from their homelands. Notice which group of immigrants was largest in more states than any other group.

Most Chinese immigrants became railroad laborers, but others worked as farmers, peddlers, and local merchants.

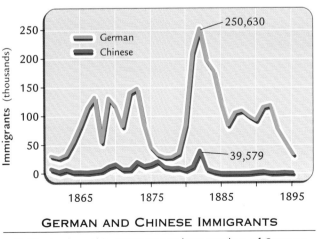

GERMAN AND CHINESE IMMIGRANTS

Political upheaval in Germany sent huge numbers of Germans to the United States in the early 1880s. Chinese immigrants outnumbered all others of non-European ancestry until 1882, when the Chinese Exclusion Act was passed.

71

Railroads Transform the West

- The first transcontinental railroad was completed in 1869. It cut cross-country travel time from 26 days to 7 days.

- Federal subsidies helped pay for Western railroads. Railroads, in turn, made it easier to settle the West.

- Trains carried cattle to Eastern markets and supplies to Western settlers.

- Railroad expansion helped destroy the buffalo (formally called the North American bison). Cattle replaced buffalo on the range and provided meat for fast-growing Eastern cities.

Building Western railroads was hard, hot work. Most of the labor was performed by Chinese and Irish immigrants.

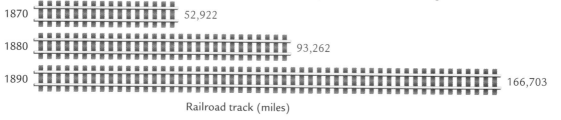

1860   30,626

1870   52,922

1880   93,262

1890   166,703

Railroad track (miles)

MILES OF RAILROAD TRACK

After 1860 all railroad track was the same gauge, or width: 4 feet, 8½ inches. Now a single train could go anywhere track had been laid. The growing U.S. steel industry provided all the track railroads needed to expand.

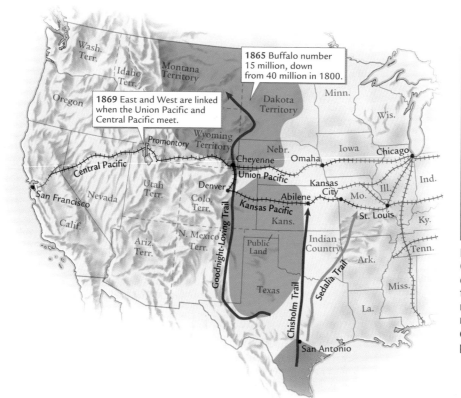

1865 Buffalo number 15 million, down from 40 million in 1800.

1869 East and West are linked when the Union Pacific and Central Pacific meet.

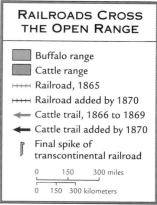

RAILROADS CROSS THE OPEN RANGE

- Buffalo range
- Cattle range
- Railroad, 1865
- Railroad added by 1870
- Cattle trail, 1866 to 1869
- Cattle trail added by 1870
- Final spike of transcontinental railroad

0   150   300 miles
0   150   300 kilometers

Buffalo roamed freely on the Great Plains until their range was cut in two by trails used by settlers traveling west. The transcontinental railroads, following a similar route, made the split permanent. Find the eastern part of the rail network on page 53.

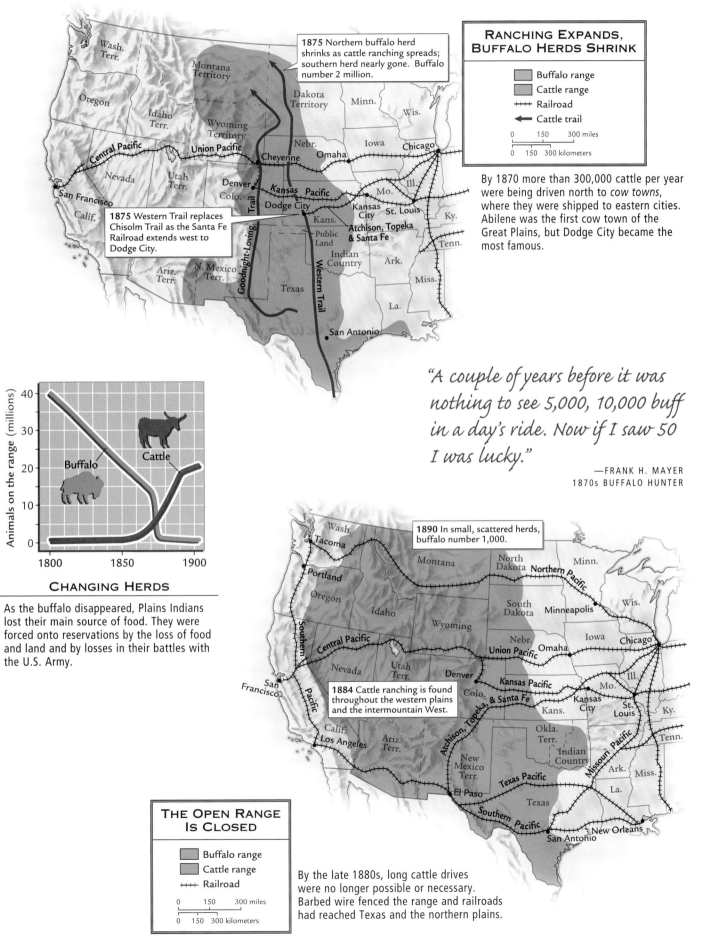

1875 Northern buffalo herd shrinks as cattle ranching spreads; southern herd nearly gone. Buffalo number 2 million.

RANCHING EXPANDS, BUFFALO HERDS SHRINK

- Buffalo range
- Cattle range
- ┼┼┼┼ Railroad
- ← Cattle trail

0   150   300 miles
0   150   300 kilometers

By 1870 more than 300,000 cattle per year were being driven north to *cow towns*, where they were shipped to eastern cities. Abilene was the first cow town of the Great Plains, but Dodge City became the most famous.

1875 Western Trail replaces Chisolm Trail as the Santa Fe Railroad extends west to Dodge City.

"A couple of years before it was nothing to see 5,000, 10,000 buff in a day's ride. Now if I saw 50 I was lucky."

—FRANK H. MAYER
1870s BUFFALO HUNTER

CHANGING HERDS

As the buffalo disappeared, Plains Indians lost their main source of food. They were forced onto reservations by the loss of food and land and by losses in their battles with the U.S. Army.

1890 In small, scattered herds, buffalo number 1,000.

1884 Cattle ranching is found throughout the western plains and the intermountain West.

THE OPEN RANGE IS CLOSED

- Buffalo range
- Cattle range
- ┼┼┼┼ Railroad

0   150   300 miles
0   150   300 kilometers

By the late 1880s, long cattle drives were no longer possible or necessary. Barbed wire fenced the range and railroads had reached Texas and the northern plains.

73

Using Indian Lands to Feed the Nation

After the Civil War, nearly 250,000 Indians lived on the western prairies and the Great Plains, a region Eastern settlers believed useless for farming.

To encourage citizens to settle the Plains, the Homestead Act of 1862 offered settlers 160 acres of free land.

Indians fought these intruders, but were weakened by the loss of the buffalo. By 1880 the army had forced most Plains Indians onto reservations.

By 1900, 500,000 settlers farmed the Plains, growing food to help feed the cities of the East.

"The West begins where the average annual rainfall drops below twenty inches."

—BERNARD DE VOTO
U.S. HISTORIAN

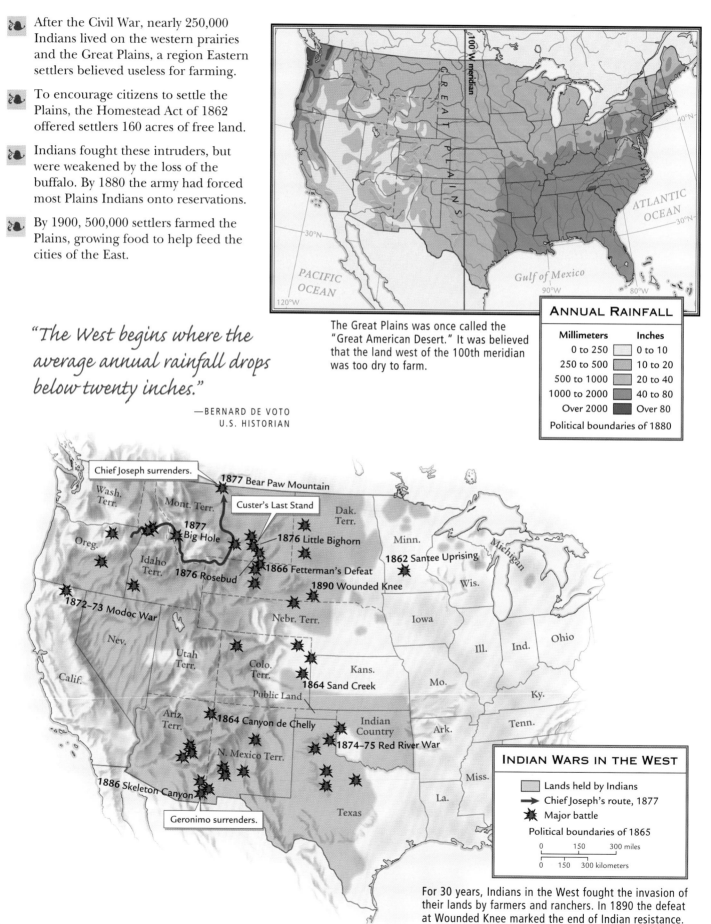

The Great Plains was once called the "Great American Desert." It was believed that the land west of the 100th meridian was too dry to farm.

ANNUAL RAINFALL

Millimeters	Inches
0 to 250	0 to 10
250 to 500	10 to 20
500 to 1000	20 to 40
1000 to 2000	40 to 80
Over 2000	Over 80

Political boundaries of 1880

Chief Joseph surrenders.
1877 Bear Paw Mountain
Custer's Last Stand
1877 Big Hole
1876 Little Bighorn
1876 Rosebud
1866 Fetterman's Defeat
1862 Santee Uprising
1890 Wounded Knee
1872–73 Modoc War
1864 Sand Creek
1864 Canyon de Chelly
1874–75 Red River War
1886 Skeleton Canyon
Geronimo surrenders.

Wash. Terr. · Mont. Terr. · Dak. Terr. · Minn. · Michigan · Oreg. · Idaho Terr. · Wis. · Nebr. Terr. · Iowa · Nev. · Utah Terr. · Colo. Terr. · Kans. · Mo. · Ill. · Ind. · Ohio · Ky. · Calif. · Ariz. Terr. · N. Mexico Terr. · Indian Country · Ark. · Tenn. · Public Land · Miss. · La. · Texas

INDIAN WARS IN THE WEST

Lands held by Indians
Chief Joseph's route, 1877
Major battle

Political boundaries of 1865

| 0 | 150 | 300 miles |
| 0 | 150 | 300 kilometers |

For 30 years, Indians in the West fought the invasion of their lands by farmers and ranchers. In 1890 the defeat at Wounded Knee marked the end of Indian resistance.

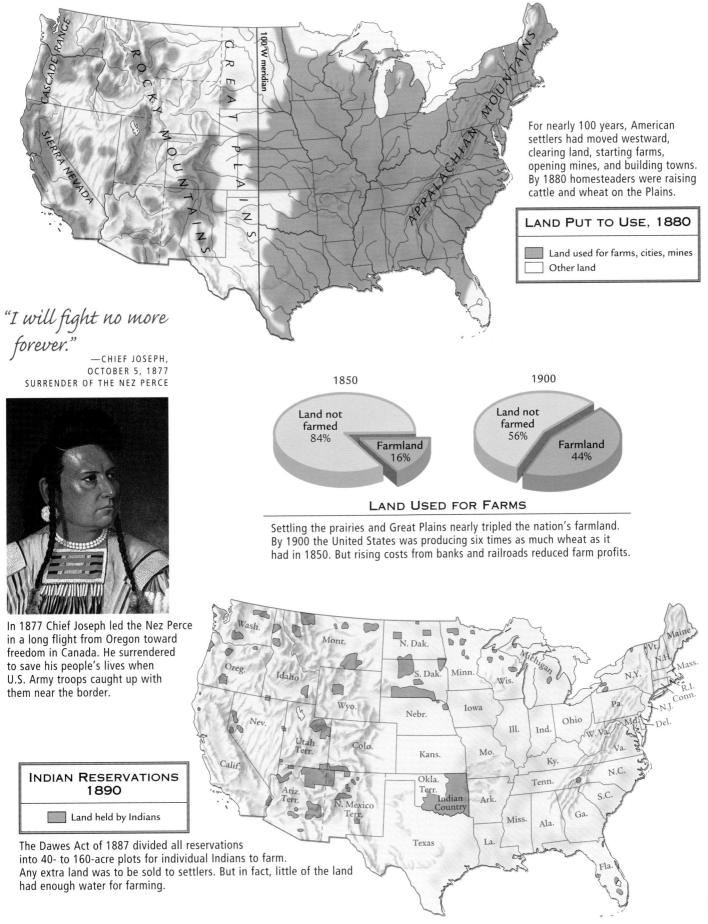

For nearly 100 years, American settlers had moved westward, clearing land, starting farms, opening mines, and building towns. By 1880 homesteaders were raising cattle and wheat on the Plains.

LAND PUT TO USE, 1880

Land used for farms, cities, mines
Other land

"I will fight no more forever."

—CHIEF JOSEPH,
OCTOBER 5, 1877
SURRENDER OF THE NEZ PERCE

1850

Land not farmed 84%
Farmland 16%

1900

Land not farmed 56%
Farmland 44%

LAND USED FOR FARMS

Settling the prairies and Great Plains nearly tripled the nation's farmland. By 1900 the United States was producing six times as much wheat as it had in 1850. But rising costs from banks and railroads reduced farm profits.

In 1877 Chief Joseph led the Nez Perce in a long flight from Oregon toward freedom in Canada. He surrendered to save his people's lives when U.S. Army troops caught up with them near the border.

INDIAN RESERVATIONS 1890

Land held by Indians

The Dawes Act of 1887 divided all reservations into 40- to 160-acre plots for individual Indians to farm. Any extra land was to be sold to settlers. But in fact, little of the land had enough water for farming.

75

Mining the Raw Materials for Industry

- Whenever gold was discovered in the United States, miners arrived from all over the world. Few became rich, but many stayed to settle the land.

- Less glamorous metals such as copper and lead provided valuable resources for Eastern factories.

- When lone miners had used up surface mines, mining companies took over with underground mining equipment.

- Purchased in 1867, Alaska went largely unnoticed for 30 years—until gold was discovered in the nearby Yukon Territory.

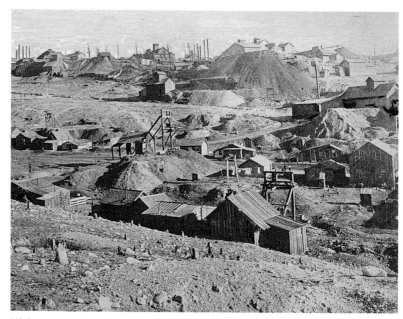

Mining companies often carried out operations at the expense of the environment. Mining by-products poisoned water and soil at the mines, downstream, and in nearby boomtowns such as Leadville, Colorado, shown in the photo above.

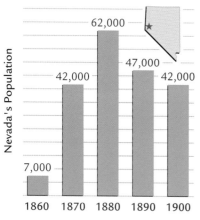

BOOM AND BUST IN NEVADA

Nevada's population boomed with the discovery of silver. But when the price of silver dropped, so did the population.

MINING THE WEST

Major Mines of the Late 1800s

- Copper
- Gold
- Lead
- Molybdenum
- Silver
- Zinc

Political boundaries of 1890

0   150   300 miles

0   150   300 kilometers

Zinc, molybdenum, and lead were added to other metals to form strong, durable *alloys*, or mixtures. Copper was valuable as a conductor of electricity.

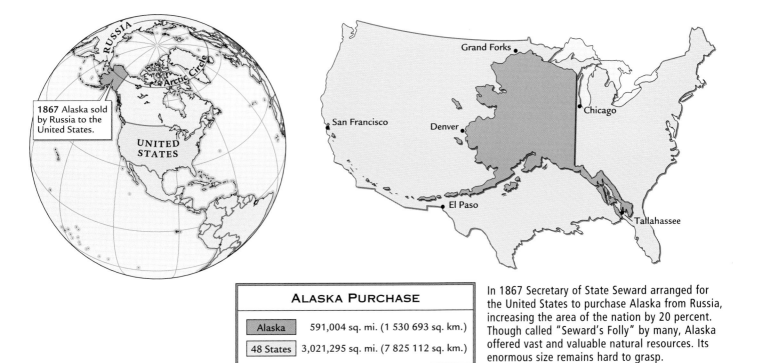

1867 Alaska sold by Russia to the United States.

ALASKA PURCHASE	
Alaska	591,004 sq. mi. (1 530 693 sq. km.)
48 States	3,021,295 sq. mi. (7 825 112 sq. km.)

In 1867 Secretary of State Seward arranged for the United States to purchase Alaska from Russia, increasing the area of the nation by 20 percent. Though called "Seward's Folly" by many, Alaska offered vast and valuable natural resources. Its enormous size remains hard to grasp.

"Gold is as plentiful as sawdust."
—ADVERTISEMENT FOR A STEAMER TO KLONDIKE COUNTRY
THE SEATTLE DAILY TIMES
JULY 14, 1897

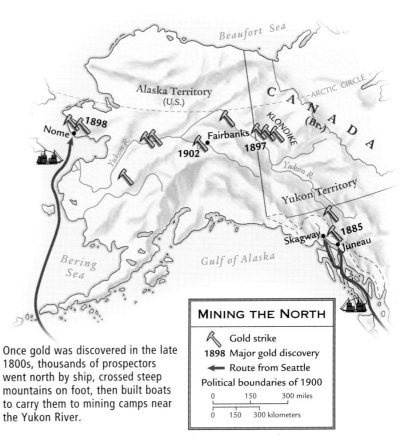

MINING THE NORTH	
⚒	Gold strike
1898	Major gold discovery
←	Route from Seattle
	Political boundaries of 1900

0   150   300 miles
0   150   300 kilometers

Once gold was discovered in the late 1800s, thousands of prospectors went north by ship, crossed steep mountains on foot, then built boats to carry them to mining camps near the Yukon River.

Miners such as the one in this hand-painted photo discovered that Alaska was more than ice and snow. Mining is still one of Alaska's leading industries.

77

Becoming an Industrial Nation

- By 1900 there were five times as many industrial workers as before the Civil War, and the United States was first in the world in factory production.

- Miners and industrial workers often worked dangerous 10-hour days, six days a week, for low pay. Labor unions sought better conditions.

- Coal powered locomotives and factories. It was also used to transform iron into steel.

- Steel was used to build machinery, railroads, steamships, and tall buildings.

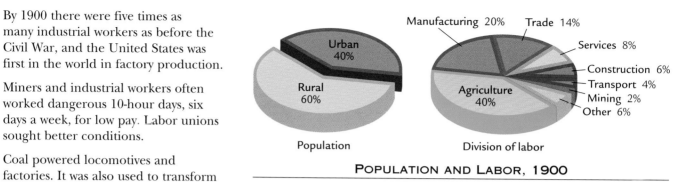

Population
Urban 40%
Rural 60%

Division of labor
Manufacturing 20% Trade 14%
Services 8%
Construction 6%
Transport 4%
Mining 2%
Other 6%
Agriculture 40%

POPULATION AND LABOR, 1900

Compare the graph of urban and rural population with the one on page 51. Industry introduced immigrants and longtime residents to new kinds of work and to life in the big city.

1890s Labor unrest grows in Western coal mines.

Chicago · Gary · Buffalo · Bethlehem · Cleveland · Youngstown · Harrisburg · Canton · Pittsburgh · Baltimore

1873 First large-scale U.S. steel mill opens near Pittsburgh.

1900 U.S. coal production is highest in the world.

Birmingham

COAL AND STEEL
- Iron deposit
- Coal deposit
- Steel-manufacturing center

By 1900 coal fueled industry, mining, and electrical power nationwide. Abundant coal, iron ore, and labor allowed the United States to become a major producer of steel.

"…there is seldom a day in the coal fields that some woman is not widowed by the mines."

—EARL W. MAYO, 1900
FRANK LESLIE'S POPULAR MONTHLY

Many coal miners were immigrants. Cave-ins, explosions, and disease made their work much more dangerous than work in factories, on railroads, and in other kinds of mines.

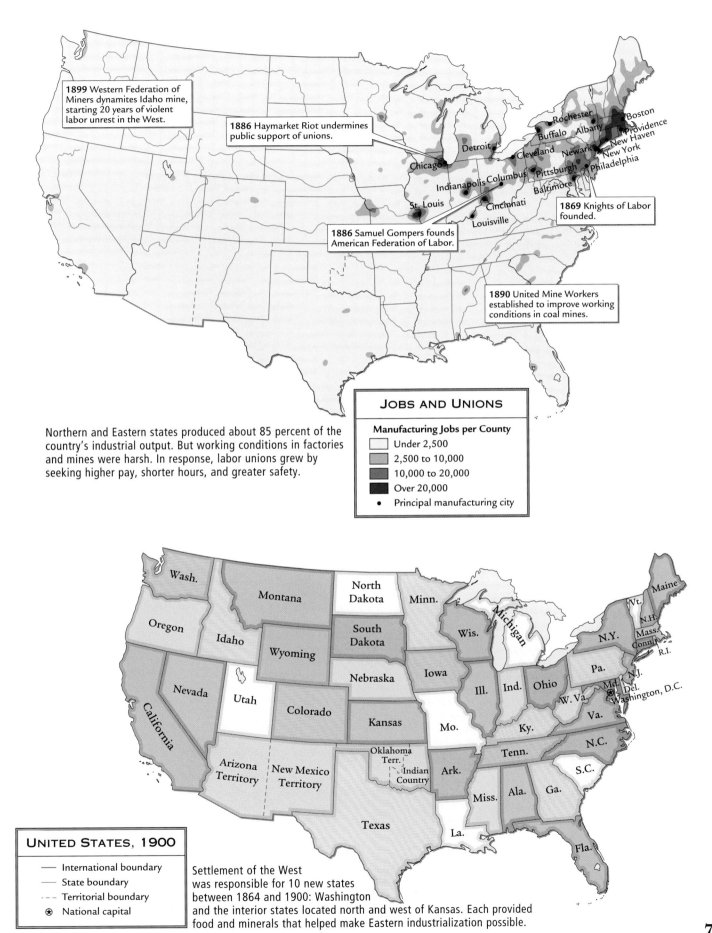

1899 Western Federation of Miners dynamites Idaho mine, starting 20 years of violent labor unrest in the West.

1886 Haymarket Riot undermines public support of unions.

1886 Samuel Gompers founds American Federation of Labor.

1869 Knights of Labor founded.

1890 United Mine Workers established to improve working conditions in coal mines.

Rochester
Buffalo · Albany · Boston
Detroit · Providence
Cleveland · Newark · New Haven
Chicago · New York
Indianapolis · Columbus · Pittsburgh · Philadelphia
St. Louis · Baltimore
Cincinnati
Louisville

Northern and Eastern states produced about 85 percent of the country's industrial output. But working conditions in factories and mines were harsh. In response, labor unions grew by seeking higher pay, shorter hours, and greater safety.

JOBS AND UNIONS

Manufacturing Jobs per County

- Under 2,500
- 2,500 to 10,000
- 10,000 to 20,000
- Over 20,000
- • Principal manufacturing city

Wash.
Montana
North Dakota
Minn.
Maine
Oregon
Idaho
South Dakota
Wis.
Michigan
Vt.
N.H.
N.Y.
Mass.
Conn.
R.I.
Wyoming
Iowa
Pa.
Nevada
Utah
Nebraska
Ill. · Ind. · Ohio
N.J.
Md. · Del.
W. Va. · Washington, D.C.
California
Colorado
Kansas
Mo.
Ky.
Va.
Arizona Territory
New Mexico Territory
Oklahoma Terr.
Indian Country
Ark.
Tenn.
N.C.
S.C.
Miss. · Ala. · Ga.
Texas
La.
Fla.

UNITED STATES, 1900

- —— International boundary
- —— State boundary
- - - - Territorial boundary
- ⊛ National capital

Settlement of the West was responsible for 10 new states between 1864 and 1900: Washington and the interior states located north and west of Kansas. Each provided food and minerals that helped make Eastern industrialization possible.

Late 1800s
Jim Crow laws passed to limit rights of African Americans.

1898
Spanish-American War involves America in Cuba and Philippines.

Hawaii becomes a U.S. possession.

★ ★ ★ ★ ★ ★ ★ ★ ★ ★ ★ ★ ★ ★ ★ ★ ★ ★ ★ **1890**   **1895**   **1900**

1890
National Park Service establishes three parks in California.

The Spanish-American War and World Power

- The United States gained recognition as a world power during the Spanish-American War.

- The Spanish-American War was fought over the independence of Cuba, a Spanish colony for 400 years.

- After the *Maine*, a U.S. warship, exploded in Havana harbor, Americans called for U.S. intervention in Cuba.

- U.S. victories over Spain brought independence to Cuba and made the Philippines a U.S. territory.

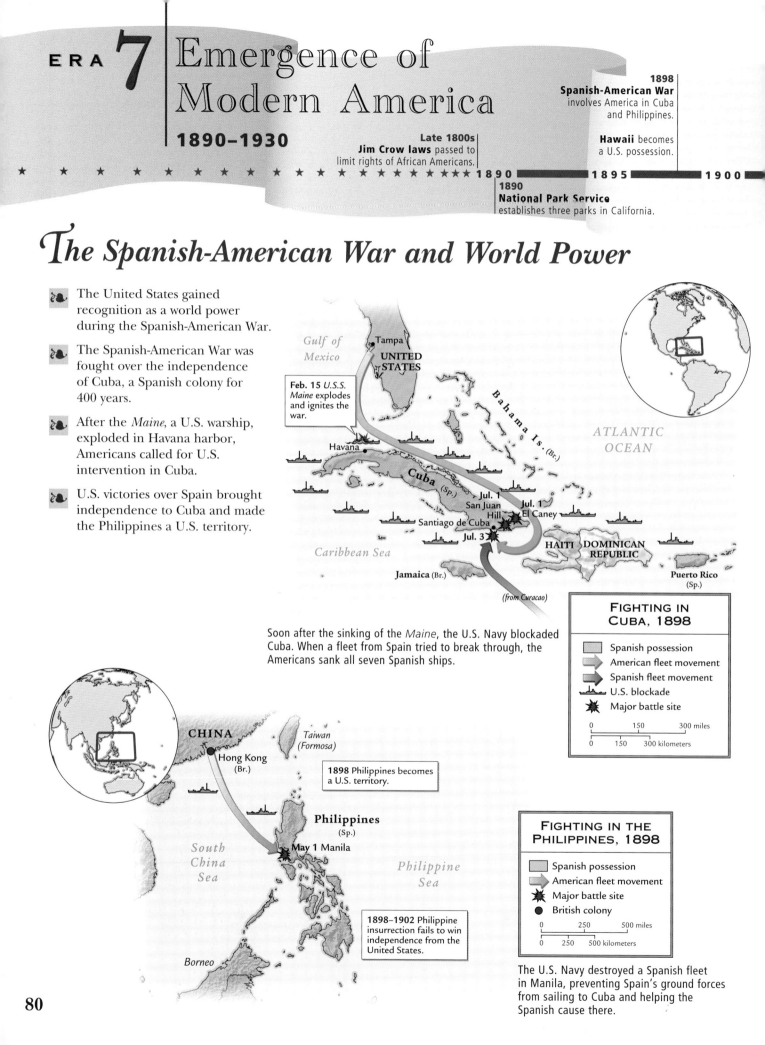

Feb. 15 U.S.S. Maine explodes and ignites the war.

Soon after the sinking of the *Maine*, the U.S. Navy blockaded Cuba. When a fleet from Spain tried to break through, the Americans sank all seven Spanish ships.

FIGHTING IN CUBA, 1898

- Spanish possession
- American fleet movement
- Spanish fleet movement
- U.S. blockade
- ✶ Major battle site

0   150   300 miles
0   150   300 kilometers

1898 Philippines becomes a U.S. territory.

1898–1902 Philippine insurrection fails to win independence from the United States.

FIGHTING IN THE PHILIPPINES, 1898

- Spanish possession
- American fleet movement
- ✶ Major battle site
- ● British colony

0   250   500 miles
0   250   500 kilometers

The U.S. Navy destroyed a Spanish fleet in Manila, preventing Spain's ground forces from sailing to Cuba and helping the Spanish cause there.

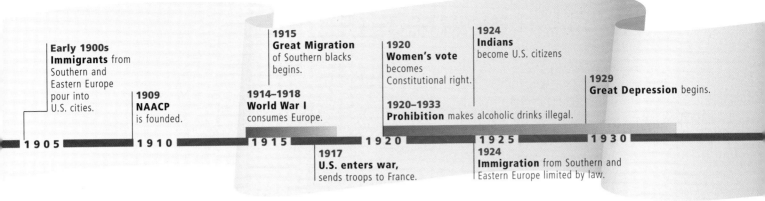

Early 1900s
Immigrants from Southern and Eastern Europe pour into U.S. cities.

1909
NAACP is founded.

1915
Great Migration of Southern blacks begins.

1914–1918
World War I consumes Europe.

1920
Women's vote becomes Constitutional right.

1920–1933
Prohibition makes alcoholic drinks illegal.

1924
Indians become U.S. citizens

1929
Great Depression begins.

1905   1910   1915   1920   1925   1930

1917
U.S. enters war, sends troops to France.

1924
Immigration from Southern and Eastern Europe limited by law.

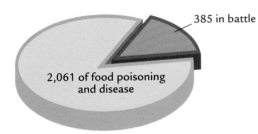

385 in battle

2,061 of food poisoning and disease

U.S. DEATHS IN THE SPANISH-AMERICAN WAR

While the superiority of the U.S. Navy kept the number of battle deaths low, tropical diseases such as malaria, dysentery, and yellow fever killed more than 2,000 troops.

Theodore Roosevelt (center) poses with his Rough Riders after winning the battle at San Juan Hill in Cuba. A few years later, Roosevelt was elected President of the United States.

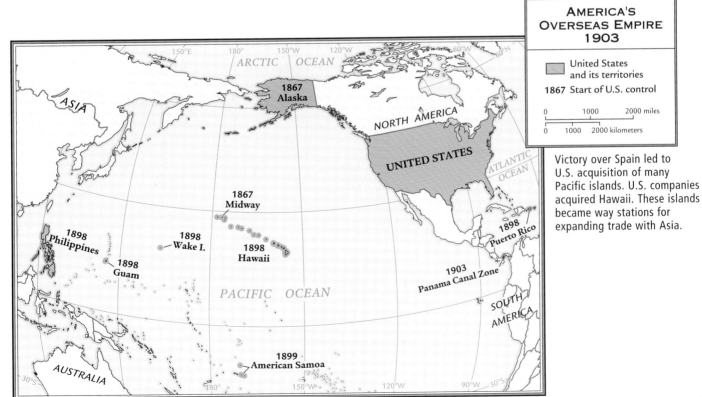

AMERICA'S OVERSEAS EMPIRE 1903

☐ United States and its territories

1867 Start of U.S. control

0   1000   2000 miles
0   1000   2000 kilometers

Victory over Spain led to U.S. acquisition of many Pacific islands. U.S. companies acquired Hawaii. These islands became way stations for expanding trade with Asia.

81

Immigration and the Growth of Cities

- Nearly 15 million immigrants entered the United States between 1895 and 1914, most of them Roman Catholics and Jews from Southern and Eastern Europe.

- Many of the new immigrants were from Italy, Russia, and Poland. They tended to settle in large cities, such as Chicago and New York.

- Settlement houses, such as Hull House in Chicago, helped immigrants adjust to life in America's cities.

- The new immigrants made the population of the United States more diverse than that of any other nation in the world.

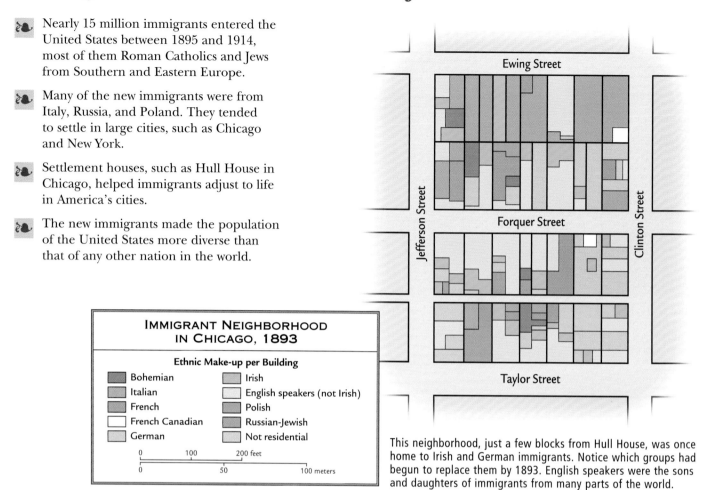

IMMIGRANT NEIGHBORHOOD IN CHICAGO, 1893

Ethnic Make-up per Building

- Bohemian
- Italian
- French
- French Canadian
- German
- Irish
- English speakers (not Irish)
- Polish
- Russian-Jewish
- Not residential

This neighborhood, just a few blocks from Hull House, was once home to Irish and German immigrants. Notice which groups had begun to replace them by 1893. English speakers were the sons and daughters of immigrants from many parts of the world.

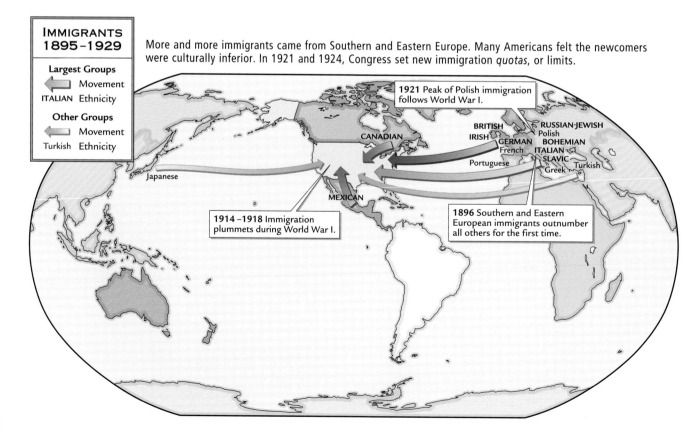

IMMIGRANTS 1895–1929

Largest Groups
- ⬅ Movement
- ITALIAN Ethnicity

Other Groups
- ⬅ Movement
- Turkish Ethnicity

More and more immigrants came from Southern and Eastern Europe. Many Americans felt the newcomers were culturally inferior. In 1921 and 1924, Congress set new immigration *quotas*, or limits.

1921 Peak of Polish immigration follows World War I.

1914–1918 Immigration plummets during World War I.

1896 Southern and Eastern European immigrants outnumber all others for the first time.

Once earlier immigrants saved enough money, they moved away from New York's Lower East Side. More recent immigrants from Southern and Eastern Europe, such as the ones in this colorized photo, moved in to replace them.

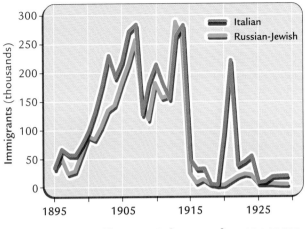

ITALIAN AND RUSSIAN-JEWISH IMMIGRANTS

Southern Italians fleeing poverty and Russian Jews fleeing religious persecution were two of the largest immigrant groups in the years before World War I.

1,041,570

- Northern & Western Europe
- Southern & Eastern Europe
- North America
- South America
- Asia

448,572

430,001

1900   1910   1920

"Nowhere in the world are so many people crowded together on one square mile as here."

—JACOB RIIS
DESCRIPTION OF AN IMMIGRANT NEIGHBORHOOD
IN NEW YORK CITY
HOW THE OTHER HALF LIVES, 1890

IMMIGRANT ORIGINS

The start of World War I in 1914 cut off most immigration by Europeans. In 1917 newly required literacy tests cut immigration still further.

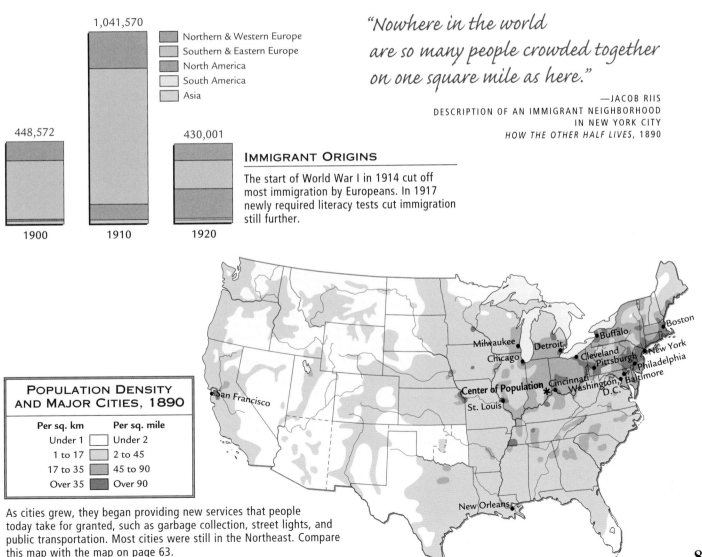

POPULATION DENSITY AND MAJOR CITIES, 1890

Per sq. km	Per sq. mile
Under 1	Under 2
1 to 17	2 to 45
17 to 35	45 to 90
Over 35	Over 90

San Francisco

Milwaukee
Chicago
Detroit
Buffalo
Boston
Cleveland
Pittsburgh
New York
Philadelphia
Center of Population
Cincinnati
Washington, D.C.
Baltimore
St. Louis

New Orleans

As cities grew, they began providing new services that people today take for granted, such as garbage collection, street lights, and public transportation. Most cities were still in the Northeast. Compare this map with the map on page 63.

The United States Enters World War I

- At first the United States resisted involvement in World War I, but eventually U.S. troops helped win the war.

- Austria-Hungary had declared war on Serbia in 1914. The rest of Europe quickly took sides in the conflict.

- On one side were the nations known as the Central Powers. On the other side were the Allies.

- Much of the fighting was done from trenches dug along two battlefronts in Europe: the Western Front and the Eastern Front.

- The United States joined the Allies in 1917. After another year of brutal trench warfare, the Central Powers surrendered.

"In one instant the entire front, as far as the eye could reach. . . was a sheet of flame."

—AMERICAN CORPORAL EUGENE KENNEDY
BATTLE OF ST. MIHIEL, SEPTEMBER 12–16, 1918

The familiar character Uncle Sam appeared on an Army recruiting poster in 1917.

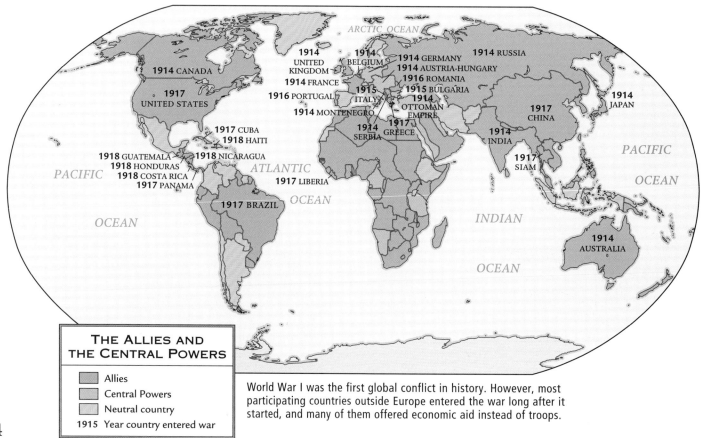

THE ALLIES AND THE CENTRAL POWERS

- Allies
- Central Powers
- Neutral country
- 1915 Year country entered war

World War I was the first global conflict in history. However, most participating countries outside Europe entered the war long after it started, and many of them offered economic aid instead of troops.

84

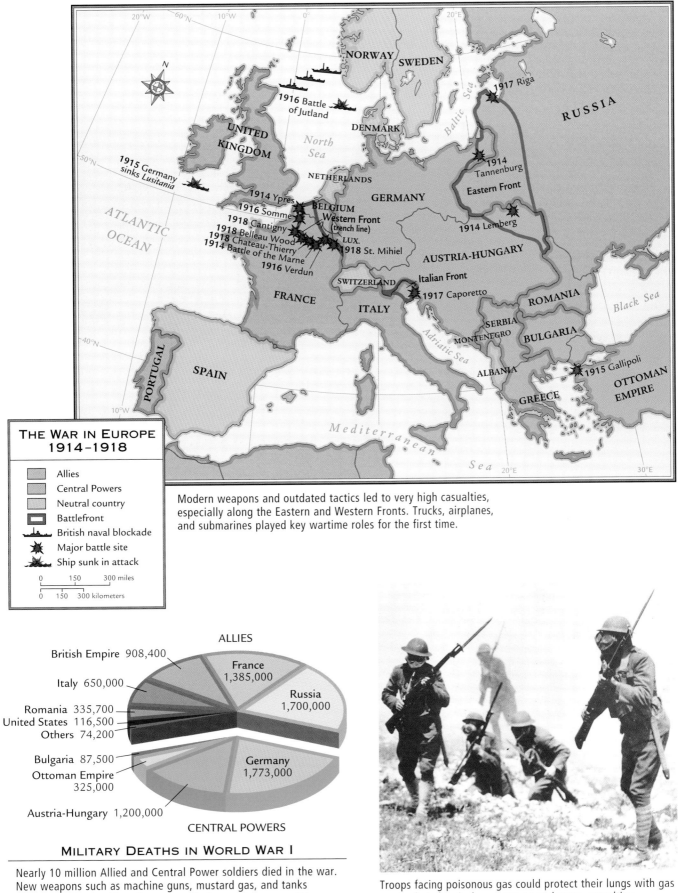

THE WAR IN EUROPE 1914–1918

- Allies
- Central Powers
- Neutral country
- Battlefront
- British naval blockade
- Major battle site
- Ship sunk in attack

0   150   300 miles
0   150   300 kilometers

Modern weapons and outdated tactics led to very high casualties, especially along the Eastern and Western Fronts. Trucks, airplanes, and submarines played key wartime roles for the first time.

MILITARY DEATHS IN WORLD WAR I

ALLIES

British Empire 908,400
Italy 650,000
Romania 335,700
United States 116,500
Others 74,200

France 1,385,000
Russia 1,700,000

Bulgaria 87,500
Ottoman Empire 325,000
Austria-Hungary 1,200,000

Germany 1,773,000

CENTRAL POWERS

Nearly 10 million Allied and Central Power soldiers died in the war. New weapons such as machine guns, mustard gas, and tanks increased the casualties. Compare with the graph on page 67.

Troops facing poisonous gas could protect their lungs with gas masks, but chemical weapons caused many casualties.

A Widespread System of Segregation

- By 1900 most African Americans were denied rights that most whites took for granted.

- In a song from the early 1800s, Jim Crow was a derogatory name for a black man. Later it became the name for a system of discrimination.

- Jim Crow laws rigidly enforced racial *segregation*, or separation, and restricted the rights of blacks.

- African Americans were forced to use separate accommodations, such as railroad cars, schools, and restrooms.

- In 1896 the Supreme Court ruled that "separate but equal" accommodations were constitutional. But accommodations for blacks and whites were in fact rarely equal.

"The problem of the Twentieth Century is the problem of the color line."

—W.E.B. DUBOIS, 1900
HISTORIAN AND SOCIOLOGIST

Segregated travel, but no voting restrictions

JIM CROW LAWS

▨	State with Jim Crow laws
1891	Year when trains and streetcars are segregated
1903	Year when black voting rights are restricted

The 15th Amendment extended the right to vote to all males over 21. In the South, however, poll taxes and literacy tests prevented most blacks from exercising those rights.

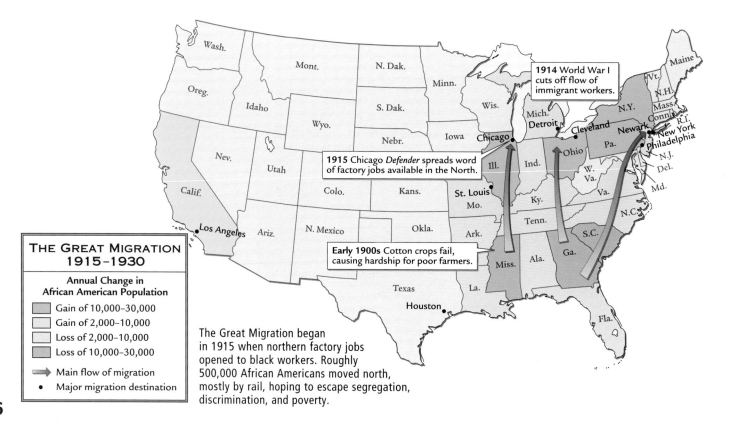

1914 World War I cuts off flow of immigrant workers.

1915 Chicago *Defender* spreads word of factory jobs available in the North.

Early 1900s Cotton crops fail, causing hardship for poor farmers.

THE GREAT MIGRATION 1915–1930

Annual Change in African American Population

▨	Gain of 10,000–30,000
▨	Gain of 2,000–10,000
▨	Loss of 2,000–10,000
▨	Loss of 10,000–30,000
→	Main flow of migration
•	Major migration destination

The Great Migration began in 1915 when northern factory jobs opened to black workers. Roughly 500,000 African Americans moved north, mostly by rail, hoping to escape segregation, discrimination, and poverty.

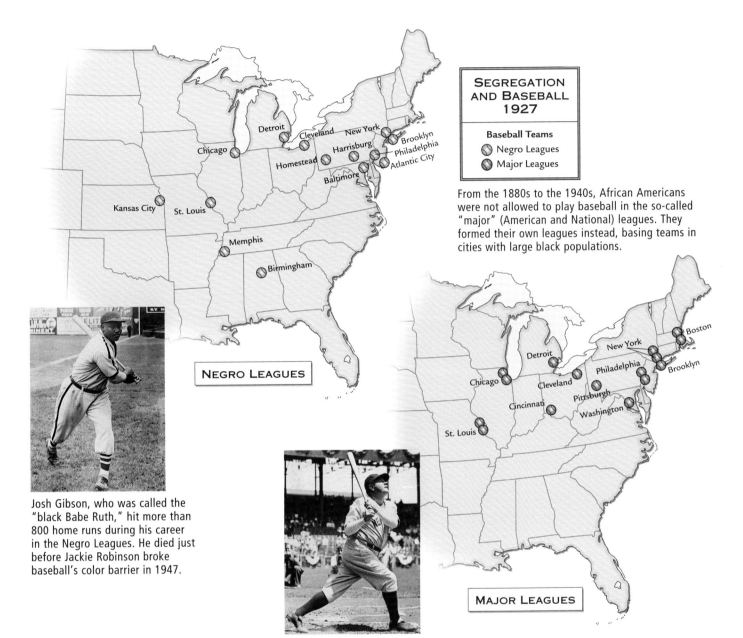

SEGREGATION AND BASEBALL 1927

Baseball Teams
- Negro Leagues
- Major Leagues

From the 1880s to the 1940s, African Americans were not allowed to play baseball in the so-called "major" (American and National) leagues. They formed their own leagues instead, basing teams in cities with large black populations.

NEGRO LEAGUES

MAJOR LEAGUES

Josh Gibson, who was called the "black Babe Ruth," hit more than 800 home runs during his career in the Negro Leagues. He died just before Jackie Robinson broke baseball's color barrier in 1947.

Babe Ruth, who hit a record 60 home runs in 1927, was the most famous baseball player of his time. Fans still wonder how their records would compare if Ruth and Gibson had played in the same league.

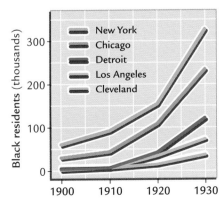

BLACK MIGRATION

During World War I, African Americans moved to cities in the North and West to start new lives with jobs in war-related industries. Even outside the South, however, blacks still faced many forms of discrimination.

Reforms Change America

- The 1910s and 1920s were decades of reform at both the state and national level.

- Between 1910 and 1930, states set limits on the amount and type of work children could perform.

- The federal government began efforts to preserve our country's scenic beauty and natural wonders.

- In 1920 the 18th Amendment prohibited the sale and manufacture of alcoholic beverages, and the 19th Amendment extended to women the right to vote.

Suffrage is the right to vote. Women called *suffragists* had fought for that right since the 1850s. In the 1910s, woman suffrage rallies drew the attention of U.S. politicians and the support of suffragists worldwide.

WOMEN GET THE VOTE

State Legislation
- 1869–1896
- 1910–1914
- 1917–1918

19th Amendment
- 1920

Many men feared that women were not knowledgeable enough to be allowed to vote. Yet women in most Western states had voted in state elections for years, helping ease such fears.

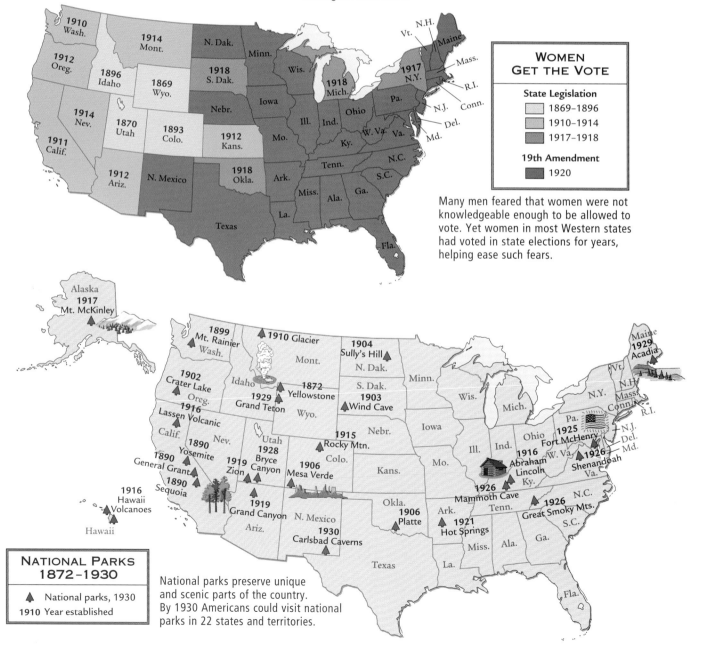

NATIONAL PARKS 1872–1930

▲ National parks, 1930
1910 Year established

National parks preserve unique and scenic parts of the country. By 1930 Americans could visit national parks in 22 states and territories.

LIMITING CHILD LABOR

Maximum Hours of Daily Work per Child, by Law

- No limit
- 11-12
- 10
- 9
- 8
- Limits vary

1890

In 1890, 20 percent of the nation's children were employed full time. The first national child labor law was declared unconstitutional by the U.S. Supreme Court in 1918. Many states then set their own limits.

1930

"I want to learn but can't when I work all the time."

—FURMAN OWENS
AGE 12, CANNOT READ,
MILLWORKER FOR FOUR YEARS

Factories hired children because they were cheaper and less demanding than adults. Most money earned by child laborers, such as those in this hand-painted photo, went to help their families.

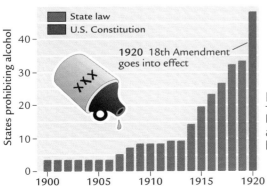

- State law
- U.S. Constitution

States prohibiting alcohol

1920 18th Amendment goes into effect

PROHIBITION

In 1920 the temperance movement and others succeeded in having alcohol banned by the 18th Amendment. The ban was unpopular, however, and in 1933 the 21st Amendment repealed the 18th.

1929–1940
Great Depression
puts millions out of work.

1932
Roosevelt (FDR)
elected President
of U.S.

1927 ★ 1930 1933

1929
Stock market crashes.

1931
Japan seizes
Manchuria.

1933
Hitler elected
Chancellor of Germany.

Prosperity Ends, Immigration Slows

- The stock market crash of 1929 introduced the Great Depression, worldwide economic hard times that lasted more than 10 years.

- In the United States, immigration dropped to its lowest level in nearly 100 years.

- At the same time, the Great Plains suffered an awful drought. The nation's breadbasket was called the "Dust Bowl" for its storms of blowing soil.

- President Franklin D. Roosevelt's New Deal policy led to agencies that created jobs and helped the needy.

"Brother, can you spare a dime?"

—YIP HARBURG
FROM A POPULAR SONG OF THE
DEPRESSION ERA

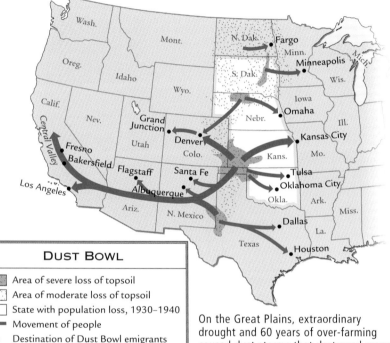

DUST BOWL

- Area of severe loss of topsoil
- Area of moderate loss of topsoil
- State with population loss, 1930–1940
- ← Movement of people
- • Destination of Dust Bowl emigrants

On the Great Plains, extraordinary drought and 60 years of over-farming caused dust storms that destroyed crops and buried fences, cars, even houses.

THE GREAT DEPRESSION

**Unemployment Rate
1929–1939**

- 15%–25%
- Over 25%
- Over 15% of people on relief, 1933
- Over 15% of banks suspended operations, 1933

At the end of 1933—the worst year of the Great Depression—over 1 million families received government assistance. The number could have been larger, but many were too proud to accept public help.

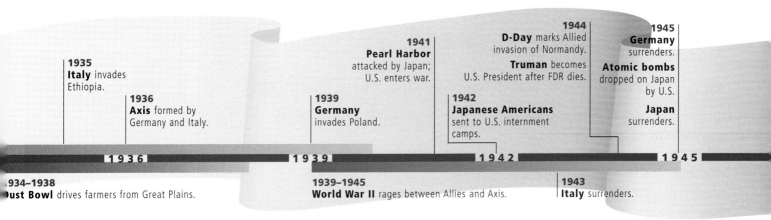

1935
Italy invades Ethiopia.

1936
Axis formed by Germany and Italy.

1941
Pearl Harbor attacked by Japan; U.S. enters war.

1939
Germany invades Poland.

1944
D-Day marks Allied invasion of Normandy.

Truman becomes U.S. President after FDR dies.

1942
Japanese Americans sent to U.S. internment camps.

1945
Germany surrenders.

Atomic bombs dropped on Japan by U.S.

Japan surrenders.

1936   1939   1942   1945

934–1938
Dust Bowl drives farmers from Great Plains.

1939–1945
World War II rages between Allies and Axis.

1943
Italy surrenders.

Millions of Americans lost jobs, homes, businesses, and savings during the Depression. Bread lines and soup kitchens run by private charities offered help to those who had lost everything.

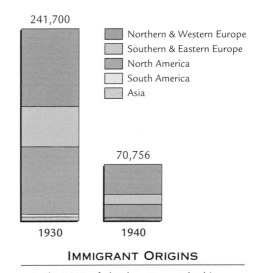

241,700

- Northern & Western Europe
- Southern & Eastern Europe
- North America
- South America
- Asia

70,756

1930   1940

IMMIGRANT ORIGINS

In the 1920s, federal quotas resulted in many prospective immigrants being turned away. During the Great Depression and World War II, the quotas went half-filled.

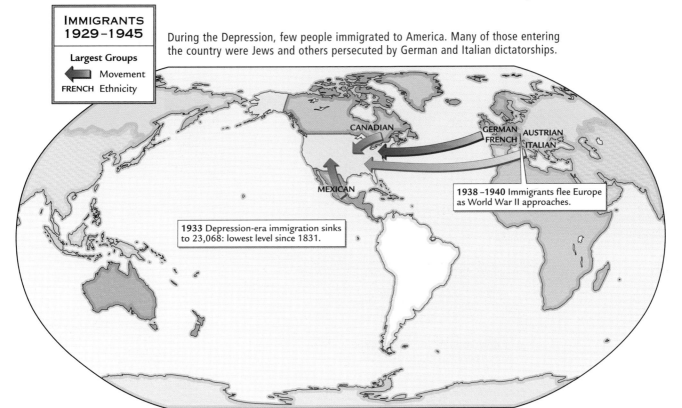

IMMIGRANTS 1929–1945

Largest Groups

← Movement
FRENCH Ethnicity

During the Depression, few people immigrated to America. Many of those entering the country were Jews and others persecuted by German and Italian dictatorships.

CANADIAN

GERMAN FRENCH   AUSTRIAN ITALIAN

MEXICAN

1938–1940 Immigrants flee Europe as World War II approaches.

1933 Depression-era immigration sinks to 23,068: lowest level since 1831.

Onset of World War II

- 🔖 The worldwide Depression helped promote militaristic governments in Germany, Italy, and Japan.

- 🔖 These countries soon began threatening their neighbors. When Germany invaded Poland in 1939, the world again went to war.

- 🔖 The United Kingdom and France led the Allies against the Axis Powers—Germany, Italy, and, later, Japan.

- 🔖 Though most Americans favored the Allies, the United States at first remained neutral.

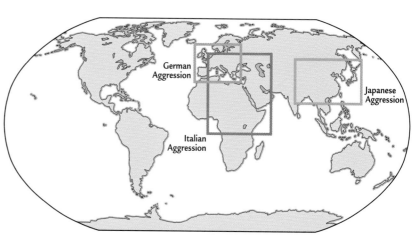

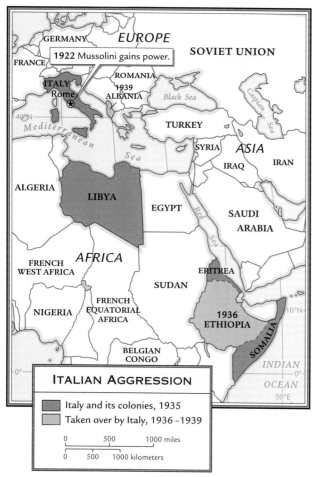

ITALIAN AGGRESSION

▨	Italy and its colonies, 1935
▨	Taken over by Italy, 1936–1939

0   500   1000 miles

0   500   1000 kilometers

Benito Mussolini came to power by promising Italians economic prosperity and military prestige. He pursued these goals through territorial expansion in Africa.

In 1936 Benito Mussolini and Adolf Hitler, the dictators of Italy and Germany, formed the Axis to impose their military and political might on the world. Japan joined the Axis in 1940.

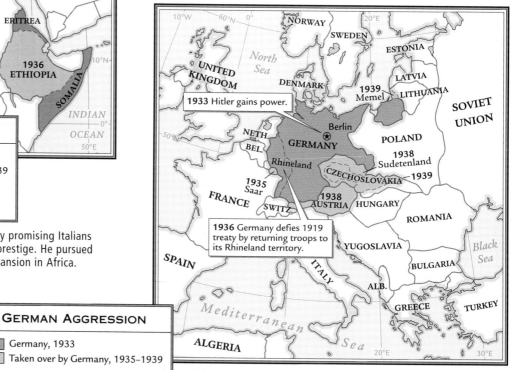

GERMAN AGGRESSION

▨	Germany, 1933
▨	Taken over by Germany, 1935–1939

0   250   500 miles

0   250   500 kilometers

Adolf Hitler vowed to avenge the humiliations suffered by Germany after World War I. First Germany took back lands it had lost in WWI. Then it began seizing other countries.

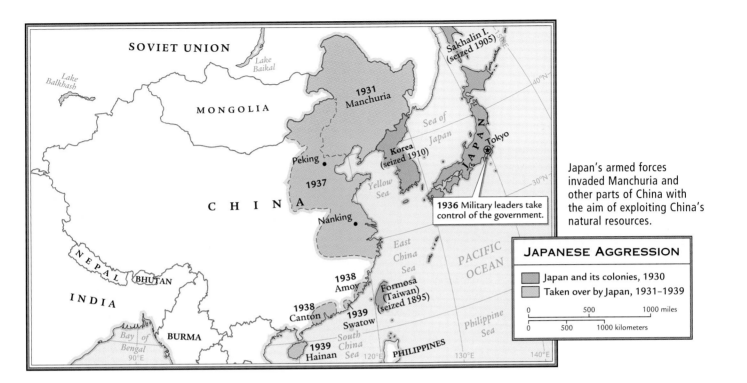

Japan's armed forces invaded Manchuria and other parts of China with the aim of exploiting China's natural resources.

JAPANESE AGGRESSION

- Japan and its colonies, 1930
- Taken over by Japan, 1931–1939

Axis troops overcame all early resistance. After Germany took France in 1940, the United Kingdom fought on alone. The Soviet Union joined the Allies only after it was invaded by Germany in June of 1941.

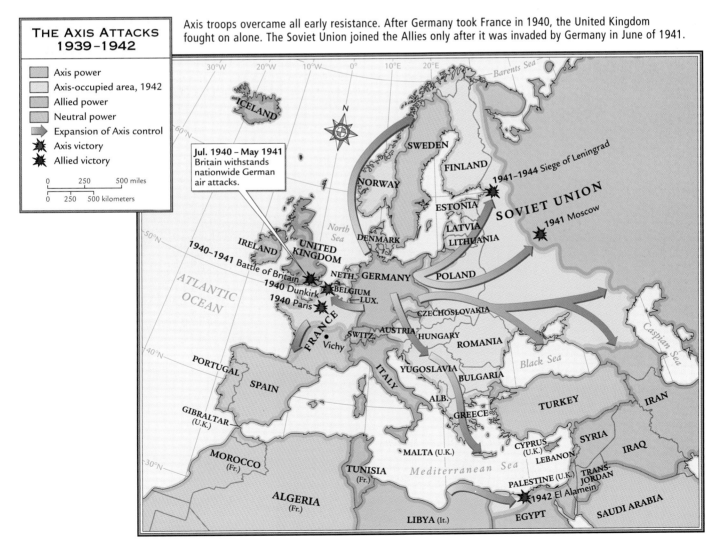

THE AXIS ATTACKS 1939–1942

- Axis power
- Axis-occupied area, 1942
- Allied power
- Neutral power
- Expansion of Axis control
- Axis victory
- Allied victory

America Enters the War

- In 1941 Japan attacked the U.S. Pacific fleet at Pearl Harbor. The United States declared war on Japan the next day. Germany then declared war on the United States.

- Although 12 million people eventually joined the armed forces, in 1941 the U.S. military was not prepared for war.

- Recruits and draftees needed months of intense military training to prepare them for combat in both Europe and the Pacific.

- Distrusted because of their ancestry, more than 100,000 Japanese Americans were relocated from the West Coast to inland internment camps. Most lost their homes.

Nearly 1,200 men lost their lives on the *U.S.S. Arizona* alone when Japan attacked Pearl Harbor. Many American planes and most large warships stationed at Pearl Harbor were damaged or destroyed.

JAPAN ATTACKS U.S. BASES

- Japan (Axis)
- Occupied by Japan
- United States and U.S. territory
- Other Allied power
- Neutral power
- → Advance to U.S. territory
- ✸ Japanese attacks

Dec. 8, 1941 Wake I. (U.S.)

Dec. 8, 1941 Guam (U.S.)

Dec. 7, 1941 Japanese warplanes attack Pearl Harbor.

Dec. 10, 1941 Japanese troops invade the Philippines.

Japan struck the only obstacle to its further expansion in the Pacific—the U.S. Pacific fleet. Most of the fleet was based in Hawaii.

Oahu
Wheeler Field
Bellows Field
Pearl Harbor
Honolulu

✸ Bombed military base

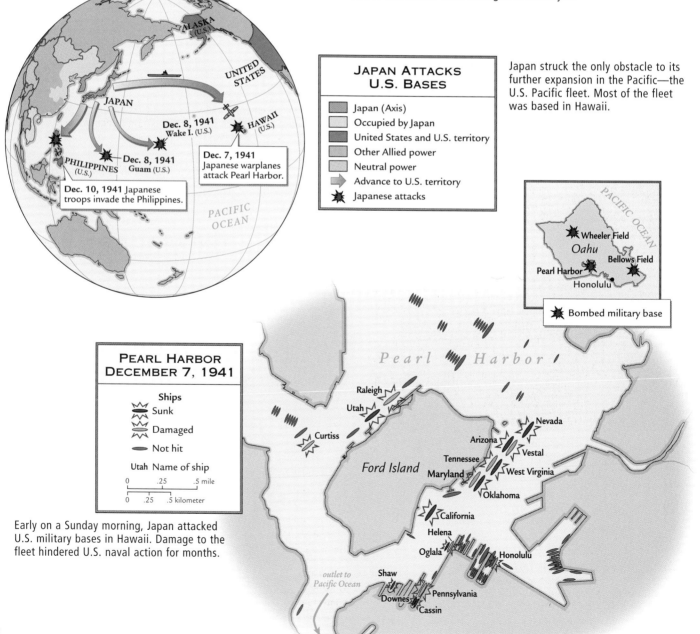

PEARL HARBOR DECEMBER 7, 1941

Ships
- Sunk
- Damaged
- Not hit

Utah Name of ship

0 — .25 — .5 mile
0 — .25 — .5 kilometer

Early on a Sunday morning, Japan attacked U.S. military bases in Hawaii. Damage to the fleet hindered U.S. naval action for months.

Pearl Harbor

Raleigh
Utah
Curtiss
Nevada
Arizona
Vestal
Tennessee
West Virginia
Ford Island
Maryland
Oklahoma
California
Helena
Oglala
Honolulu
Shaw
Pennsylvania
Downes
Cassin

outlet to Pacific Ocean

BASIC TRAINING CAMPS

- ★ Army, major sites
- ✈ Army Air Corps, major sites
- Navy
- Marine Corps
- Rolla Selected training site

New recruits to the armed forces underwent weeks of training at boot camps before being sent to war. Most camps were in the South, where the weather allowed year-round training.

All Japanese American families along the West Coast were relocated, even though none had committed acts of spying or sabotage. German and Italian Americans escaped such treatment.

"I didn't understand what I'd done. I was a native-born American citizen. I'd lived all my life in America."

—SYLVIA KOBAYASHI, JAPANESE AMERICAN
RELOCATED TO MINIDOKA, IDAHO

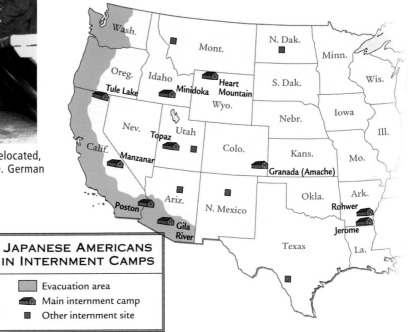

JAPANESE AMERICANS IN INTERNMENT CAMPS

- Evacuation area
- Main internment camp
- Other internment site

While their families lived in crowded barracks, surrounded by barbed wire and armed guards, many Japanese Americans fought for their country. The 442nd Regiment, all Japanese American, was the most decorated unit in U.S. history.

95

Fighting the War in Europe

- The Allies halted German advances in 1942, then went on the offensive to reverse earlier Axis gains.

- Allied advances pushed Axis troops out of France, Italy, and the Soviet Union. Italy surrendered on September 3, 1943.

- By 1945 the conflict had become a true world war, involving nearly 60 nations from six continents.

- In 1945 Allied troops fought their way toward Berlin from the east, west, and south. Germany surrendered on May 7.

Aerial bombings played a key role throughout the war. Both Axis and Allied bombers, such as the B-24s in this painting, attacked transportation routes, military facilities, and factories, many located in crowded cities.

Victories in Stalingrad and North Africa were turning points of the war and opened the way to Allied advances by land and by sea. Fierce fighting continued for over two years before the Axis fell.

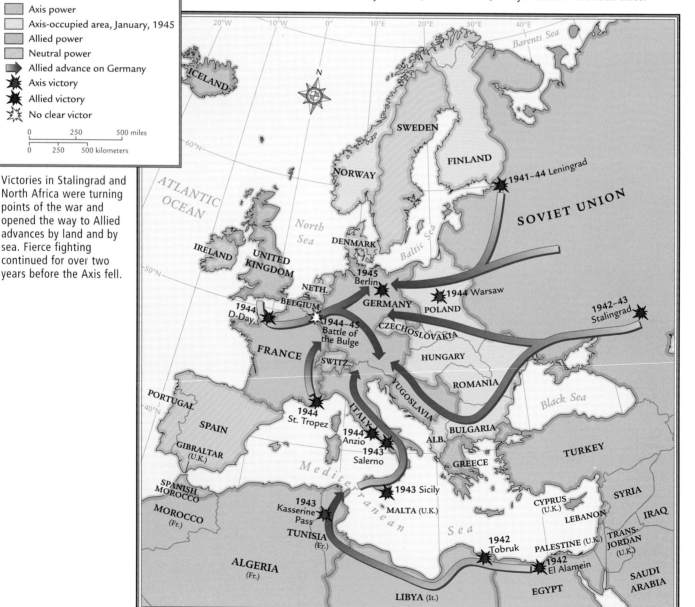

VICTORY IN EUROPE 1942–1945

- Axis power
- Axis-occupied area, January, 1945
- Allied power
- Neutral power
- Allied advance on Germany
- Axis victory
- Allied victory
- No clear victor

0   250   500 miles
0   250   500 kilometers

20°W 10°W 0° 10°E 20°E 30°E 40°E

Barents Sea

ICELAND

N

SWEDEN

NORWAY   FINLAND

ATLANTIC OCEAN

1941–44 Leningrad

SOVIET UNION

North Sea   Baltic Sea

60°N

DENMARK

IRELAND   UNITED KINGDOM

50°N

NETH.   1945 Berlin

BELGIUM   GERMANY   1944 Warsaw

1944 D-Day   POLAND

1944–45 Battle of the Bulge   CZECHOSLOVAKIA   1942–43 Stalingrad

FRANCE   SWITZ.   HUNGARY

PORTUGAL   40°N   YUGOSLAVIA   ROMANIA   Black Sea

SPAIN   1944 St. Tropez   ITALY   BULGARIA

GIBRALTAR (U.K.)   1944 Anzio   ALB.   TURKEY

SPANISH MOROCCO   1943 Salerno   GREECE   CYPRUS (U.K.)   SYRIA

Mediterranean   1943 Sicily   LEBANON   IRAQ

MOROCCO (Fr.)   1943 Kasserine Pass   MALTA (U.K.)   PALESTINE (U.K.)   TRANS-JORDAN (U.K.)

TUNISIA (Fr.)   Sea   1942 Tobruk

ALGERIA (Fr.)   1942 El Alamein   SAUDI ARABIA

LIBYA (It.)   EGYPT

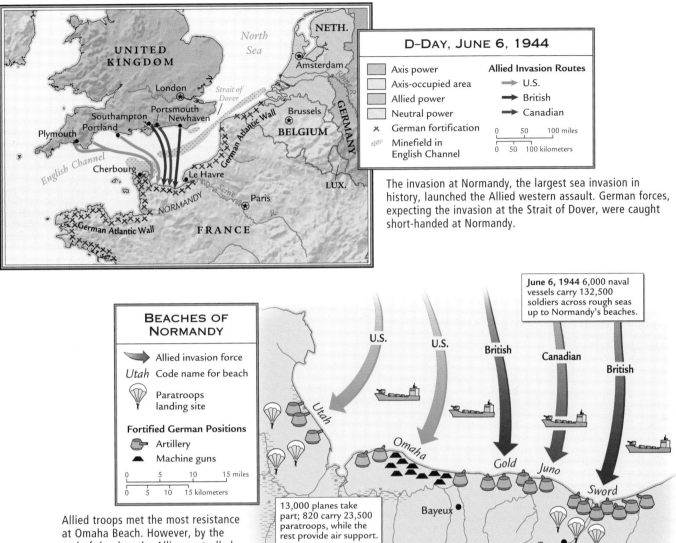

D-DAY, JUNE 6, 1944

- Axis power
- Axis-occupied area
- Allied power
- Neutral power
- × German fortification
- Minefield in English Channel

Allied Invasion Routes
- → U.S.
- → British
- → Canadian

0   50   100 miles
0   50   100 kilometers

The invasion at Normandy, the largest sea invasion in history, launched the Allied western assault. German forces, expecting the invasion at the Strait of Dover, were caught short-handed at Normandy.

June 6, 1944 6,000 naval vessels carry 132,500 soldiers across rough seas up to Normandy's beaches.

BEACHES OF NORMANDY

- Allied invasion force
- *Utah* Code name for beach
- Paratroops landing site

Fortified German Positions
- Artillery
- ▲ Machine guns

0   5   10   15 miles
0   5   10   15 kilometers

Allied troops met the most resistance at Omaha Beach. However, by the end of the day, the Allies controlled all five beaches in Normandy.

13,000 planes take part; 820 carry 23,500 paratroops, while the rest provide air support.

Allied troops faced deadly fire from German artillery as their landing craft fought through the waves to the beaches of Normandy, as in this hand-painted photo.

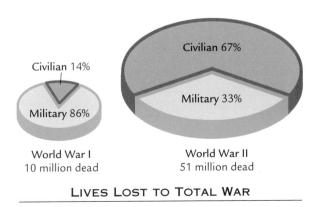

Civilian 14%
Military 86%

World War I
10 million dead

Civilian 67%
Military 33%

World War II
51 million dead

LIVES LOST TO TOTAL WAR

Worldwide, World War II took more lives, mostly civilians, than any other war. Among the civilian dead were 13 million killed in Nazi concentration camps, about half of them Jews killed during the Holocaust. See the graphs on pages 67 and 85.

Ending the War in the Pacific

- As the land war raged in Europe, fighting intensified in the Pacific and the war effort intensified at home.

- At home, the entire country aided the war effort, which created jobs and brought the United States out of the Great Depression.

- Abroad in the Pacific, aircraft carriers and U.S. Marines pushed westward toward Japan.

- In August 1945, U.S. planes dropped atomic bombs on Hiroshima and Nagasaki. Japan soon surrendered.

- Its key role in the Allied victory in World War II made the United States a superpower.

The character "Rosie the Riveter" became a symbol of women working in wartime industrial jobs. Riveting planes was just one of many jobs women performed to contribute to the war effort.

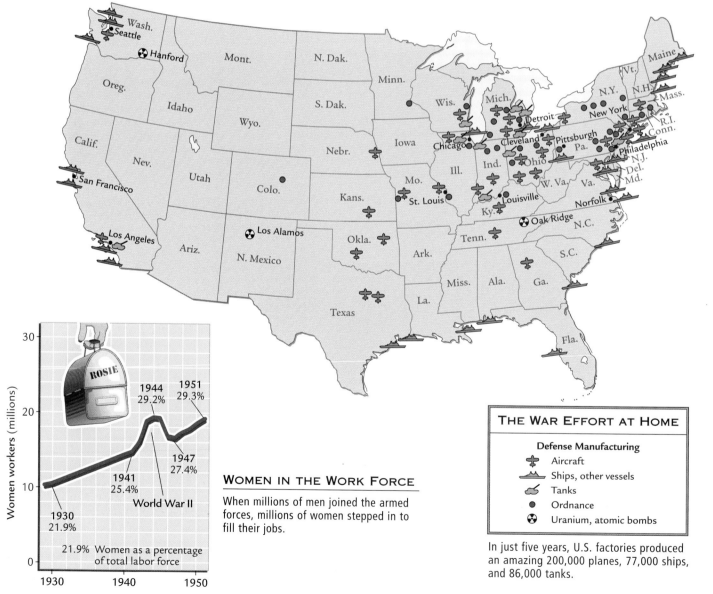

WOMEN IN THE WORK FORCE

When millions of men joined the armed forces, millions of women stepped in to fill their jobs.

Women workers (millions)

- 1930 21.9%
- 1941 25.4%
- World War II
- 1944 29.2%
- 1951 29.3%
- 1947 27.4%

21.9% Women as a percentage of total labor force

THE WAR EFFORT AT HOME

Defense Manufacturing
- Aircraft
- Ships, other vessels
- Tanks
- Ordnance
- Uranium, atomic bombs

In just five years, U.S. factories produced an amazing 200,000 planes, 77,000 ships, and 86,000 tanks.

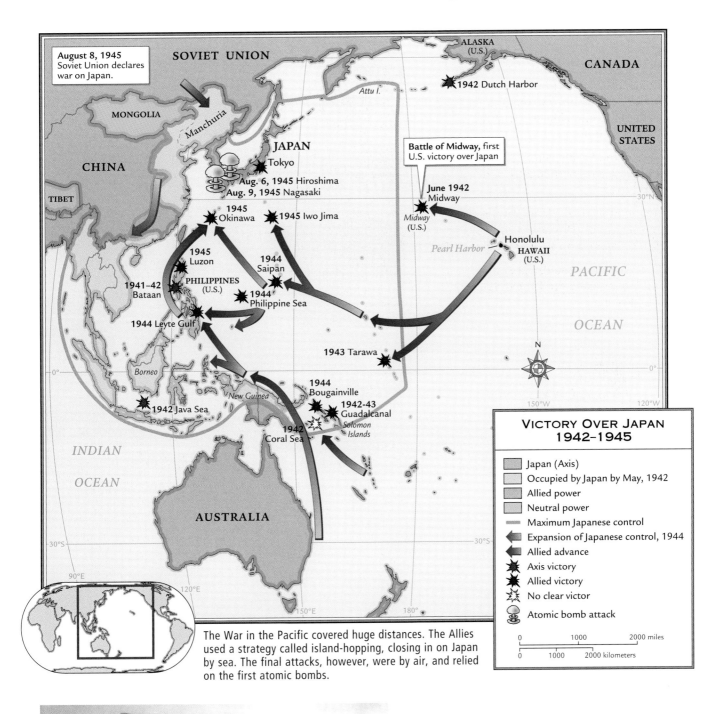

August 8, 1945
Soviet Union declares
war on Japan.

SOVIET UNION

ALASKA
(U.S.)

CANADA

MONGOLIA

Manchuria

Attu I.

1942 Dutch Harbor

CHINA

JAPAN

UNITED
STATES

TIBET

Tokyo

Aug. 6, 1945 Hiroshima
Aug. 9, 1945 Nagasaki

Battle of Midway, first
U.S. victory over Japan

30°N

1945
Okinawa

1945 Iwo Jima

June 1942
Midway

Midway
(U.S.)

1945
Luzon

1944
Saipan

Honolulu
HAWAII
(U.S.)

PHILIPPINES
(U.S.)

Pearl Harbor

1941–42
Bataan

1944
Philippine Sea

PACIFIC

1944 Leyte Gulf

OCEAN

1943 Tarawa

0°

Borneo

1944
Bougainville

New Guinea

1942 Java Sea

1942–43
Guadalcanal

1942
Coral Sea

Solomon
Islands

N

INDIAN

OCEAN

AUSTRALIA

30°S

30°S

90°E

120°E

150°E

180°

150°W

120°W

**VICTORY OVER JAPAN
1942–1945**

	Japan (Axis)
	Occupied by Japan by May, 1942
	Allied power
	Neutral power
——	Maximum Japanese control
←	Expansion of Japanese control, 1944
←	Allied advance
✴	Axis victory
✴	Allied victory
✳	No clear victor
💣	Atomic bomb attack

0   1000   2000 miles
0   1000   2000 kilometers

The War in the Pacific covered huge distances. The Allies
used a strategy called island-hopping, closing in on Japan
by sea. The final attacks, however, were by air, and relied
on the first atomic bombs.

U.S. Marines fought Japanese troops on Okinawa for
two months. The bloody battle was seen as a preview
of far deadlier combat to come if the Allies had to
invade Japan. Hoping to make an invasion unnecessary,
President Truman ordered that atomic bombs be
dropped on Japan.

1945
World War II ends.
United Nations founded.
Cold War begins.

1949
NATO unites Western nations against Soviet attack.

1950–1953
Korean War fought to a standstill.

★ ★ ★ ★ ★ ★ ★ ★ ★ ★ ★ ★ ★ ★ ★ ★ ★★★ **1940** | **1945** | **1950**

1941
Great Migration of blacks resumes, lasts to 1970.

1946
Baby Boom begins, continues to 1964.

American Troops Fight the Korean War

🐚 After World War II, Japanese control of Korea ended. U.S. troops occupied the South, Soviet troops the North. In 1948 each side set up its own government.

🐚 In June 1950, Communist North Korea invaded South Korea. The United States led a coalition of United Nations troops against the invaders.

🐚 An armistice ended the war in January 1953. It left Korea divided almost exactly as it had been before the war.

🐚 The Korean War was the first military fight of the Cold War, a struggle between democratic and Communist countries.

The devastation of war forced many Koreans from their homes. These young refugees help their mother as they flee from the danger of a nearby battle.

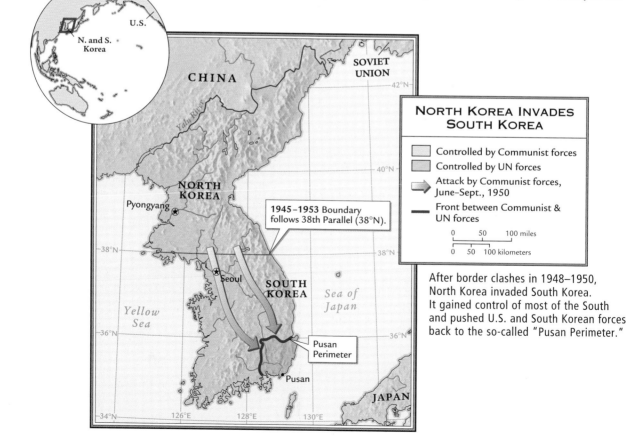

NORTH KOREA INVADES SOUTH KOREA

☐ Controlled by Communist forces
☐ Controlled by UN forces
➡ Attack by Communist forces, June–Sept., 1950
▬ Front between Communist & UN forces

0 50 100 miles
0 50 100 kilometers

1945–1953 Boundary follows 38th Parallel (38°N).

After border clashes in 1948–1950, North Korea invaded South Korea. It gained control of most of the South and pushed U.S. and South Korean forces back to the so-called "Pusan Perimeter."

100

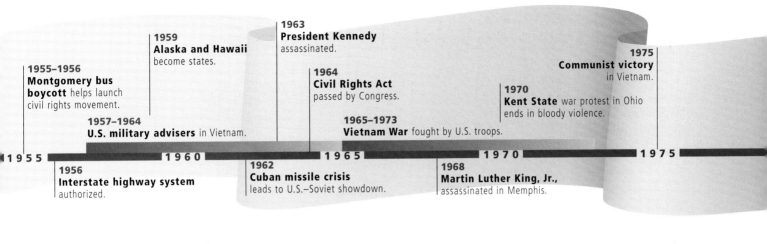

1955–1956
Montgomery bus boycott helps launch civil rights movement.

1959
Alaska and Hawaii become states.

1963
President Kennedy assassinated.

1964
Civil Rights Act passed by Congress.

1975
Communist victory in Vietnam.

1970
Kent State war protest in Ohio ends in bloody violence.

1957–1964
U.S. military advisers in Vietnam.

1965–1973
Vietnam War fought by U.S. troops.

1 9 5 5   1 9 6 0   1 9 6 5   1 9 7 0   1 9 7 5

1956
Interstate highway system authorized.

1962
Cuban missile crisis leads to U.S.–Soviet showdown.

1968
Martin Luther King, Jr., assassinated in Memphis.

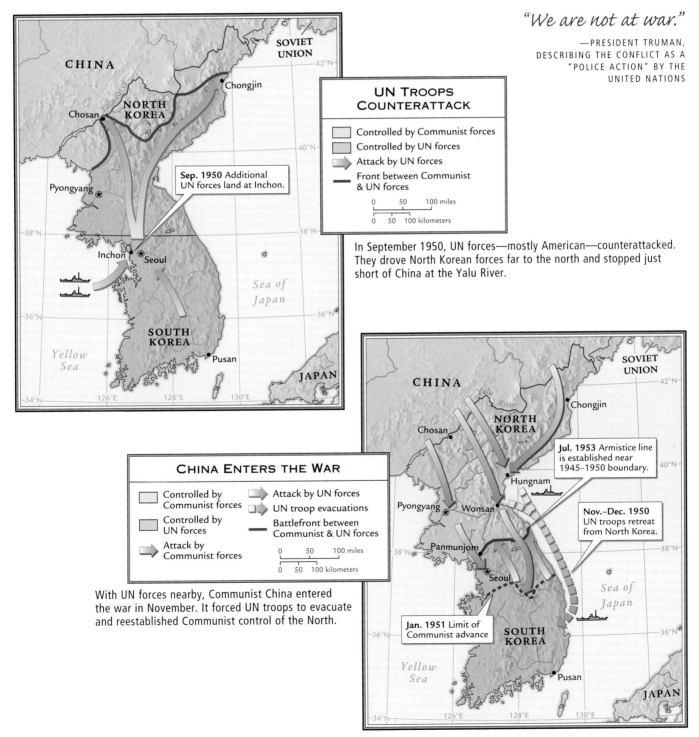

"We are not at war."

—PRESIDENT TRUMAN, DESCRIBING THE CONFLICT AS A "POLICE ACTION" BY THE UNITED NATIONS

UN TROOPS COUNTERATTACK

- Controlled by Communist forces
- Controlled by UN forces
- → Attack by UN forces
- — Front between Communist & UN forces

0   50   100 miles
0   50   100 kilometers

Sep. 1950 Additional UN forces land at Inchon.

In September 1950, UN forces—mostly American—counterattacked. They drove North Korean forces far to the north and stopped just short of China at the Yalu River.

CHINA ENTERS THE WAR

- Controlled by Communist forces
- Controlled by UN forces
- → Attack by Communist forces
- ⇒ Attack by UN forces
- ⇒ UN troop evacuations
- — Battlefront between Communist & UN forces

0   50   100 miles
0   50   100 kilometers

With UN forces nearby, Communist China entered the war in November. It forced UN troops to evacuate and reestablished Communist control of the North.

Jul. 1953 Armistice line is established near 1945–1950 boundary.

Nov.–Dec. 1950 UN troops retreat from North Korea.

Jan. 1951 Limit of Communist advance

101

Superpowers Face Off in the Cold War

- The alliances of the Cold War were led by two superpowers: the democratic United States and the Communist Soviet Union, an outgrowth of Russia.

- Democratic alliances included NATO in Europe and North America and CENTO in Asia.

- Communist nations joined the Warsaw Pact in Eastern Europe. After 1949, China was also a Communist country.

- In the most perilous moment of the Cold War, the Cuban Missile Crisis brought the two superpowers to the brink of nuclear war.

During the 1950s, Americans were so worried about the possibility of nuclear war that schoolchildren regularly practiced atomic bomb drills.

Both the United States and the Soviet Union stockpiled nuclear weapons. Each reasoned that fear of retaliation would keep the other from firing the first missile. This policy was known as MAD—Mutual Assured Destruction.

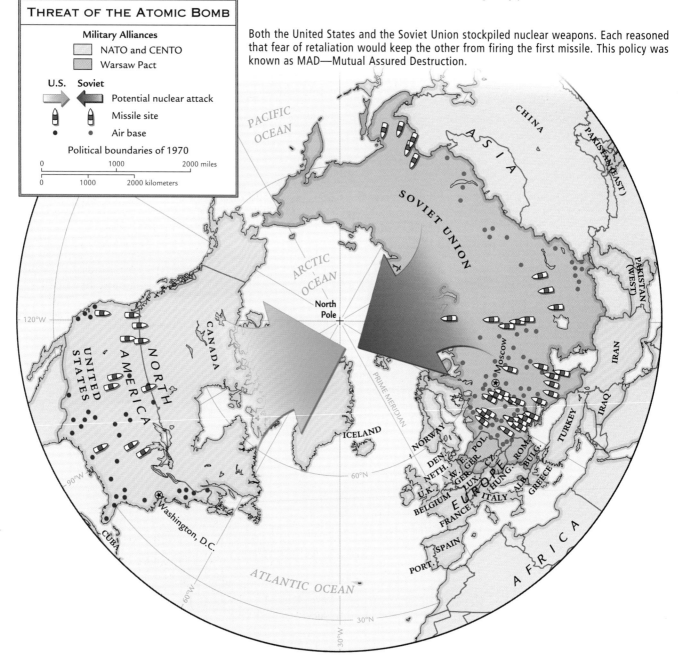

THREAT OF THE ATOMIC BOMB

Military Alliances
- NATO and CENTO
- Warsaw Pact

U.S. Soviet
- Potential nuclear attack
- Missile site
- Air base

Political boundaries of 1970

0   1000   2000 miles
0   1000   2000 kilometers

IRON CURTAIN 1946–1989

- Warsaw Pact member
- Other Communist nation
- NATO member
- Neutral nation
- Iron Curtain
- ⊕ Divided city

Political boundaries of 1989

0   250   500 miles
0   250   500 kilometers

The Communist countries of Eastern Europe and the NATO democracies of the West were isolated from one another for decades after World War II. The term "Iron Curtain" symbolized this rigid and hostile division.

When the Soviet Union installed nuclear missiles in Cuba, the United States used a naval quarantine to force their removal. The world watched, expecting nuclear war. After several tense days, the Soviets finally backed down and removed the missiles.

CUBAN MISSILE CRISIS 1962

- Cuba
- United States and U.S. territory
- Extent of U.S. quarantine
- Soviet arms shipment
- U.S. military base
- Soviet missile site

0   200   400 miles
0   200   400 kilometers

Oct. 1962 Ships carrying Soviet armaments honor U.S. quarantine.

103

Baby Boom and Suburban Growth

- After World War II, the United States grew in both area and population.

- Alaska and Hawaii became states in 1959, increasing the area of the United States by more than 600,000 square miles.

- Returning troops by the millions got married and started families, creating a "baby boom."

- Suburbs boomed too, made accessible by a recovering economy and by federal financing of new highways and low-cost mortgages.

Millions of babies were born in the years immediately following World War II. Growing families and affordable mortgages created a demand for millions of new suburban homes.

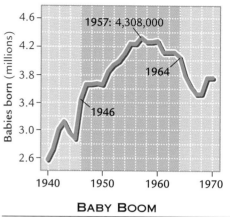

BABY BOOM

Americans born during the years 1946–1964 were called the "Baby Boom" generation. Far more babies were born in those years than during the generations before or after.

Distant Alaska and Hawaii had grown familiar to Americans during World War II. After the war, Alaska was valued for its forests and minerals, Hawaii as a tourist destination. In 1959 they became the 49th and 50th states.

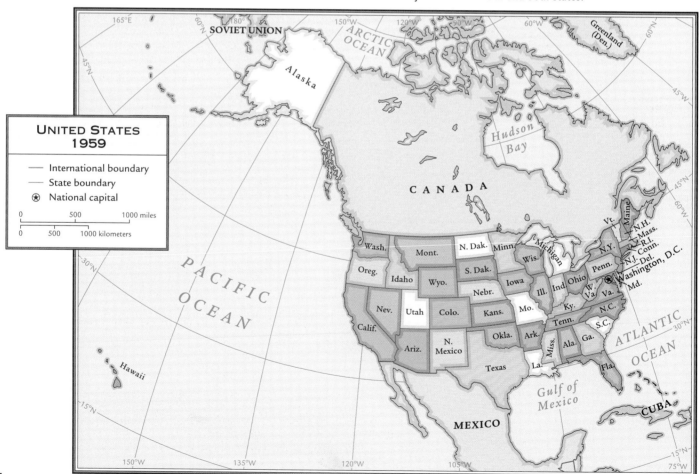

UNITED STATES 1959

— International boundary
— State boundary
⊛ National capital

0   500   1000 miles
0   500   1000 kilometers

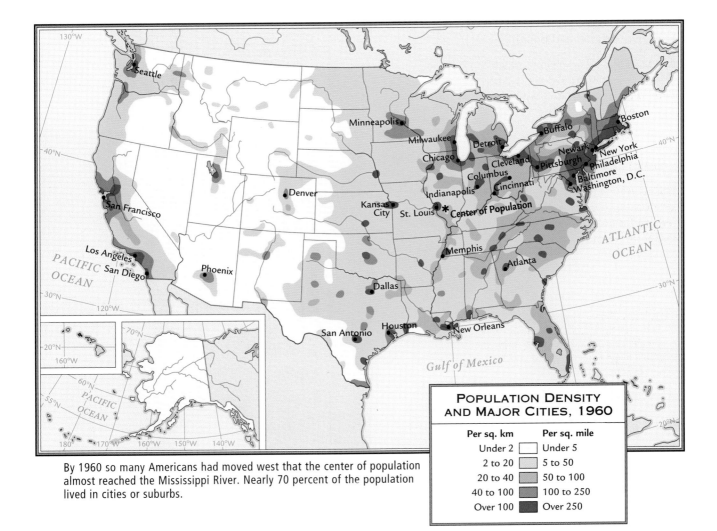

POPULATION DENSITY AND MAJOR CITIES, 1960

Per sq. km	Per sq. mile
Under 2	Under 5
2 to 20	5 to 50
20 to 40	50 to 100
40 to 100	100 to 250
Over 100	Over 250

By 1960 so many Americans had moved west that the center of population almost reached the Mississippi River. Nearly 70 percent of the population lived in cities or suburbs.

GROWTH OF A SUBURBAN CORRIDOR

- Residential
- Commercial, industrial, institutional
- Vacant or abandoned land
- 494 Interstate highway
- Other road

0 .5 1 mile
0 .5 1 kilometer

Suburbs near big cities grew along new freeways, such as Interstate 494 south of Minneapolis. Vacant land was soon replaced by businesses built to provide goods and services to the growing suburban population.

1953

1962

1971

In Search of the American Dream

- After World War II, millions of immigrants and citizens sought better lives in the United States.

- More and more immigrants came from Latin America and Asia.

- Between 1940 and 1970, more than 5 million blacks left the South to escape racial discrimination and to seek opportunity elsewhere.

- The contrast between the fight for freedom during World War II and the lack of freedom at home helped launch the civil rights movement.

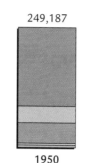

249,187 — 1950
265,398 — 1960
373,326 — 1970

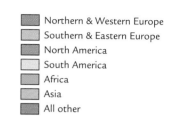

- Northern & Western Europe
- Southern & Eastern Europe
- North America
- South America
- Africa
- Asia
- All other

IMMIGRANT ORIGINS

By 1970 immigrants from the Americas, Africa, and Asia far outnumbered those from Europe.

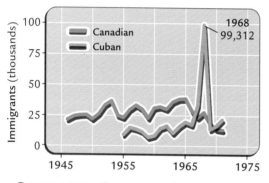

CUBAN AND CANADIAN IMMIGRANTS

Cuban refugees surged to the United States in 1959, gaining immigrant status in 1968. In contrast, steady numbers of Canadians moved to the United States until 1965, when immigration laws changed.

1968
99,312

Canadian
Cuban

Immigrants (thousands)
100 / 75 / 50 / 25 / 0
1945 / 1955 / 1965 / 1975

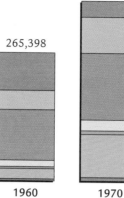

Thousands of refugees fled Cuba after the Communist revolution there in 1959. Most eventually gained immigrant status and sought citizenship in the United States.

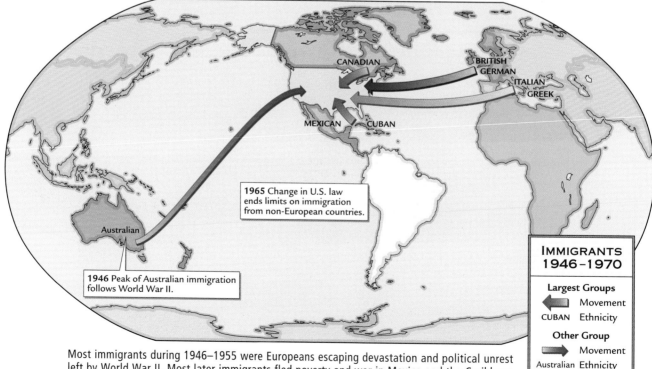

CANADIAN
BRITISH
GERMAN
ITALIAN
GREEK
MEXICAN
CUBAN
Australian

1965 Change in U.S. law ends limits on immigration from non-European countries.

1946 Peak of Australian immigration follows World War II.

IMMIGRANTS 1946–1970

Largest Groups
⬅ Movement
CUBAN Ethnicity

Other Group
➡ Movement
Australian Ethnicity

Most immigrants during 1946–1955 were Europeans escaping devastation and political unrest left by World War II. Most later immigrants fled poverty and war in Mexico and the Caribbean.

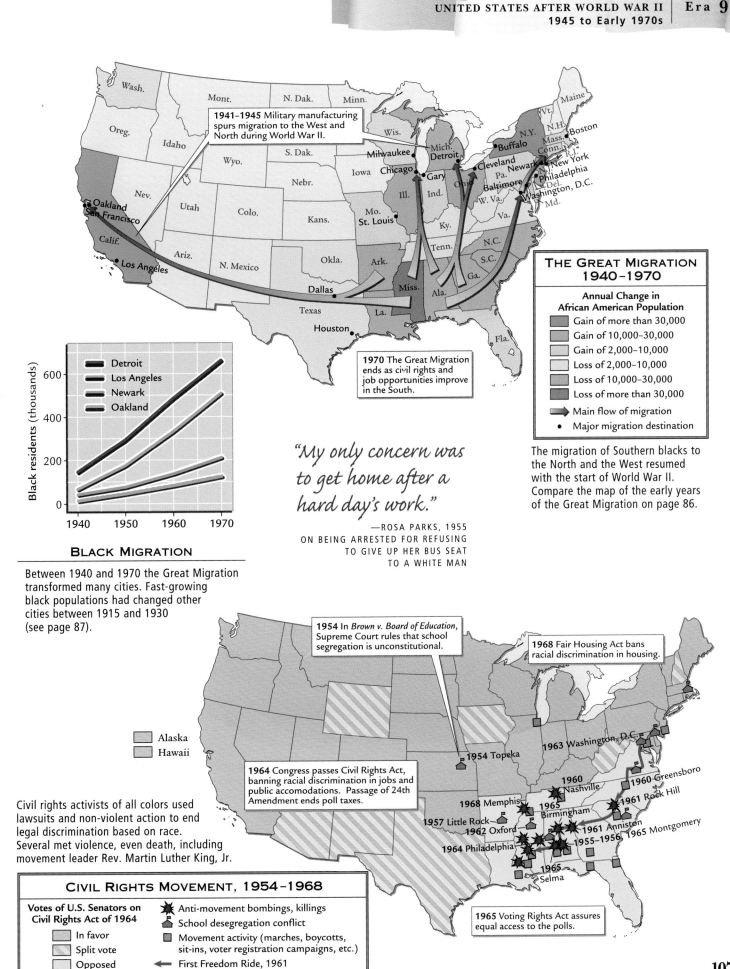

1941–1945 Military manufacturing spurs migration to the West and North during World War II.

1970 The Great Migration ends as civil rights and job opportunities improve in the South.

THE GREAT MIGRATION 1940–1970

Annual Change in African American Population

Gain of more than 30,000
Gain of 10,000–30,000
Gain of 2,000–10,000
Loss of 2,000–10,000
Loss of 10,000–30,000
Loss of more than 30,000

⇨ Main flow of migration
• Major migration destination

The migration of Southern blacks to the North and the West resumed with the start of World War II. Compare the map of the early years of the Great Migration on page 86.

"My only concern was to get home after a hard day's work."

—ROSA PARKS, 1955
ON BEING ARRESTED FOR REFUSING TO GIVE UP HER BUS SEAT TO A WHITE MAN

Black residents (thousands)

Detroit
Los Angeles
Newark
Oakland

600
400
200
0

1940 1950 1960 1970

BLACK MIGRATION

Between 1940 and 1970 the Great Migration transformed many cities. Fast-growing black populations had changed other cities between 1915 and 1930 (see page 87).

1954 In *Brown v. Board of Education*, Supreme Court rules that school segregation is unconstitutional.

1968 Fair Housing Act bans racial discrimination in housing.

Alaska
Hawaii

1964 Congress passes Civil Rights Act, banning racial discrimination in jobs and public accomodations. Passage of 24th Amendment ends poll taxes.

1954 Topeka
1963 Washington, D.C.
1960 Nashville
1960 Greensboro
1961 Rock Hill
1968 Memphis
1965 Birmingham
1957 Little Rock
1962 Oxford
1961 Anniston
1964 Philadelphia
1955–1956 Montgomery
1965 Montgomery
1965 Selma

Civil rights activists of all colors used lawsuits and non-violent action to end legal discrimination based on race. Several met violence, even death, including movement leader Rev. Martin Luther King, Jr.

CIVIL RIGHTS MOVEMENT, 1954–1968

Votes of U.S. Senators on Civil Rights Act of 1964

In favor
Split vote
Opposed

✹ Anti-movement bombings, killings
⬔ School desegregation conflict
▪ Movement activity (marches, boycotts, sit-ins, voter registration campaigns, etc.)
← First Freedom Ride, 1961

1965 Voting Rights Act assures equal access to the polls.

The Vietnam War Ends an Era

- In 1957 U.S. military advisers went to assist capitalist South Vietnam, which faced a growing Communist rebellion.

- In 1965 the United States committed troops to fight against both the Viet Cong rebels and Communist North Vietnam, which supported them.

- As the war went on, Americans at home became dissatisfied. Lack of support for the war eventually led to the withdrawal of U.S. troops in 1973.

- Without the assistance of American troops, South Vietnam fell to Communist forces in 1975.

Helicopters were the workhorses of the Vietnam War. They were used to spot the enemy, defend ground troops, transport soldiers and supplies, and evacuate the dead and wounded.

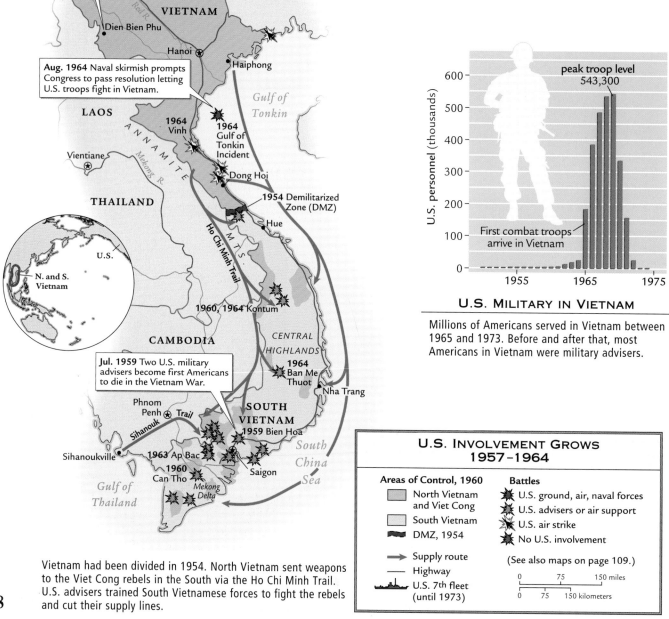

May 1954 Vietnamese rebels defeat French; a divided Vietnam gains independence from France.

Aug. 1964 Naval skirmish prompts Congress to pass resolution letting U.S. troops fight in Vietnam.

Jul. 1959 Two U.S. military advisers become first Americans to die in the Vietnam War.

NORTH VIETNAM
CHINA
Red R.
Dien Bien Phu
Hanoi
Haiphong
Gulf of Tonkin
LAOS
1964 Vinh
1964 Gulf of Tonkin Incident
Vientiane
Mekong R.
A N N A M I T E
Dong Hoi
1954 Demilitarized Zone (DMZ)
THAILAND
Hue
Ho Chi Minh Trail
M T S.
U.S.
N. and S. Vietnam
1960, 1964 Kontum
CAMBODIA
CENTRAL HIGHLANDS
1964 Ban Me Thuot
Nha Trang
Phnom Penh
Trail
Sihanouk Trail
SOUTH VIETNAM
1959 Bien Hoa
Sihanoukville
1963 Ap Bac
1960 Can Tho
Saigon
South China Sea
Gulf of Thailand
Mekong Delta

U.S. MILITARY IN VIETNAM

peak troop level
543,300

First combat troops arrive in Vietnam

U.S. personnel (thousands)
600
500
400
300
200
100
0

1955   1965   1975

Millions of Americans served in Vietnam between 1965 and 1973. Before and after that, most Americans in Vietnam were military advisers.

U.S. INVOLVEMENT GROWS 1957–1964

Areas of Control, 1960
- North Vietnam and Viet Cong
- South Vietnam
- DMZ, 1954
- Supply route
- Highway
- U.S. 7th fleet (until 1973)

Battles
- U.S. ground, air, naval forces
- U.S. advisers or air support
- U.S. air strike
- No U.S. involvement

(See also maps on page 109.)

0   75   150 miles
0   75   150 kilometers

Vietnam had been divided in 1954. North Vietnam sent weapons to the Viet Cong rebels in the South via the Ho Chi Minh Trail. U.S. advisers trained South Vietnamese forces to fight the rebels and cut their supply lines.

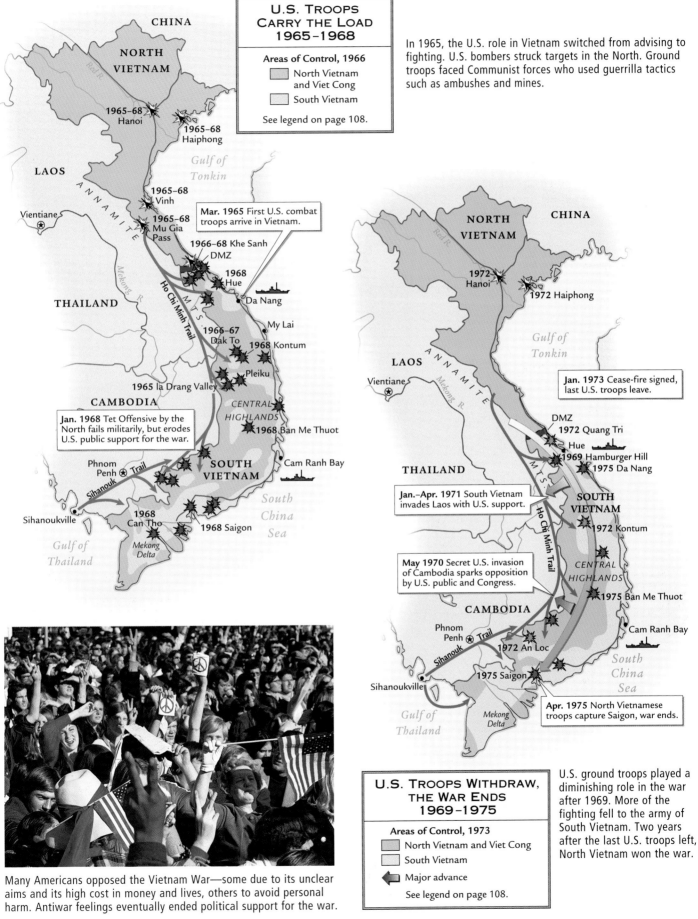

U.S. TROOPS CARRY THE LOAD 1965–1968

Areas of Control, 1966

- North Vietnam and Viet Cong
- South Vietnam

See legend on page 108.

In 1965, the U.S. role in Vietnam switched from advising to fighting. U.S. bombers struck targets in the North. Ground troops faced Communist forces who used guerrilla tactics such as ambushes and mines.

Mar. 1965 First U.S. combat troops arrive in Vietnam.

Jan. 1968 Tet Offensive by the North fails militarily, but erodes U.S. public support for the war.

CHINA
NORTH VIETNAM
LAOS
THAILAND
CAMBODIA
SOUTH VIETNAM

1965–68 Hanoi
1965–68 Haiphong
Gulf of Tonkin
1965–68 Vinh
Vientiane
1965–68 Mu Gia Pass
1966–68 Khe Sanh
DMZ
1968 Hue
Da Nang
My Lai
1966–67 Dak To
1968 Kontum
Pleiku
1965 Ia Drang Valley
CENTRAL HIGHLANDS
1968 Ban Me Thuot
Cam Ranh Bay
Phnom Penh
Sihanouk Trail
Sihanoukville
1968 Can Tho
1968 Saigon
Mekong Delta
Gulf of Thailand
South China Sea
Red R.
Mekong R.
Ho Chi Minh Trail
ANNAMITE MTS.

U.S. TROOPS WITHDRAW, THE WAR ENDS 1969–1975

Areas of Control, 1973

- North Vietnam and Viet Cong
- South Vietnam
- Major advance

See legend on page 108.

Jan. 1973 Cease-fire signed, last U.S. troops leave.

Jan.–Apr. 1971 South Vietnam invades Laos with U.S. support.

May 1970 Secret U.S. invasion of Cambodia sparks opposition by U.S. public and Congress.

Apr. 1975 North Vietnamese troops capture Saigon, war ends.

CHINA
NORTH VIETNAM
LAOS
THAILAND
CAMBODIA
SOUTH VIETNAM

1972 Hanoi
1972 Haiphong
Gulf of Tonkin
Vientiane
DMZ
1972 Quang Tri
Hue
1969 Hamburger Hill
1975 Da Nang
1972 Kontum
CENTRAL HIGHLANDS
1975 Ban Me Thuot
Cam Ranh Bay
Phnom Penh
Sihanouk Trail
Sihanoukville
1972 An Loc
1975 Saigon
Mekong Delta
Gulf of Thailand
South China Sea
Red R.
Mekong R.
Ho Chi Minh Trail
ANNAMITE MTS.

U.S. ground troops played a diminishing role in the war after 1969. More of the fighting fell to the army of South Vietnam. Two years after the last U.S. troops left, North Vietnam won the war.

Many Americans opposed the Vietnam War—some due to its unclear aims and its high cost in money and lives, others to avoid personal harm. Antiwar feelings eventually ended political support for the war.

ERA 10 Contemporary United States

1969 to Present

1969
Richard M. Nixon
sworn in as President.

1969
U.S. astronauts
land on moon.

1973
Vietnam War ends
for U.S. with pullout.

1973
Oil embargo
results in gas
shortages.

1977
Love Canal
reveals danger
of toxic waste.

1978
**First foreign
auto plant**
in U.S. opens.

1968 · 1972 · 1976

Oil, Arms, and U.S. Foreign Policy

- Beginning in the late 1900s, the United States played a dominant role in international affairs.

- Conflicts erupted in the Middle East and near the Caribbean during and after U.S. involvement in the Vietnam War.

- Arab nations refused to ship oil to the United States and others that backed Israel during the 1973 Yom Kippur War.

- In Cold War disputes closer to home, U.S. policy supported opponents of Communism.

- Foreign terrorists attacked U.S. landmarks, embassies, and civilians beginning in the 1990s and killed thousands of people on Sept. 11, 2001.

In the early 1970s, like now, the United States was dependent on foreign oil—it used more oil than it produced. During the 1973–1974 oil embargo, gasoline prices rose and quantities were rationed.

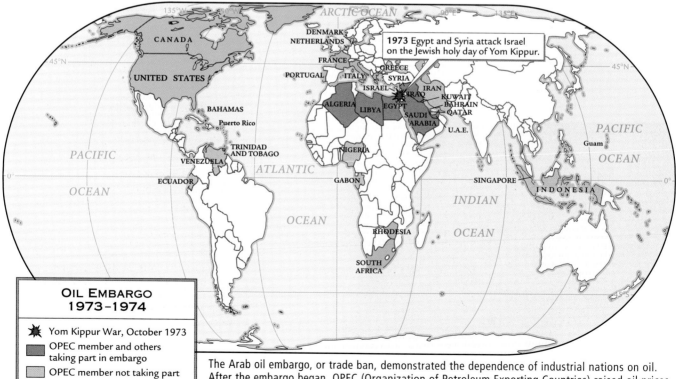

1973 Egypt and Syria attack Israel on the Jewish holy day of Yom Kippur.

OIL EMBARGO 1973-1974

- ✸ Yom Kippur War, October 1973
- OPEC member and others taking part in embargo
- OPEC member not taking part
- Embargoed country

The Arab oil embargo, or trade ban, demonstrated the dependence of industrial nations on oil. After the embargo began, OPEC (Organization of Petroleum Exporting Countries) raised oil prices, contributing to inflation and economic recession in the United States.

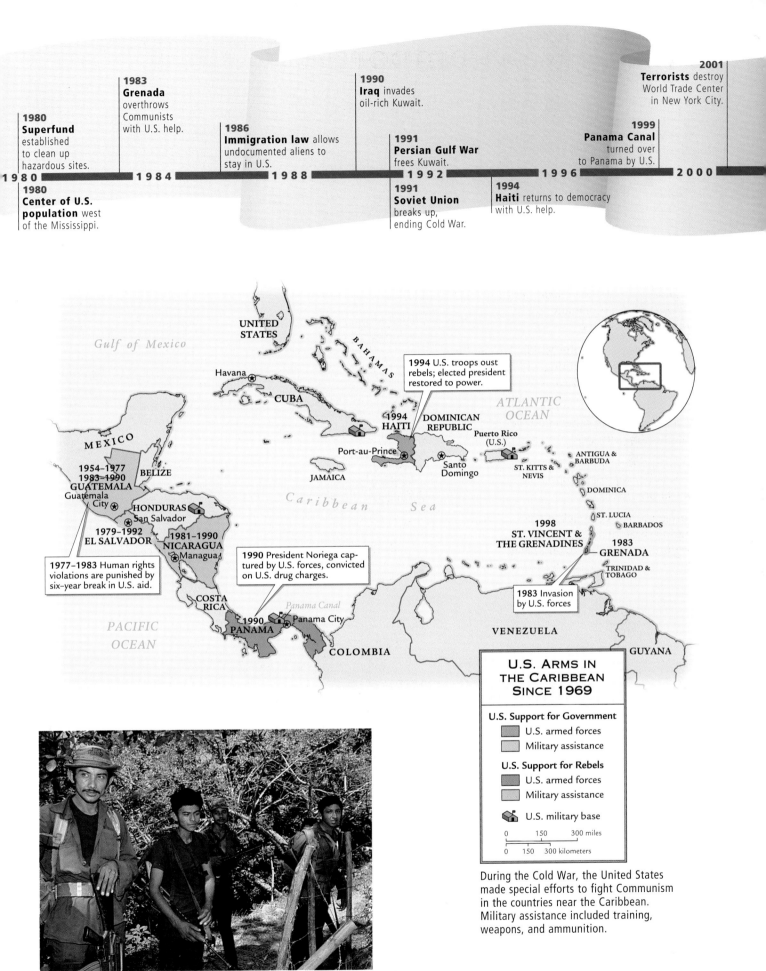

1980
Superfund established to clean up hazardous sites.

1983
Grenada overthrows Communists with U.S. help.

1986
Immigration law allows undocumented aliens to stay in U.S.

1990
Iraq invades oil-rich Kuwait.

1991
Persian Gulf War frees Kuwait.

2001
Terrorists destroy World Trade Center in New York City.

1999
Panama Canal turned over to Panama by U.S.

1980 ▬ 1984 ▬ 1988 ▬ 1992 ▬ 1996 ▬ 2000 ▬

1980
Center of U.S. population west of the Mississippi.

1991
Soviet Union breaks up, ending Cold War.

1994
Haiti returns to democracy with U.S. help.

1994 U.S. troops oust rebels; elected president restored to power.

1977–1983 Human rights violations are punished by six-year break in U.S. aid.

1990 President Noriega captured by U.S. forces, convicted on U.S. drug charges.

1983 Invasion by U.S. forces

U.S. ARMS IN THE CARIBBEAN SINCE 1969

U.S. Support for Government
- U.S. armed forces
- Military assistance

U.S. Support for Rebels
- U.S. armed forces
- Military assistance

- U.S. military base

0   150   300 miles
0   150   300 kilometers

During the Cold War, the United States made special efforts to fight Communism in the countries near the Caribbean. Military assistance included training, weapons, and ammunition.

In Nicaragua, the United States assisted rebel forces; in El Salvador, the government. Rebel troops, such as these guerrillas in El Salvador, often were no older than U.S. high school students.

111

The United States in the World of the 1990s

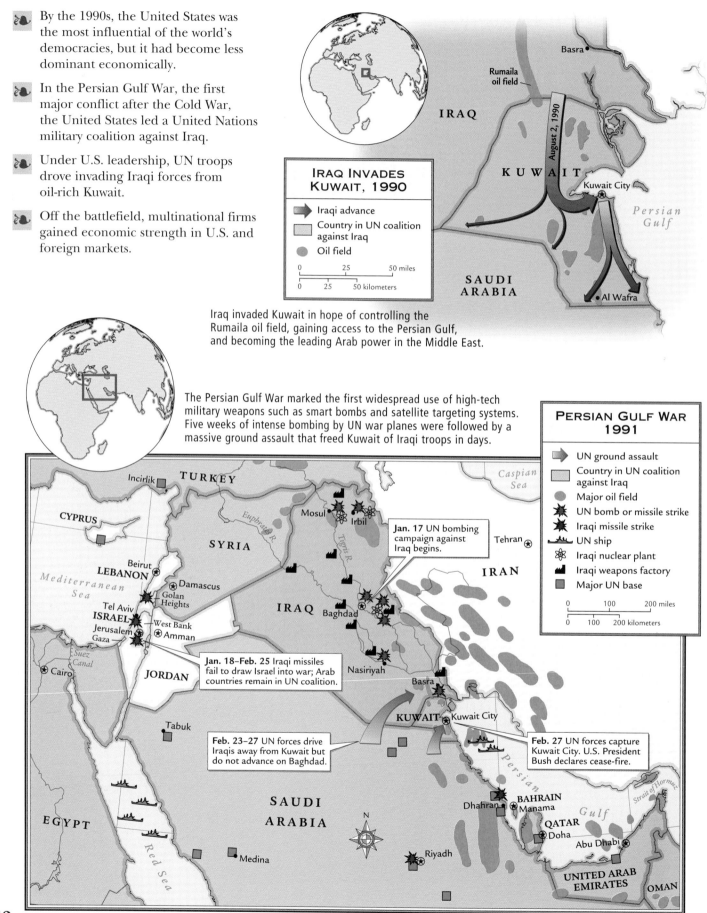

- By the 1990s, the United States was the most influential of the world's democracies, but it had become less dominant economically.

- In the Persian Gulf War, the first major conflict after the Cold War, the United States led a United Nations military coalition against Iraq.

- Under U.S. leadership, UN troops drove invading Iraqi forces from oil-rich Kuwait.

- Off the battlefield, multinational firms gained economic strength in U.S. and foreign markets.

IRAQ INVADES KUWAIT, 1990

→ Iraqi advance
⬜ Country in UN coalition against Iraq
● Oil field

0   25   50 miles
0   25   50 kilometers

Iraq invaded Kuwait in hope of controlling the Rumaila oil field, gaining access to the Persian Gulf, and becoming the leading Arab power in the Middle East.

The Persian Gulf War marked the first widespread use of high-tech military weapons such as smart bombs and satellite targeting systems. Five weeks of intense bombing by UN war planes were followed by a massive ground assault that freed Kuwait of Iraqi troops in days.

PERSIAN GULF WAR 1991

→ UN ground assault
⬜ Country in UN coalition against Iraq
● Major oil field
✸ UN bomb or missile strike
✹ Iraqi missile strike
⚓ UN ship
⚛ Iraqi nuclear plant
🏭 Iraqi weapons factory
⬜ Major UN base

0   100   200 miles
0   100   200 kilometers

Jan. 17 UN bombing campaign against Iraq begins.

Jan. 18–Feb. 25 Iraqi missiles fail to draw Israel into war; Arab countries remain in UN coalition.

Feb. 23–27 UN forces drive Iraqis away from Kuwait but do not advance on Baghdad.

Feb. 27 UN forces capture Kuwait City. U.S. President Bush declares cease-fire.

112

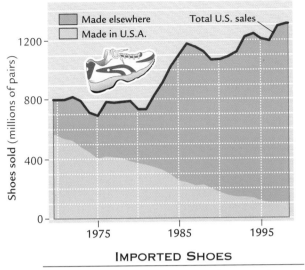

IMPORTED SHOES

From the 1970s on, sales of new shoes rose faster than the population. More and more brands are made outside the United States.

Specialized shoes for different sports help account for rising shoe sales. Children and teenagers are among the main consumers of athletic shoes.

WHAT MAKES A CAR AMERICAN?

Automobile Plants

- American company
- ▲ Foreign company (U.S. plants only)
- ■ Jointly owned by American and foreign companies

Many U.S. companies now make cars abroad because of lower labor costs or to reduce shipping costs to foreign markets. At the same time, many foreign companies hire Americans to build and sell cars in the United States.

Using Our Environment

- As the 1900s drew to a close, Americans were using and abusing more of the country's natural resources.

- Irrigation allowed farming in more places and increased crop yields, but it strained water supplies.

- Many technological advances left hazardous wastes that endangered human, animal, and plant life.

- Farming, logging, and development had used all but a small share of the country's original forests and grasslands.

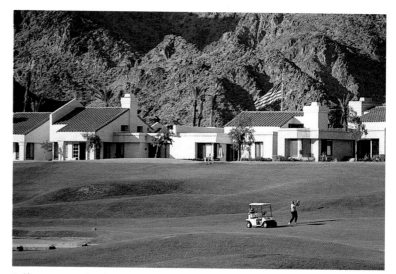

Golf courses and palm trees in most parts of the southwestern United States, such as these near Palm Springs, California, depend on water pumped from deep underground or carried by canals from far-off rivers.

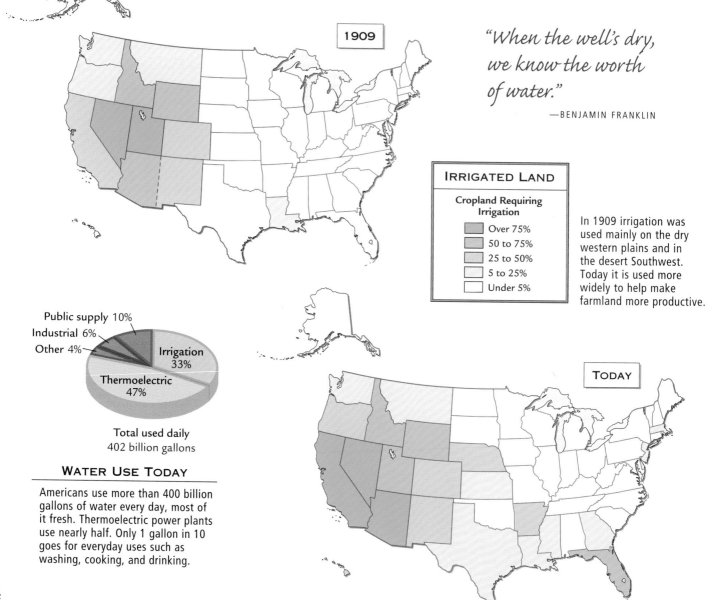

1909

"When the well's dry, we know the worth of water."

—BENJAMIN FRANKLIN

IRRIGATED LAND

Cropland Requiring Irrigation

- Over 75%
- 50 to 75%
- 25 to 50%
- 5 to 25%
- Under 5%

In 1909 irrigation was used mainly on the dry western plains and in the desert Southwest. Today it is used more widely to help make farmland more productive.

Public supply 10%
Industrial 6%
Other 4%
Irrigation 33%
Thermoelectric 47%

Total used daily
402 billion gallons

WATER USE TODAY

Americans use more than 400 billion gallons of water every day, most of it fresh. Thermoelectric power plants use nearly half. Only 1 gallon in 10 goes for everyday uses such as washing, cooking, and drinking.

TODAY

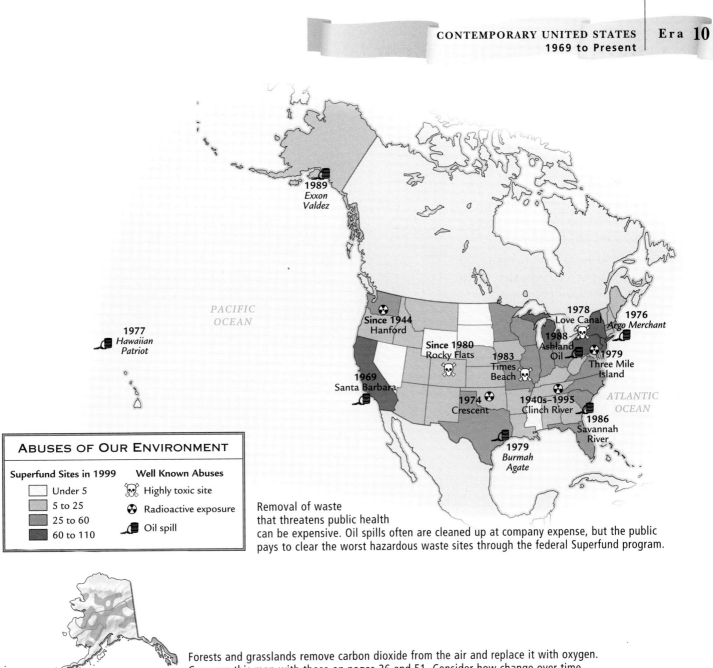

ABUSES OF OUR ENVIRONMENT

Superfund Sites in 1999

- Under 5
- 5 to 25
- 25 to 60
- 60 to 110

Well Known Abuses

- ☠ Highly toxic site
- ☢ Radioactive exposure
- 🛢 Oil spill

PACIFIC OCEAN

1989
Exxon Valdez

1977
Hawaiian Patriot

Since 1944
Hanford

Since 1980
Rocky Flats

1969
Santa Barbara

1974
Crescent

1983
Times Beach

1940s–1995
Clinch River

1979
Burmah Agate

1978
Love Canal

1988
Ashland Oil

1979
Three Mile Island

1976
Argo Merchant

1986
Savannah River

ATLANTIC OCEAN

Removal of waste
that threatens public health
can be expensive. Oil spills often are cleaned up at company expense, but the public
pays to clear the worst hazardous waste sites through the federal Superfund program.

Forests and grasslands remove carbon dioxide from the air and replace it with oxygen.
Compare this map with those on pages 26 and 51. Consider how change over time
may have affected the atmosphere.

FOREST AND GRASSLAND TODAY

- Forest
- Grassland

A Growing and Shifting Population

 In 1990 about 250 million people lived in the United States.

Retirees and families headed by Baby Boomers moved to new communities and new regions.

Three-fourths of U.S. residents lived in or near cities, mostly in the suburbs that now spread far beyond urban centers.

After 1990 many parts of the West and South grew substantially, while other regions lost population.

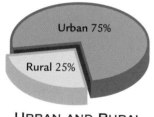

URBAN AND RURAL POPULATION, 1990

During the 1900s, America changed from a rural to an urban—and suburban—nation. Compare this graph with the one on page 78.

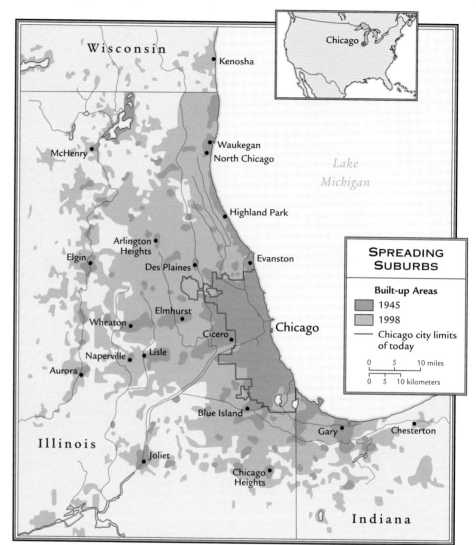

SPREADING SUBURBS

Built-up Areas
- 1945
- 1998
- Chicago city limits of today

0   5   10 miles
0   5   10 kilometers

Ever since the end of World War II, new houses have grown larger and the size of the average family has fallen. In cities like Chicago, suburban areas spread quickly as a result, even with slow population growth. For a closer look at a similar area, see page 105.

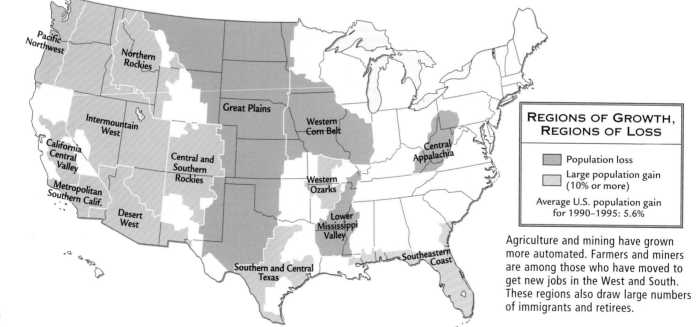

REGIONS OF GROWTH, REGIONS OF LOSS

- Population loss
- Large population gain (10% or more)

Average U.S. population gain for 1990–1995: 5.6%

Agriculture and mining have grown more automated. Farmers and miners are among those who have moved to get new jobs in the West and South. These regions also draw large numbers of immigrants and retirees.

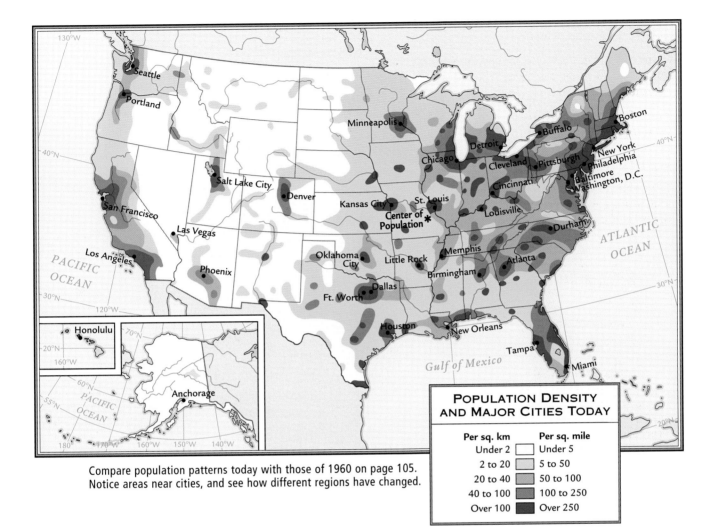

Compare population patterns today with those of 1960 on page 105.
Notice areas near cities, and see how different regions have changed.

**POPULATION DENSITY
AND MAJOR CITIES TODAY**

Per sq. km	Per sq. mile
Under 2	Under 5
2 to 20	5 to 50
20 to 40	50 to 100
40 to 100	100 to 250
Over 100	Over 250

A new housing boom began after the end of economic
recessions in the late 1970s and early 1980s. By 1990
nearly half of the U.S. population lived in suburbs.
Many others lived in fast-growing cities such as
Las Vegas, shown above.

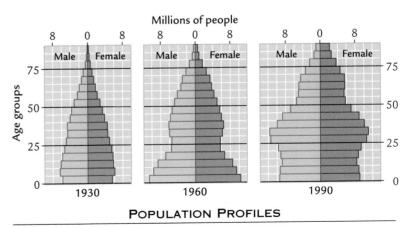

POPULATION PROFILES

Each profile shows that year's total population divided into groups by age,
and within age groups by sex. The U.S. population is not only growing larger,
it is also growing older. (Everyone 85 or older is included in the top bar.)

117

The Changing Face of America

🕊 In the late 1900s, immigration continued to make the U.S. population more diverse.

🕊 By 1990 over 8 percent of the U.S. population was foreign-born, the highest level in 50 years.

🕊 The majority of immigrants to the United States were no longer from Europe, but from Asia and Latin America.

🕊 Immigrants from the Philippines, South Korea, Vietnam, China, and especially Mexico were the most numerous.

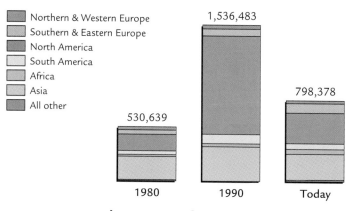

- Northern & Western Europe
- Southern & Eastern Europe
- North America
- South America
- Africa
- Asia
- All other

1980: 530,639
1990: 1,536,483
Today: 798,378

IMMIGRANT ORIGINS

In 1986 a new law offered immigrant status to people who had been U.S. residents for years without immigration papers.

While most immigrants came from Asia and Latin America, there were also large numbers of voluntary immigrants from Africa—for the first time in history.

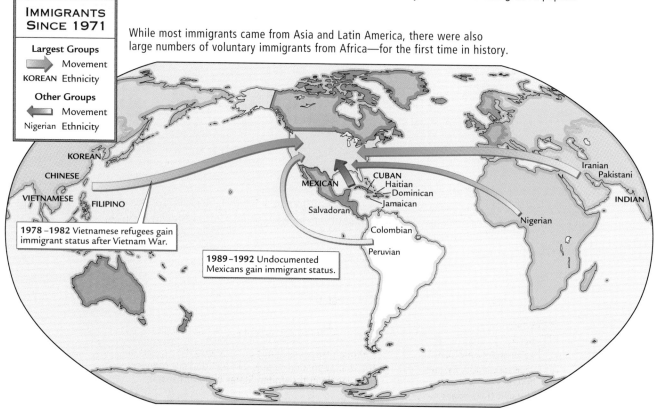

IMMIGRANTS SINCE 1971

Largest Groups
➡ Movement
KOREAN Ethnicity

Other Groups
⬅ Movement
Nigerian Ethnicity

KOREAN
CHINESE
VIETNAMESE
FILIPINO

MEXICAN
CUBAN
Haitian
Dominican
Jamaican
Salvadoran
Colombian
Peruvian

Iranian
Pakistani
INDIAN
Nigerian

1978–1982 Vietnamese refugees gain immigrant status after Vietnam War.

1989–1992 Undocumented Mexicans gain immigrant status.

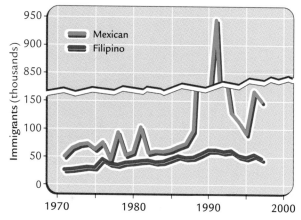

Immigrants (thousands)

- Mexican
- Filipino

MEXICAN AND FILIPINO IMMIGRANTS

Nearly 1 million Mexicans gained immigrant status in 1991. In most years, Filipinos are among the largest immigrant groups entering the United States.

Many Mexicans who gained immigrant status after 1986 later became U.S. citizens.

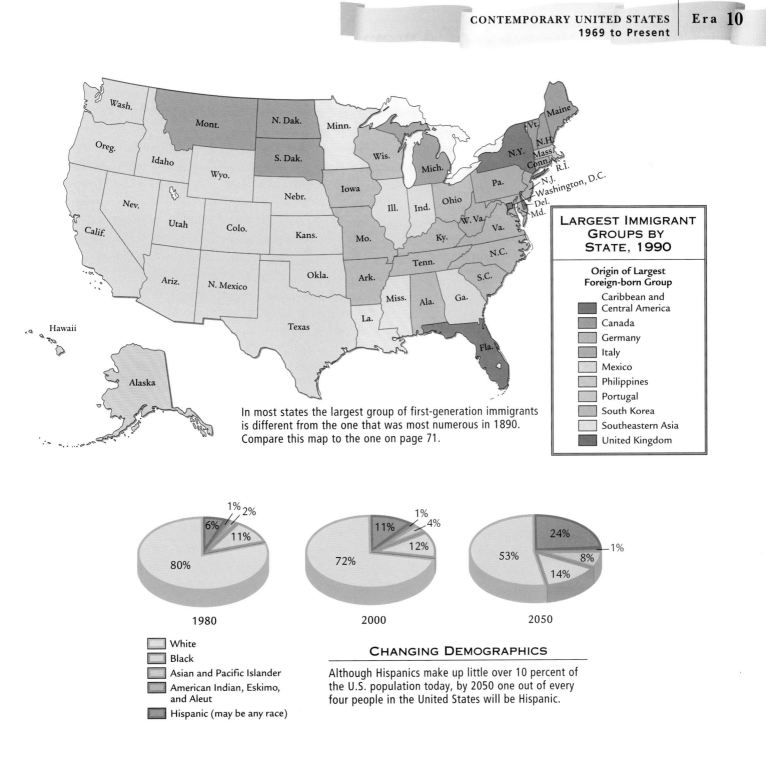

LARGEST IMMIGRANT GROUPS BY STATE, 1990

Origin of Largest Foreign-born Group

- Caribbean and Central America
- Canada
- Germany
- Italy
- Mexico
- Philippines
- Portugal
- South Korea
- Southeastern Asia
- United Kingdom

In most states the largest group of first-generation immigrants is different from the one that was most numerous in 1890. Compare this map to the one on page 71.

1980 — 80%, 11%, 6%, 2%, 1%

2000 — 72%, 12%, 11%, 4%, 1%

2050 — 53%, 24%, 14%, 8%, 1%

- White
- Black
- Asian and Pacific Islander
- American Indian, Eskimo, and Aleut
- Hispanic (may be any race)

CHANGING DEMOGRAPHICS

Although Hispanics make up little over 10 percent of the U.S. population today, by 2050 one out of every four people in the United States will be Hispanic.

"Everyone is kneaded out of the same dough, but not baked in the same oven."

—FOLK SAYING

High school students today are part of a population that is different from that of their grandparents. Two generations from now the population of the United States will be still more diverse.

Glossary

abolition Overthrow of slavery.

Allies 1. Nations that fought the Central Powers in World War I. Included France, Russia, the United Kingdom, and the United States. 2. Nations that fought the Axis Powers in World War II. Included France, the Soviet Union, the United Kingdom, and the United States.

annex To add territory to a place with established boundaries, such as a city or country.

armistice Temporary agreement between two or more countries to stop fighting. A truce.

Articles of Confederation The first constitution of the United States, ratified in 1777 and replaced in 1788 by the Constitution. It granted fewer powers to the national government and more to the states than the Constitution did.

Axis Powers Nations that fought the Allies in World War II. Included Germany, Italy, and Japan.

blockade Isolation of a place by ships or troops to prevent people and goods from entering or leaving.

boomtown Town that experiences rapid population growth.

boundary Shared border separating places such as states or countries. When two places do not agree on the location of their shared boundary, the boundary is said to be disputed.

boycott Method of expressing political or social disfavor by refusing to buy products, patronize businesses, or use services.

casualty Person killed, wounded, captured, or missing in action after a battle or war.

center of population Place within a country where equal numbers of people live to the North, South, East, and West.

Central Powers Nations that fought the Allies in World War I. Included Germany, Austria-Hungry, and the Ottoman Empire.

cession Territory surrendered by one country to another as a result of a war or treaty.

charter Document issued by a government to create a smaller unit of government or other institution and to define its rights and responsibilities.

civil rights Freedoms guaranteed to U.S. citizens by the Constitution.

civil war War between two groups or regions of the same country.

Cold War Political and military tension between Communist and democratic nations following World War II. It stopped short of open warfare between its main adversaries, the United States and the Soviet Union.

colony Settlement or region governed by a distant parent country.

Communism System of government ownership and controls of the property and equipment used for producing food, goods, and services. Communist countries generally do not have democratic governments.

compromise Method of settling differences in which both sides agree to give up some of their demands.

Confederate States of America The 11 Southern states that seceded from the United States during the Civil War. Also called the Confederacy.

constitution Document that sets forth the powers, duties, and structure of a government. The U.S. Constitution was ratified in 1788 and has been amended more than 25 times.

contiguous Connected or touching.

country 1. Land with one government. 2. Large region, such as the "Oregon Country."

Crusade One of eight wars between 1096 and 1270 when Christian armies from Europe tried to win control of Palestine (the "Holy Land") from its Muslim rulers.

culture group Ethnic, racial, religious, or Indian group.

D-Day Abbreviation for the "designated day" of a military offensive. Usually refers to the Allied invasion of Normandy during World War II.

democracy 1. Government by the people, in which citizens vote in free elections. 2. Country with a democratic system of government.

depression Severe drop in a country's economy that causes rising unemployment and falling prices.

drought Long period of unusually low rainfall.

emigrant Person who leaves one region or country to settle in another.

empire Set of nations or territories sharing a single ruler.

Fall Line Imaginary line connecting a series of waterfalls where rivers drop from the Piedmont to the Atlantic Coastal Plain. It marks the farthest point that boats traveling upstream from the Atlantic can reach.

famine Severe and widespread shortage of food.

federation Group or union of people, groups, or states under a central leadership.

Filipino Person from the Philippines.

front Forward line of an army, often where the army faces its opponent.

gap Opening through mountains. A pass.

glacier Large, slow-moving mass of ice formed from a long-lasting accumulation of snow.

guerrilla Member of a military unit who fights in territory occupied by enemy forces. Guerrilla fighters usually use surprise tactics.

highland Large area of mountains or elevated land.

Hispanic U.S. citizen or resident who is of Spanish or Latin American descent. In some areas of the United States, the terms "Latino" and "Latina" (for a woman or girl) are preferred over "Hispanic."

homestead Land claimed by a settler.

Ice Age Period of history when ice sheets cover huge regions of the earth's surface. Ice Ages last thousands of years and cause sea level to drop as large amounts of ocean water freeze.

ice sheet Expanse of ice one to three miles thick that covers a large part of the earth.

immigrant Person who enters a new country to settle there permanently.

Indian Term commonly used to refer to Native Americans. Columbus called the native people he encountered "Indians," because he believed he had reached the Indies.

Indies European term for the islands and mainland of Southeast Asia, India, and coastal China. Today "East Indies" mainly refers to the islands of Southeast Asia and "West Indies" to the islands in and near the Caribbean Sea.

indigo Plant from which blue dye can be made.

internment camp Location where large numbers of people are confined for political or military reasons, usually during wartime.

irrigate To supply dry land with water by artificial means, usually for farming.

Jim Crow laws State and local legislation, found mostly in the South, designed to discriminate against and suppress the rights of African Americans. Most Jim Crow laws were overturned or dropped during the 1950s and 1960s.

labor union Organization created to protect the rights and safety of workers in their workplace, and to negotiate employment contracts on their behalf.

literacy test Assessment of a person's ability to read and write.

Manifest Destiny The 19th-century belief that the United States had the right and the duty to expand westward to the Pacific.

migration Mass movement of people from one region to another.

military adviser Person who instructs foreign armed forces on military strategy, tactics, and procedure, and who may participate in battle.

mission Religious facility used as a base for promoting the spread of Christianity.

Mormon Believer in the Bible and the Book of Mormon. Member of a Mormon congregation.

nation Large group of people bound together by shared culture, history, or geography; often but not always the citizens of a country.

New World Continents west of the Atlantic Ocean; North and South America.

North Atlantic Treaty Organization (NATO) Defensive military alliance established in 1949 to discourage attacks by the Soviet Union and Soviet-occupied Eastern Europe. Early members included Canada, the United States and 13 countries of Western Europe.

occupy To control another country by maintaining a military force there.

Old World Continents east of the Atlantic Ocean. Europe, Asia, and Africa.

ordnance Combat equipment such as ammunition, weapons, and vehicles.

Organization of Petroleum Exporting Countries (OPEC) Economic alliance of oil-producing countries, created in 1960 to set and control worldwide oil prices.

Panama Canal Zone Strip of land crossing the Isthmus of Panama from which the United States administered and operated the Panama Canal; U.S. territory from 1903 to 1979.

piedmont 1. Gently sloping land along the foot of a mountain or mountain range. 2. **Piedmont** Region between the Appalachian Mountains and the Atlantic Coastal Plain

plain Broad area of land that is gently rolling or almost flat.

plateau Elevated plain, usually with at least one steeply dropping or rising side. Some plateaus ar heavily eroded.

poll tax Fee that must be paid before a person can vote. Designed to prevent Southern blacks from voting.

population density Number of people per square mile or square kilometer.

quota Limit or maximum number.

rainfall Rain or the equivalent amount of water from snow, sleet, and hail. Annual rainfall is the total for a typical year.

range 1. Connected line of mountains. 2. Open land where cattle, buffalo, or other livestock wander and graze.

ratify To formally approve.

Reconstruction Period from 1865 to 1877 when former Confederate states were readmitted to the Union and subject to federal control following the Civil War.

reform Action intended to solve a country's social problems and improve the conditions of its citizens.

refugee Person who flees a country due to war, political oppression, or religious persecution.

relief Financial or other assistance provided by the government to those in need.

republic Country whose leader is elected by the citizens or their chosen representatives.

reservation Land set aside by a government, especially land set aside for Native Americans.

revolution Overthrow of a country's government by citizens of that country.

rural Belonging to the countryside, as opposed to towns and cities.

sea ice Ice floating on the sea. Some sea ice forms a permanent cover near the North Pole, while other sea ice is seasonal.

secede To formally leave a union.

segregate To separate from others.

settlement 1. Newly established community or colony. 2. The act of establishing homes in a new place.

sharecropper Person who farms the land of another and pays rent with an agreed share of the harvested crops.

siege Period when an army surrounds a city or other place to force it to surrender.

sit-in Method of protest by demonstrators who seat themselves in a public place and refuse to move.

slave Person who is owned by another and is forced to work without pay.

slavery Practice of owning slaves.

state Part of a country with laws and leaders of its own. The United States consists of 50 states.

suburban Relating to the ring of smaller towns that make up the outer part of an urban area.

superpower Influential nation with internationally dominant military power. Usually used to describe the United States and the Soviet Union during the Cold War.

tactics Maneuvers used to achieve a military goal.

territory 1. Part of a country that does not have the full rights of a state or province. 2. Any large region, often with poorly defined boundaries.

textile Cloth, usually knitted or woven.

topsoil Surface layer of earth that includes organic matter necessary to nourish plants.

trade Business of selling and buying products.

transcontinental Crossing a continent.

treaty Formal agreement between two or more countries, usually dealing with peace or trade.

Underground Railroad Not a true railroad, but an escape route and series of hiding places to help runaway slaves reach the free states or Canada.

undocumented Without the documents required by law to live in a foreign country.

Union 1. A short name for the United States of America. 2. The Northern and Western states that remained part of the United States during the Civil War. 3. See labor union.

United Nations International organization that includes most countries of the world. Created in 1948 to resolve world problems peacefully.

urban Consisting of towns or cities. The opposite of rural.

viceroyalty Province governed by a viceroy (governor).

Warsaw Pact Defensive military alliance established in 1955 to discourage attacks by NATO; treaty that created the alliance. Early members included the Soviet Union and seven Eastern European countries under its control.

State Facts

State	Capital	Largest City	Admitted to Union (order)	U.S. House Members	Population	Rank in Population	1990 % Urban	Area in Sq. Mi. Sq. Km	Rank in Area	Postal Abbrev.
ALABAMA	Montgomery	Birmingham	1819 (22)	7	4,351,999	23	60	51,718 133 950	29	AL
ALASKA	Juneau	Anchorage	1959 (49)	1	614,010	48	68	591,004 1 530 693	1	AK
ARIZONA	Phoenix	Phoenix	1912 (48)	6	4,668,631	21	88	114,007 295 276	6	AZ
ARKANSAS	Little Rock	Little Rock	1836 (25)	4	2,538,303	33	54	53,183 137 742	27	AR
CALIFORNIA	Sacramento	Los Angeles	1850 (31)	52	32,666,550	1	93	158,648 410 896	3	CA
COLORADO	Denver	Denver	1876 (38)	6	3,970,971	24	82	104,100 269 618	8	CO
CONNECTICUT	Hartford	Bridgeport	1788 (5)	6	3,274,069	29	79	5,006 12 966	48	CT
DELAWARE	Dover	Wilmington	1787 (1)	1	743,603	45	73	2,026 5 246	49	DE
FLORIDA	Tallahassee	Jacksonville	1845 (27)	23	14,915,980	4	85	58,681 151 982	22	FL
GEORGIA	Atlanta	Atlanta	1788 (4)	11	7,642,207	10	63	58,930 152 627	21	GA
HAWAII	Honolulu	Honolulu	1959 (50)	2	1,193,001	41	89	6,459 16 729	47	HI
IDAHO	Boise	Boise	1890 (43)	2	1,228,684	40	57	83,574 216 456	13	ID
ILLINOIS	Springfield	Chicago	1818 (21)	20	12,045,326	5	85	56,343 145 928	24	IL
INDIANA	Indianapolis	Indianapolis	1816 (19)	10	5,899,195	14	65	36,185 93 720	38	IN
IOWA	Des Moines	Des Moines	1846 (29)	5	2,862,447	30	61	56,276 145 754	25	IA
KANSAS	Topeka	Wichita	1861 (34)	4	2,629,067	32	69	82,282 213 110	14	KS
KENTUCKY	Frankfort	Louisville	1792 (15)	6	3,936.499	25	52	40,411 104 665	37	KY
LOUISIANA	Baton Rouge	New Orleans	1812 (18)	7	4,368,967	22	68	47,720 123 593	31	LA
MAINE	Augusta	Portland	1820 (23)	2	1,244,250	39	45	33,128 85 801	39	ME
MARYLAND	Annapolis	Baltimore	1788 (7)	8	5,134,808	19	81	10,455 27 077	42	MD
MASSACHUSETTS	Boston	Boston	1788 (6)	10	6,147,132	13	84	8,262 21 398	45	MA
MICHIGAN	Lansing	Detroit	1837 (26)	16	9,817,242	8	71	58,513 151 548	23	MI
MINNESOTA	St. Paul	Minneapolis	1858 (32)	8	4,725,419	20	70	84,397 218 587	12	MN
MISSISSIPPI	Jackson	Jackson	1817 (20)	5	2,752,092	31	47	47,695 123 530	32	MS
MISSOURI	Jefferson City	Kansas City	1821 (24)	9	5,438,559	16	69	69,709 180 546	19	MO

State	Capital	Largest City	Admitted to Union (order)	U.S. House Members	Population	Rank in Population	1990 % Urban	Area in Sq. Mi. Sq. Km	Rank in Area	Postal Abbrev.
MONTANA	Helena	Billings	1889 (41)	1	880,453	44	53	147,047 380 849	4	MT
NEBRASKA	Lincoln	Omaha	1867 (37)	3	1,662,719	38	66	77,359 200 358	15	NE
NEVADA	Carson City	Las Vegas	1864 (36)	2	1,746,898	36	88	110,567 286 367	7	NV
NEW HAMPSHIRE	Concord	Manchester	1788 (9)	2	1,185,048	42	51	9,283 24 044	44	NH
NEW JERSEY	Trenton	Newark	1787 (3)	13	8,115,011	9	89	7,790 20 175	46	NJ
NEW MEXICO	Santa Fe	Albuquerque	1912 (47)	3	1,736,931	37	73	121,599 314 939	5	NM
NEW YORK	Albany	New York City	1788 (11)	31	18,175,301	3	84	49,112 127 200	30	NY
NORTH CAROLINA	Raleigh	Charlotte	1789 (12)	12	7,546,493	11	50	52,672 136 421	28	NC
NORTH DAKOTA	Bismarck	Fargo	1889 (39)	1	638,244	47	53	70,704 183 123	17	ND
OHIO	Columbus	Columbus	1803 (17)	19	11,209,493	7	74	41,328 107 040	35	OH
OKLAHOMA	Oklahoma City	Oklahoma City	1907 (46)	6	3,346,713	27	68	69,903 181 048	18	OK
OREGON	Salem	Portland	1859 (33)	5	3,281,974	28	71	97,052 251 365	10	OR
PENNSYLVANIA	Harrisburg	Philadelphia	1787 (2)	21	12,001,451	6	69	45,310 117 351	33	PA
RHODE ISLAND	Providence	Providence	1790 (13)	2	988,480	43	86	1,213 3 142	50	RI
SOUTH CAROLINA	Columbia	Columbia	1788 (8)	6	3,835,962	26	55	31,117 80 593	40	SC
SOUTH DAKOTA	Pierre	Sioux Falls	1889 (40)	1	738,171	46	50	77,122 199 744	16	SD
TENNESSEE	Nashville	Memphis	1796 (16)	9	5,430,621	17	61	42,146 109 158	34	TN
TEXAS	Austin	Houston	1845 (28)	30	19,759,614	2	80	266,874 691 201	2	TX
UTAH	Salt Lake City	Salt Lake City	1896 (45)	3	2,099,758	34	87	84,905 219 902	11	UT
VERMONT	Montpelier	Burlington	1791 (14)	1	590,883	49	32	9,615 24 903	43	VT
VIRGINIA	Richmond	Virginia Beach	1788 (10)	11	6,791,345	12	69	40,598 105 149	36	VA
WASHINGTON	Olympia	Seattle	1889 (42)	9	5,689,263	15	76	68,126 176 446	20	WA
WEST VIRGINIA	Charleston	Charleston	1863 (35)	3	1,811,156	35	36	24,231 62 759	41	WV
WISCONSIN	Madison	Milwaukee	1848 (30)	9	5,223,500	18	66	56,145 145 414	26	WI
WYOMING	Cheyenne	Cheyenne	1890 (44)	1	480,907	50	65	97,818 253 349	9	WY

Index

Homestead, city in Pennsylvania, 87
Homestead Act of 1862, 74
Honolulu, capital of Hawaii, 6, 94, 117, 122
Hopewell, early Native American empire, 16
Hormuz, Strait of, Persian Gulf, 112
Horn, Cape, South America, 13, 54
Horseshoe Bend, battle in Mississippi, 48
Houston, city in Texas, 7, 53, 86, 90, 105, 117
Hudson, Henry, explorer for England and
    Netherlands, 22, 30
Hudson Bay, Canada, 13, 22
Hudson River, New York, 9
Hue, city in South Vietnam, 109
Humboldt River, Nevada, 8, 50, 56
Hungary, country in Europe, 11, 19, 93, 96,
    102-103, 113
Huron, Indian nation, 26, 36
Huron, Lake, North America, 9, 48, 52

I

Ice Ages, long period of cold climate, 14-16
Iceland, island country in Atlantic Ocean, 11,
    15, 22
Idaho, U.S. state and terr., 6, 79, 122
Illinois, U.S. state and terr., 7, 42, 51, 122
Inca, early Native American empire, 16, 23, 28
Inchon, landing site in South Korea, 101
Incirlik, military base in Turkey, 112
Independence, city in Missouri, 7, 56
India, country in Asia, 10-11, 18, 20-21, 84, 118
Indian Country. *See* Indian Territory
Indian Ocean, 12-13, 18, 20-21
Indian Territory, past U.S. terr., 49, 59, 63
Indiana, U.S. state, 7, 42, 51, 122
Indianapolis, capital of Indiana, 7, 59, 79, 105, 122
Indies, region of Asia, 20-22, 28
Indonesia, country in Asia, 10, 110
internment camps, 95
Inuit, Native American cultural group, 16, 119
Iowa, Indian nation, 26, 48-49
Iowa, U.S. state, 7, 60, 63, 122
Iran, country in Middle East, 11, 102, 110, 112, 118
Iraq, country in Middle East, 11, 102, 110, 112
Irbil, city in Iraq, 112
Ireland, country in Europe, 11, 19, 58, 70-72, 82
Iron Curtain, political barrier of Cold War, 103
Iroquois, Indian confederation, 26, 29, 36, 38
Israel, country in Middle East, 11, 110, 112
Italy, country in Europe, 11, 18, 84-85, 92-93, 96,
    103, 110
    immigrants from, 70, 82-83, 91, 106, 119
Iwo Jima, World War II battle in the Pacific, 99

J

Jackson, capital of Mississippi, 7, 65-66, 122
Jamaica, island country in Caribbean Sea, 11, 28,
    34, 45, 118
James River, Virginia, 8, 25, 31
Jamestown, British settlement in Virginia, 25, 29,
    31-32
Japan, country in Asia, 10, 82, 84, 92-95, 98-99
Japan, Sea of, Pacific Ocean, 12, 93, 100-101
Japanese Americans, 94-95
Java Sea, World War II battle near Borneo, 99
Jefferson, Thomas, U.S. President, 46
Jefferson City, capital of Missouri, 7, 122
Jerusalem, city in Israel, 112
Jews, religious group, 33, 82-83, 91, 97, 110
Jim Crow, laws of racial segregation, 86
Jordan, country in Middle East, 11, 112
Joseph, Chief, Nez Perce leader, 74-75

Juneau, capital of Alaska, 6, 77, 122
Jutland, naval battle near Denmark, 85

K

Kanem, past kingdom in Africa, 17
Kansa, Indian nation, 26, 49
Kansas, U.S. state and terr., 6-7, 60-61, 63, 122
Kansas City, city in Missouri, 7, 72-73, 87, 90, 105, 117
Kansas-Nebraska Act (1854), 60-61
Kelso, city in Washington, 57
Kennedy, John F., U.S. President, 101
Kentucky, U.S. state and terr., 7, 37, 42, 51, 122
Kenya, country in Africa, 11, 113
Khe Sanh, battle in South Vietnam, 109
Kickapoo Indians, Indian nation, 48-49
King, Rev. Martin Luther, Jr., 101, 107
King Philip's War, conflict in New England, 29
Klondike, mining region in the Yukon, 77
Kontum, battles in South Vietnam, 108-109
Korea, past country in Asia, 93
Korean War, 67, 100-101
Kuwait, country in Middle East, 11, 110, 112

L

La Crosse, city in Wisconsin, 7, 53
labor unions, 78-79
Lansing, capital of Michigan, 7, 122
Laos, country in Asia, 10, 108-109
Laredo, city in Texas, 6, 44
Las Vegas, city in Nevada, 6, 117
Lazarus, Emma, U.S. poet, 70
Leadville, mining town in Colorado, 76
Lebanon, country in Middle East, 11
Lee, Robert E., Confederate general, 68
Lenape, Indian nation, 48
Leningrad, site of World War II siege in Soviet
    Union, 93, 96
Lewis, Meriwether, U.S. explorer, 46-47
Lexington, battle in Massachusetts, 38
Leyte Gulf, World War II battle in Philippines, 99
Liberia, country in Africa, 11, 84
Libya, country in Africa, 11, 92, 96, 110
Lincoln, Abraham, U.S. President, 60-62, 64, 66, 68
Lincoln, capital of Nebraska, 7, 123
Lisbon, capital of Portugal, 17-21, 24
Little Bighorn, Indian Wars battle in Montana, 74
Little Rock, capital of Arkansas, 7, 66-67, 107,
    117, 122
Logan, city in Utah Territory, 57
London, capital of Britain, 19, 39
Long, Stephen, U.S. explorer, 50
Long Island, New York, U.S., 9, 38
Los Angeles, city in California, 6, 44, 54, 56, 73,
    86-87, 90, 105, 107, 117
Louisiana, U.S. state and terr. and French colony,
    7, 29, 44-45, 47, 51, 122
Louisiana Purchase, territorial acquisition, 46
Louisville, city in Kentucky, 7, 53, 62, 79, 95, 117
Lusitania, ship sunk in World War I, 85
Luxembourg, country in Europe, 11, 85, 92, 96, 103
Luzon, World War II battle in Philippines, 99

M

Madison, capital of Wisconsin, 7, 123
Mahican, Indian nation, 36
Maine, U.S. state, 7, 51, 55, 60, 63, 122
Mali, country in Africa, 11
Mali, past empire in Africa, 15, 17
Manama, capital of Bahrain, 112
Manassas. *See* Bull Run
Manchuria, region of China, 93, 99

Mandan, Indian nation, 26, 47
Manifest Destiny, U.S. foreign policy, 54-55
Manila, capital of Philippines, 10, 80
Marne, World War I battle in France, 85
Maryland, U.S. state and British colony, 7, 32-33,
    41, 122
Massachusetts, U.S. state and British colony, 7,
    32-33, 40-41, 122
Maya, early Native American empire, 14, 16
Medina, city in Saudi Arabia, 112
Mediterranean Sea, 13, 17-20, 24, 112
Mekong River, Asia, 108-109
Memphis, city in Tennessee, 7, 62, 87, 105, 107, 117
Merced River, California, 57
Mexican Cession, territorial acquisition, 54-55
Mexico, country in North America, 10-11, 37,
    44-45, 50, 54
    immigrants from, 71, 82, 91, 106, 118-119
Mexico City, capital of Mexico, 10, 28, 30, 54
Mexico, Gulf of, Atlantic Ocean, 13, 23, 48, 54, 64
Miami, city in Florida, 7, 103, 117
Miami, Indian nation, 48-49
Michigan, U.S. state and terr., 7, 51, 60, 122
Michigan, Lake, United States, 9, 48, 116
Middle Colonies, colonial region, 32, 38
Midway, island terr. in Pacific Ocean, 81, 99
Milwaukee, city in Wisconsin, 7, 53, 83, 105, 107
Minneapolis, city in Minnesota, 7, 90, 105, 117
Minnesota, U.S. state and terr., 7, 63, 122
Mississippi, U.S. state and terr., 7, 51, 69, 122
Mississippi River, 9, 23, 40, 42, 46-50, 56, 64-68
Mississippian, Native American empire, 14, 16
Missouri, U.S. state and terr., 7, 51, 60, 63, 122
Missouri Compromise (1820), 60
Missouri River, United States, 8-9, 46-47, 52, 56, 76
Mobile, city in Alabama, 7, 53
Mobile Bay, Civil War battle site in Alabama, 9, 67
Modoc, Indian nation, 26, 74
Mojave Desert, California, 8
Mongolia, country in Asia, 10, 18
Monmouth, battle in New Jersey, 38
Monroe, James, U.S. President, 44
Monroe Doctrine, U.S. foreign policy, 44-45
Montana, U.S. state and terr., 6, 26, 79, 123
Monterey, city in California, 6, 44, 57
Monterrey, city in Mexico, 6, 30, 54
Montgomery, capital of Alabama, 7, 107, 122
Montpelier, capital of Vermont, 7, 123
Montreal, city in Canada, 7, 31, 36, 38
Mormons, religious group, 56-57
Moscow, capital of Russia, 11, 93
Mosul, city in Iraq, 112
Mussolini, Benito, Italian dictator, 92
Mutual Assured Destruction, nuclear policy, 102
My Lai, site of massacre in South Vietnam, 109

N

Naches Pass, Washington, 56-57
Nacogdoches, city in New Spain, 44
Nagasaki, city in Japan, 98-99
Naples, city in Italy, 17, 19
Narváez, Pánfilo de, Spanish explorer, 23
Nashville, capital of Tennessee, 7, 42, 65-67, 123
Nassau, naval battle in the Bahamas, 39
National Association for the Advancement of
    Colored People, civil rights group, 81
national parks, 88
NATO, democratic alliance, 102-103
Navajo, Indian nation, 26
Nebraska, U.S. state and terr., 6-7, 60-61, 79, 123
Netherlands, country in Europe, 11, 19, 24, 92, 96,
    103, 110